D1351723

6/16/-

FELDSPARS

FELDSPARS

Tom. F. W. Barth

Professor, Mineralogisk-Geologisk Museum
Oslo, Norway

WILEY – INTERSCIENCE
a division of John Wiley & Sons Inc.
NEW YORK   LONDON   SYDNEY   TORONTO

UNIVERSITY LIBRARY
2 1 OCT 1970
LANCASTER

Copyright © 1969 John Wiley & Sons Inc.
All rights reserved. No part of this book may
be reproduced by any means, nor transmitted,
nor translated into a machine language without
the written permission of the publisher.

Library of Congress catalog card number 68–57147

SBN 471 05430 5

Printed in Great Britain at the Pitman Press, Bath

70/   3191

Preface

Knowledge of the rock-making feldspars is essential to all students of physical geology, mineralogy, petrography, petrology, crystallography and geochemistry. The last decade has seen spectacular advances in feldspar mineralogy, and progress is now so fast that during the writing of this book new data, concepts and theories had constantly to be considered. Still more recent information appeared while the book was in production, which could only in part be incorporated in the present work.

All available data on feldspar are collected and discussed here for the first time, but description of determinative methods are deliberately left out. The x-ray methods are commonplace; but optical methods are more specialized and have a long tradition and hence the literature on the subject is very large. The triclinic symmetry allowing infinite variations in

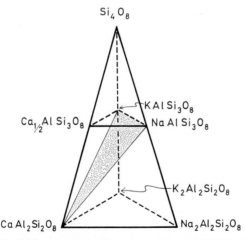

FIGURE 1 The feldspar composition space composed of the oxides SiO_2, Al_2O_3, CaO, Na_2O and K_2O. The shaded plane represents the traditional composition plane for the feldspars, but both $Ca_{\frac{1}{4}}AlSi_3O_8$ (= Schwantke's molecule) and $Na_2Al_2Si_2O_8$ (= nepheline molecule) manifestly enter into the feldspar lattices and throw the composition into three dimensional space. See K. Perry, *Lithos*, **1** (1968), p. 201.

shape and position of the optical indicatrix makes the feldspars particularly amenable to this treatment. In a modern comprehensive treatise the optical properties and the technique of their determination have been systematically presented and explained by C. Burri, R. L. Parker and E. Wenk (in cooperation with H. R. Wenk) in *Die optische Orientierung der Plagioclase* (Birkhäuser, Basel and Stuttgart, 1967) with 17 diagrams and plates for the determination of the plagioclases by universal stage methods. Further treatment in the present book is therefore unnecessary.

Eventually a few words may be said about the rapidly developing crystal chemistry and geochemistry of feldspars: The chief molecules of natural feldspars are $K[AlSi_3O_8]$, $Na[AlSi_3O_8]$ and $Ca[Al_2Si_2O_8]$, but recent computations and experiments have proved that relatively considerable amounts of $Ca_{\frac{1}{2}}[AlSi_3O_8]$ and of $Na_2[Al_2Si_2O_8]$ also may be present, see figure 1. Ionic substitution of many kinds is common in the feldspar lattice. The large cations may be replaced by $[H_3O]$, $[NH_4]$, Rb, Cs, Sr, Ba, Pb, Tl, but in natural feldspar only Ba enters in great amounts —a pure Ba feldspar (celsian) is known as a rarity. The four co-ordinated small cations (Al and Si) may be replaced by Fe, Ge, Ga, (Sc), and B. The rare boron analogue (= redmergnerite) occurs as a pure mineral; in K feldspars up to 12% Fe feldspars exists in solid solution; Ge, and Ga, enter but in traces, although pure compounds can be made in the laboratory. Many of these chemically unusual feldspar compounds exhibit interesting properties, and a further study of them will shed much light on the physical chemistry of the common feldspars.

Tom. F. W. Barth

Contents

Introduction xi

1 General Mineralogy and Classification of the Rock-forming Feldspars

1.1 Potassium Feldspars 2
   1.11 Monoclinic potassium feldspar: orthoclase and sanidine . 2
   1.12 Triclinic potassium feldspar: microcline and adularia . 4
1.2 Sodium Feldspar: Albite 10
   1.21 Silica deficient albite: Anemousite 12
1.3 Calcium Feldspar: Anorthite 13
   1.31 Lime deficient anorthite: Schwantke's molecule . . 14
1.4 The Feldspar Series 15
   1.41 Alkali feldspar 15
      1.411 Solid solutions 15
      1.412 Perthites and antiperthites 17
   1.42 Sodium–calcium feldspars or plagioclases . . . 30
      1.421 General 30
      1.422 High- and low-temperature variants . . . 37
      1.423 Intermediate plagioclases 41
   1.43 Ternary feldspars (anorthoclases, sanidines) . . 43
1.5 Summary of Occurrence and Formation 46
   References 51

2 Survey of Pseudosymmetry and Twinning

2.1 Pseudosymmetry 60
2.2 Twinning Laws 61
   2.21 Normal twins 62
   2.22 Parallel twins 62
   2.23 Complex twins 63
2.3 Twin Boundaries 65
2.4 Rhombic Section 68
2.5 Genesis of Twins 75
   References 83

3 The Structures of the Feldspars

3.1 Survey of the Crystal Structure 88
   3.11 Introduction 88

3.12 Types of structure 92
3.13 The atomic positions within the unit cell of sanidine . 93
3.14 Megaw's notations for feldspar structures . . . 96
3.15 Albite and microcline 98
3.16 Anorthite 100
  3.161 Body-centred anorthite 100
  3.162 Primitive anorthite 100
3.17 Disorder or anisotropic temperature vibration . . . 101
3.2 The Structures of the Alkali Feldspars . . . 102
3.21 Potassium feldspars 102
  3.211 The structures of the variants 102
  3.212 The names of the variants of potassium feldspar . . 112
  3.213 Stability and frequency of the structural variants . 114
  3.214 The problem of adularia 118
3.22 Sodium feldspar 120
  3.221 On the monoclinic sodium feldspar . . . 123
3.23 Alkali feldspar mixed crystals. 125
  3.231 Summary 133
3.3 The Structure of Anorthite 134
3.4 The Structure of the Plagioclases 135
References 140

4 **Physical Properties of Feldspars**

4.1 Hardness 147
4.2 Density of Crystals and Glasses 151
4.21 Alkali feldspars 154
4.22 Plagioclases 158
4.23 Ternary feldspars 163
4.24 Feldspar glasses 165
4.3 Thermal Expansion 171
4.4 Elastic Constants 181
4.41 Compressibility 181
4.42 Elastic constants 182
4.43 Tensile strength 183
4.44 Shear strength 183
4.45 Velocities of compressional waves 183
4.46 Viscosity 185
References 186

5 **Thermodynamic Properties of Feldspars**

5.1 Thermochemical Data 189

5.11 Data for $KAlSi_3O_8$ 192

5.12 Data for $NaAlSi_3O_8$ 194

5.13 Data for $CaAl_2Si_2O_8$ 197

5.14 The alkali feldspar series $NaAlSi_3O_8$–$KAlSi_3O_8$ solid
solutions 199

5.15 The plagioclase series $NaAlSi_3O_8$–$CaAl_2Si_2O_8$ solid solutions 201

5.16 The partial free energy of albite and orthoclase in alkali
feldspar   201

5.2 Solubility and Alteration of Feldspars   201

5.3 Phase Equilibria and Melting in Feldspars   206

5.31 General   206

5.32 The temperature of melting   209

5.33 Solid–solid transformations   224

References   234

6 **Historical Notes and Old Names**

References   247

Author Index 253

Subject Index 259

Introduction

Feldspars are the most important of all rock-forming substances and are the most studied minerals in the world. They are found under a wide variety of geological conditions, and are more widespread than any other mineral group. Because of their ubiquity and predominance over other minerals the classification of rocks is to a large extent based upon the quantity and kind of the feldspars present.

There is no mineral group which has been studied more thoroughly in the past, and yet there is no mineral group which has presented, and still presents to the mineralogist so many puzzling problems. Thus, in classical mineralogy much speculation persisted, and various hypotheses were advanced to explain the complete isomorphism and the formation of mixed crystals between $NaAlSi_3O_8$ and $CaAl_2Si_2O_8$. Again, in the K-feldspars the relations between monoclinic orthoclase and triclinic microcline were highly conjectural, likewise the relations sanidine–adularia. Many other problems existed and some of them have remained standing puzzles in contemporary mineralogy.

During the last thirty years x-ray crystal structure investigations have revealed that feldspar systems afford remarkable examples of order/ disorder relations, diffusive transformations as well as other kinds of polymorphism, viz. reconstructive, displacive, enantiotropic and mono-tropic. Mixed-crystal series of various types are known, some show a wide compositional range at high temperatures, and exsolve in peculiar ways at lower temperatures, others are almost insoluble in each other at any temperature; each type exhibits a characteristic phase equilibrium diagram reflecting the complexities of the several crystallochemical relations.

Modern experimental and diagnostic techniques have intensified the study of feldspar, and during the last decades no other mineral group has yielded so much valuable information.

1

General Mineralogy and Classification of the Rock-forming Feldspars

There are three† chemical molecules in the rock-forming feldspars:

1. The orthoclase‡ molecule (Or) $KAlSi_3O_8$
2. The albite molecule (Ab) $NaAlSi_3O_8$
3. The anorthite molecule (An) $CaAl_2Si_2O_8$

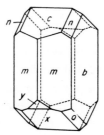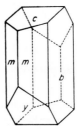

FIGURE 1.1 Usual forms of orthoclase

These are described as potassium feldspar, sodium feldspar and calcium feldspar respectively. At elevated temperatures there are complete

---

† Small amounts of Ba, Sr, Fe and Rb feldspars may also be present. The role of the molecules $NaAlSiO_4$ and $Ca_{\frac{1}{2}}AlSi_3O_8$ will be discussed on pp. 12 and 14 respectively.

‡ The symbol Or customarily applies to the chemical substance $KAlSi_3O_8$ regardless of the actual mineral, whether microcline or orthoclase.

mixed-crystal series between Ab and Or (the alkali feldspars), and between Ab and An (the plagioclase feldspars). But there is very little solid solution between Or and An at any temperature.

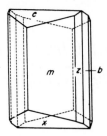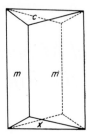

FIGURE 1.2 Adularia types of orthoclase

Although some feldspars exhibit monoclinic and others triclinic symmetry, they are very similar in habit and crystal structure.

Name and symbol		Symmetry	$a:b:c$	α	β	γ
Orthoclase	Or	Monoclinic	0·658:1:0·555	90°	116° 00′	90°
Microcline	Or	Triclinic	0·660:1:0·558	90° 40′	115° 50′	87° 40′
Albite	Ab	Triclinic	0·636:1:0·561	94° 20′	116° 35′	87° 40′
Anorthite	An	Triclinic	0·635:1:0·557	93° 10′	115° 50′	91° 15′

1.1 POTASSIUM FELDSPARS

1.11 Monoclinic potassium feldspar: orthoclase and sanidine $KAlSi_3O_8$

Orthoclase as a mineral name may be used for any monoclinic K-feldspar including sanidine. Sanidine is restricted to glassy monoclinic crystals usually embedded in unaltered volcanic rocks, Na is always

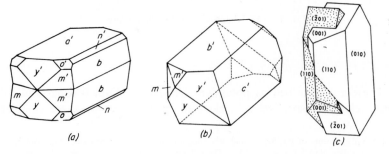

FIGURE 1.3 The three most common twins in orthoclase. (*a*) Manebach; (*b*) Baveno; (*c*) Carlsbad

present. Soda sanidine contains 40–60% albite in solid solution. Ordinary or common orthoclase is opaque white or reddish, non-glassy, but occasionally translucent. It occurs in a great variety of massive rocks and crystalline schists and is usually perthitic (see section 1.412). The crystals are often prismatic or platy with the prism m (110) and the pinacoid b (010) dominating, the base c (001) and x ($\bar{1}01$) are common;

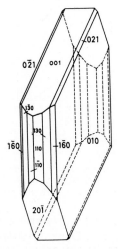

FIGURE 1.4 Sanidine from trachytic lava, Monte Cimino, Viterbo near Rome, Italy. (After Zambonini, *Z. Krist.*, **34**, 1901)

frequently observed are also y ($\bar{2}01$), n (021), o ($\bar{1}11$) and z (130). Sanidine is often tabular parallel to (010), hence the name ($\sigma\alpha\nu\iota\varsigma$ = tablet: see figure 1.4).

Twinning is common according to the Carlsbad, Baveno and Manebach laws, see figure 1.3.

Cleavage: c (001) perfect, b (010) somewhat less so, the two cleavages are inclined at 90° (=orthoclasic); m (110) imperfect. Parting sometimes parallel to a (100), also to a hemi-orthodome ($\bar{h}0l$), approximately ($\bar{8}01$) = murchisonite parting.

An examination of the topology of the crystal structure shows that the cleavages (001) and (010) break the smallest possible number of tetrahedral bonds per unit area. It is worthy of note that these two cleavages break only those bonds which link one chain of four-rings to adjacent chains, while any other cleavage must break bonds within the four-rings themselves. The parting ($\bar{8}01$) is explained by being nearly perpendicular to the axis of maximum thermal expansion.

Fracture conchoidal to uneven. Brittle. Hardness = 6. Specific gravity = 2·54–2·57. Lustre vitreous, on c (001) often pearly. Colourless, white, pale, yellow–brown, flesh red, grey, rarely green.

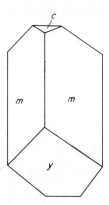

FIGURE 1.5 Orthoclase cryptoperthite with schiller; from larvikite, Oslo area, Norway. (After Rose, *Z. Geol. Ges.*, **1,** 377, 1849.) This is the typical habit of phenocrysts in rhomb porphyries

Iso-orthoclase is an optically positive orthoclase. It has been found in granitic gneiss in three localities. Duparc (1904) observed $+2V$ small and variable. Barth (1933) and Tsuboi (1936) found large optic angles varying on both sides of 90°. Lacroix (1927) found an optically positive sanidine in tahitite lava; it probably represents a ternary feldspar.

Authigenic potassium feldspar is usually apparently monoclinic (but may be triclinic), non-perthitic, and takes only very small amounts of other feldspars into solid solution: K_2O—16·4%, Na_2O—0·2%, CaO—0·2%. However, in rare cases, it may be highly enriched in iron (Thorez and Michot, 1964), see p. 50.

Orthoclase has a wide distribution and is present in a variety of rocks, particularly in igneous rocks and in high-temperature metamorphites. It has also been found in meteorites (Bunch and Olsen, 1967).

1.12 Triclinic potassium feldspar: microcline and adularia

Breithaupt (1830) introduced the name microcline for 'orthoclases' that did not cleave at a right angle. Des Cloizeaux proved that the twin lamellae in microcline exhibited triclinic optics.

By submicroscopic twinning a monoclinic symmetry would be counterfeited (hypothesis of Mallard, 1881, Michel-Lévy, 1879). It was therefore generally believed that orthoclase and microcline were identical minerals.

FIGURE 1.6 Orthoclase porphyroblast from augen gneiss, Feda, S. Norway.
Crystal is 5 cm long

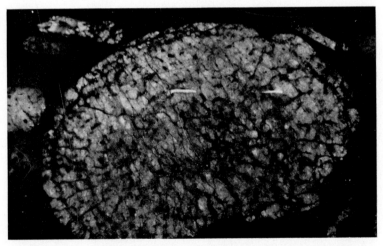

FIGURE 1.7 Authigenic orthoclase, Peko Mine, Northern Territory, Australia. A large ovoid-shaped colloidal accretion which has now crystallized
with optical continuity to feldspar. A radial and concentric shrinkage
crack pattern is well developed. Largest dimension = 2·5 cm. (From
Elliston, 1966)

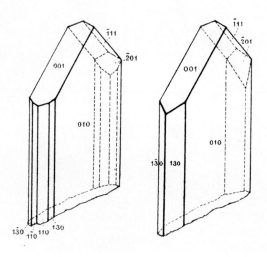

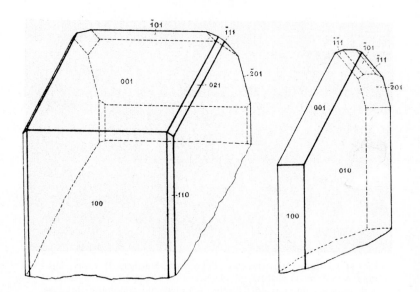

FIGURE 1.8 Untwinned crystals of microcline from druses in pegmatite dikes, Langesundfjord, Norway. (From Brögger, 1890)

Subsequent x-ray studies have shown, however, that orthoclase and microcline differ in the order–disorder relations of the Al–Si ions in the crystal lattice. Consequently, they represent two different modifications of the compound $KAlSi_3O_8$ (see section 3.211). Microcline is stable at lower temperatures, orthoclase at elevated temperatures (section 3.213). By sufficiently slow cooling orthoclase will therefore invert to microcline, a fact that becomes visible through the formation of two sets of microscopically small twin lamellae representing a peculiar combination of the albite and pericline law (= the microcline twin law or M-twin, see p. 73) producing the characteristic cross-hatching in polarized light. Other common twins are, as in orthoclase, Carlsbad, Baveno and Manebach, see figure 1.3.

Microclines of different 'triclinicity' exist; there are all transitions from the 'maximum microcline' to truly monoclinic orthoclase (see section 3.213). It is almost always perthitic (see section 1.412).

The great majority of microclines from granite, gneiss and crystalline schists are M-twinned, indicating that they are secondary after orthoclase.

FIGURE 1.9 Typical microcline twinning: cross-twins on the albite and pericline law seen approximately normal to the (001) face ($\times$ 10, crossed nicols). The white spots inside the microcline are film perthites. In the lower right corner myrmekite is seen

Prior to the twin development the crystals were monoclinic or nearly so. The twinning is a consequence of the monoclinic–triclinic inversion (see p. 79). Primary untwinned microcline, and microclines exhibiting twins with irregular composition faces are found as rarities in pegmatites and in some low-temperature rocks, as, for example, chlorite schists, see figure 2.5.

The face development, cleavage and parting are as in orthoclase.

Colour: clear, white, grey, yellowish, brick red.

Amazonite is bright green. Flawless crystals are used as gemstones; as a rule they are maximum microclines, an exception is the monoclinic amazonite from the Pack Alp, Austria (Makart and Preisinger, 1965). The cause of the colour is doubtful. According to Przibram (1956) the colour is induced by irradiation, it disappears with heating as already observed by Des Cloizeaux (1876); Oftedal (1957) found the colour to disappear at $270°$c. Zavaritsky (1943), Parker and others (1963) suggest a relation between colour intensity (white, pink, green) and rubidium content (Rb_2O from $0·06$ to $1·0\%$). The content of lead also correlates with the colour (Catanzaro and Gast, 1960): green microclines in pegmatites contain lead in the range 240–500 ppm, whereas all samples which are not green contain less than 100 ppm. Zhirov and Stishov (1965) found that green colour does not relate to Rb or Tl but is caused by structural defects arising from the replacement of 2K by Pb. The coupled substitution of K + Si by Pb + Al has no colour effect.

Isomicrocline is an optically positive microcline first recognized in granitic gneisses of the Fichtelgebirge by Luczizky (1905). It was found by Anderson (see Anderson and Maclelland, 1937) in granite of the Northern Inyo Range, California–Nevada: ($Or_{72}Ab_{26}An_2$) with $(+)2V = 64–89°$, $\alpha = 1·518$, $\beta = 1·520$, $\gamma = 1·524$. Emerson (1964) investigated feldspars from the same rock but was unable to find it; 50 potassium feldspars investigated by him gave $(-)2V = 61–89°$.

In gneisses from southern Switzerland, Gysin (1948) found microclines with $2V$ both positive and negative close to $90°$, and, in one locality, Reinhard (1964) recorded $(+)2V = 80°$. In Precambrian granite gneisses of the Baikal Highlands, Kazakov (1956) found that about one-fourth of the microclines investigated were positive with $(+)2V = 70–90°$.

Adularia is usually transparent or milky-white, and often opalescent with a pearly bluish lustre on a face nearly parallel to (100) (= moonstone).

The predominant forms are *m* (110) and *x* ($\bar{1}01$). The base (001) is frequently very small or absent, see figures 1.2 and 1.5. Manebach and Baveno twins are common but Carlsbad has never been observed.

Adularia is weakly triclinic, or apparently monoclinic; the interaxial angles α and γ may differ by a few minutes, or a few tens of minutes of arc from 90°. Irregular variations are found in different parts of the same crystal. The triclinicity is usually highest where the (110) and ($\bar{1}$10) faces or the (1$\bar{1}$0) and ($\bar{1}\bar{1}$0) faces meet. In some crystals, the optic variations range from those of sanidine to those of maximum microcline (Chaisson, 1950; Laves, 1950), see p. 118.

Monoclinic adularia usually give streak-shaped, satellitic x-ray defraction spots indicating the presence of triclinic (beside many monoclinic) domains. Nissen and Bollmann (1966) could observe these domains on electron transmission micrographs.

Adularia is often almost pure K-feldspar, but it typically has a relatively high content of barium corresponding to about 0·2–4·0 mole per cent celsian. The sodium content varies, and usually corresponds to about 3–13% albite.

Although adularia forms at moderate to very low temperatures, it seems probable that it crystallized with apparent monoclinic symmetry, i.e. as high-temperature orthoclase (orthoclase HT), and that a slow change toward higher triclinicity took place later. This is supported by observations on 'adularization' of low-temperature albite (albite LT) which, according to Tane (1962), may be described by the simplified relation:

$$\text{albite LT} + \text{K}^+ \rightarrow \text{orthoclase HT} + \text{Na}^+$$

This transformation was also performed experimentally by Wyart and Sabatier (1956b).

The typical occurrences of adularia are in fissures in crystalline schists, particularly in the region of the Swiss Alps.

Moonstone is a cryptoperthite which, if flawless and of special quality, is used as a gemstone (e.g. moonstones from Ceylon). It emits a characteristic bluish to milky-white lustre which arises when the dimensions and spacings of the submicroscopically small perthite lamellae are comparable to the wavelengths of visible light. The diffuseness of the lustre is ascribed to irregularities in the orthoclase–albite boundaries, and the bluish-white hue indicates that the lamellae vary considerably in thickness, so that all visible wavelengths will suffer some interference (see Raman and others, 1950).

Direct observations on moonstone with an electron microscope (Fleet and Ribbe, 1963, Nissen and Bollman, 1966) revealed alternating, irregular sheets of orthoclase and low albite, approximately parallel to ($\bar{6}$01) and widely varying in thickness, but usually a few thousand angstrom units thick. The albite sheets are finely twinned parallel to (010)—the composition face of the albite twin law—each twin being exactly four albite unit cells wide. They often repeat regularly over a sufficiently large distance to constitute a superstructure which gives sharp subsidiary reflections in the electron diffraction patterns.

1.2 SODIUM FELDSPAR: ALBITE NaAlSi₃O₈

The name is an allusion to the white colour (Berzelius and Gahn, 1815).

The crystallographic elements are given on p. 2. They refer to the low-temperature albite which is common in nature. Natural high-temperature 'albite' is almost always contaminated with appreciable amounts of Or and An in solid solution (Kano, 1956): these albitic mixed crystals become monoclinic at 900–1000°c. But pure albite is probably triclinic at all temperatures (see p. 124). Low albite takes almost no calcium or potassium into solid solution.

The most common faces are analogous to those of orthoclase. The crystals are often tabular parallel to (010), also elongate in the direction of the *b* axis as in the variety pericline. Pericline crystals may exhibit the faces λ ($\bar{3}\bar{3}2$) and *r* ($40\bar{3}$).

Twinning frequent after the albite law and the pericline law. The other feldspar twin laws, particularly Carlsbad, Manebach and Baveno are also observed.

Cleavage: as typical of all feldspars, *c* (001) perfect; *b* (010) less so; *m* ($1\bar{1}0$) imperfect, it may be different from *l* (110).

Fracture uneven to conchoidal. Brittle. Hardness = 6–6·5. Specific gravity 2·62–2·65. Lustre vitreous, on cleavage often pearly.

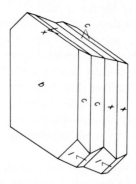

FIGURE 1.10 Albite: complex fourling from Nolla, Thusis. (From Parker and Niggli, *Mineralien der Schweizeralpen*, Wepf, Basel, 1940)

Colour: white, also occasionally bluish, reddish, green, transparent to subtranslucent.

Albite is regularly deposited from hydrothermal solutions in cavities and veins in schists of the Swiss Alps and elsewhere. Such 'Kluftalbite' is water clear and, as distinct from pericline (see below), chemically remarkably pure; only traces of K-feldspar or Ca-feldspar exist in solid solution. The content of Sr-feldspar is variable but often as high as that of Ca-feldspar. Thus, albite is strongly favoured by the partition of strontium

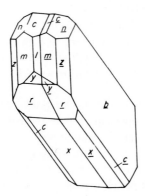

FIGURE 1.11 Albite twin, Alp Rischuna. (From Krebs, 1921)

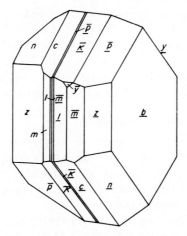

FIGURE 1.12 Complex albite–Carlsbad twin, Alp Rischuna. (From Krebs, 1921)

between the albite lattice and the aqueous solutions (analogously, adularia is favoured by the partition of barium ions).

Albite has a wide distribution in low-temperature metamorphic rocks (greenschist facies rocks). Larger bodies of almost pure albitite are not uncommon.

Albitization is a common metasomatic process in nature. Fixation of sodium by excess alumina in argillaceous slates takes place under regional metamorphic conditions at low temperatures with the formation of albite. The resulting rocks are albite–chlorite schists, phyllites, etc. Special kinds of albitization are described on p. 47.

In certain meteorites (chondrites) with very fine-grained feldspar and appreciable amounts of clinopyroxene as well as orthopyroxene, the feldspar is almost pure albite, whereas the more crystallized chondrites have more calcic plagioclase, usually with between 10 and 20 % of the anorthite component (Mason, 1965).

Clevelandite, in lamellar or leaf-like books of crystals often forming fan-shaped aggregates, represents a late hydrothermal product deposited in veins or as masses in certain granite pegmatites.

Pericline is a variety of albite, occurring in alpine veins, in rather large milky-white crystals with characteristic elongation in the direction of the b axis, see figure 2.9. The pericline twin law takes its name from this variety. The twin composition plane in pericline is characterized by the angle $\sigma = 9$–$10°$ (see section 2.4), which is smaller than that in ordinary albite (Laves and Schneider, 1956). Pericline is probably an albitized oligoclase.

Aventurine, sunstone, see pp. 40 and 241.

Authigenic albite grows in unconsolidated sediments, see p. 50. It is very pure: Na_2O—$11 \cdot 2\%$, K_2O—$0 \cdot 3\%$, CaO—$0 \cdot 2\%$. Optically it is distinguished by an axial angle $(-)$ $2V$ close to $90°$; magmatic or vein albite has a smaller value of $2V$, and the optic sign is positive. Otherwise, rare twins of the complex X–Carlsbad law are common in certain authigenic albites, see figure 2.6 (Füchtbauer, 1948, 1956).

1.21 Silica deficient albite: Anemousite

In the literature there are numerous suggestions that the standard molecules: Or, Ab, An, cannot give the express composition of the feldspar minerals. The Al/Si ratio in alkali feldspar has attracted much attention and the existence of albite with excess silica, as well as of albite deficient in silica has been proposed.

For example, Washington and Wright (1910) examined loose crystals of a labradorite-like mineral collected at Monte Rosso on the island of Linosa, east of Tunis, and found it to contain the nepheline molecule (called, by the authors, the carnegieite molecule) in solid solution; they named the mineral *anemousite*:

Or 4·5 wt. %   Ab 36·2 wt. %   An 53·8 wt. %   Ne 5·6 wt. %

Barth (1930) announced a member of the same mineral series to occur in some undersaturated Pacific lavas, (see p. 45).

Ernst and Nieland (1934) reinvestigated the feldspars of Linosa. They reported chemically normal labradorite crystals exhibiting high-temperature optics. However, as emphasized already by Washington and Wright, the variations in the chemical composition must be of considerable magnitude. According to Ernst and Nieland the optic axial angle, $2V_y$, varies in the range 77–97°, and the index β varies from 1·5487 to 1·5611 (Na-light); the values would differ from crystal to crystal rather than within a single crystal. It is not surprising, therefore, if the material analysed by Washington was somewhat different from that analysed twenty-five years later.

Muir (1955) studied an additional feldspar from Linosa and published an analysis which, in his opinion, could be reconciled with the normal plagioclase formula. But actually, like the analyses of Washington and Wright, it shows significant deviations from classical stoichiometry which are removed by including the carnegieite molecule in solid solution.

1.3 CALCIUM FELDSPAR: ANORTHITE CaAl₂Si₂O₈

The name comes from $\alpha\nu o\rho\theta o\varsigma$, oblique, an allusion to the triclinic symmetry (Rose, 1823).

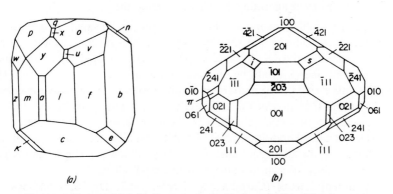

(a)   *(b)*

FIGURE 1.13 Anorthite. (*a*) From an inclusion in andesite of the Aranyer Mountains, Siebenbürgen, Moravia. (vom Rath, *Pogg. Ann.*, **147**, 1872); (*b*) From Vesuvius. (vom Rath, *Pogg. Ann.*, **138**, 1869)

The crystallographic elements are given on p. 2. The face development and habit differ somewhat from the other feldspars. In addition to the common faces listed under orthoclase (p. 3), the following are worthy of note: a (100), γ (013), e (021), n ($0\bar{2}1$), κ ($0\bar{2}3$), z ($1\bar{3}0$), f (130), π ($\bar{1}\bar{3}1$), q ($\bar{2}03$), t (201), o ($\bar{1}\bar{1}1$), p ($\bar{1}11$), o' ($1\bar{1}1$), p' (111), g ($\bar{2}21$), u ($\bar{2}\bar{2}1$), v ($\bar{2}\bar{4}1$), w ($\bar{2}41$), β (241), b' ($2\bar{4}1$), d ($\bar{4}\bar{2}1$), μ ($\bar{4}21$), i ($\bar{4}23$), s ($\bar{4}23$).

Cleavage and fracture as in other feldspars. Hardness $= 6$. Specific gravity 2·75–2·76. Translucent. Twinning as in albite (see p. 10).

Colour: white, greyish, reddish.

Anorthite occurs in some basic igneous rocks, rarely as a well-developed druse mineral (ejectementa of Vesuvius), in some tuffs and skarn rocks. It has been found in meteorites.

Anorthite undergoes a continuous structural transformation from room temperature to about 341°C. Above 341°C another structural variant is stable up to about 800°C. Above 800°C a third variant is stable. It is possible that these variants are related to the development of a primitive lattice, a transitional lattice, and a body-centred lattice (Bloss, 1964). Natural anorthite was found always to exhibit the primitive lattice (see p. 136), but recently Ueda and Tatekawa (1966) reported anorthites with transitional lattices occurring as phenocrysts in basalt of the Mitaki area, Sendai, Japan.

Hydrothermal experiments (Goldsmith and Ehlers, 1952) indicate that anorthite is stable in the presence of water at temperatures down to 350°C. A hexagonal polymorph of anorthite, unknown in nature, is consistently synthesized at lower temperatures.

1.31 Lime deficient anorthite: Schwantke's molecule

Schwantke (1909) proposed that K-feldspar at elevated temperatures was able to take into solid solution both Na-feldspar and a molecule of the formula $Ca_{\frac{1}{2}}AlSi_3O_8$. Upon cooling, unmixing would take place and the exsolved phases would be plagioclase and quartz.

Schwantke's ideas were elaborated by other workers. There are numerous observations that myrmekite is directly linked with perthite exsolution (see discussion in section 1.412). The theory is based on the assumption that the 'Schwantke molecule', viz. $Ca_{\frac{1}{2}}AlSi_3O_8$ exists as solid solution in high-temperature alkali feldspar. The nature of the Schwantke molecule can be explained in terms of lattice vacancies (Phillips, 1964).

Experimental work (Carman and Tuttle, 1963; Duffin, 1964; Wyart and Sabatier, 1965) proved that the extent of solid solution of this molecule at high temperatures and high vapour pressure is considerable. At 600°C both $KAlSi_3O_8$ and $NaAlSi_3O_8$ will take about 30 mole per cent of $Ca_{\frac{1}{2}}AlSi_3O_8$ into solid solution (see p. 28).

Recently, Perry (1966, 1968) has shown mathematically that the chemical analyses of feldspar cannot be recalculated satisfactorily in terms of Or, Ab, An; they require additional components, and one of them may advantageously be chosen to be $Ca_{\frac{1}{2}}AlSi_3O_8$.

It is not yet possible to discuss the role of the Schwantke molecule in natural feldspar. Although laboratory experiments prove its existence, its presence in the natural minerals, thus far, has not been directly verified by optic measurements or by specific measurements of other physical properties; the effect of this molecule on the physical constants is unknown. An extended discussion is, therefore, premature. But the development of new methods of determining the presence and the quantity of this molecule in the feldspar lattice, and research into its mode of formation and its stability relations should be watched with keen anticipation, for it will most certainly throw new light on many facets of feldspar mineralogy.

1.4 THE FELDSPAR SERIES

1.41 Alkali feldspar

The alkali feldspars are mixtures, or else mixed crystals, of potassium feldspar and sodium feldspar. At elevated temperatures they form a complete series of solid solution that is conventionally divided into three intervals: sanidine (or orthoclase), soda sanidine (or soda orthoclase), anorthoclase, see figure 1.14. They take some calcium feldspar into solid solution.

1.411 Solid solutions

Stable mixed crystals exist only at elevated temperatures. Under equilibrium conditions exsolution takes place below $\simeq 700°$c. However, the diffusion rates are low, and the undercooled mixed crystals persist indefinitely in a metastable state at room temperature. To them belong the sanidine and anorthoclases of the effusive rocks and tuffs.

The subsolidus relations are shown in figure 1.14. One end member is triclinic, the other is monoclinic. The transition point, which at room temperature is at Or_{33}, Ab_{67}, changes rapidly with temperature. The transition is spontaneous, whether induced by change in temperature or change in composition; it is therefore a typical displacive transition which leaves the aluminium distribution pattern unaffected, i.e. it is identical on either side of the transition line.

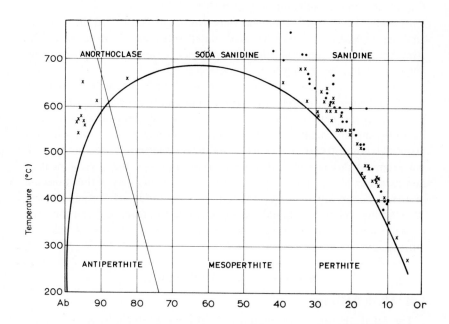

FIGURE 1.14 Subsolidus relations in the alkali feldspar series
The projection points represent the chemical composition of various rock-
forming feldspars in relation to the temperature at which they were formed
(determined by the two-feldspar thermometer). Crosses and circles refer
to triclinic phases and to monoclinic phases respectively, as they are now
observed (most of them were monoclinic at the time of formation).
The heavy curve is the solvus. Homogeneous mixed crystals are stable
above the solvus; but mixed crystals below the solvus have a higher
free energy and will eventually unmix and perthites are formed
However, the formation of perthites requires a diffusion of Na ions
against the concentration gradient. In a narrow zone on the concave
side of the solvus, this 'uphill diffusion' is impossible without the
addition of some external energy; not until the spinodal curve (not
shown in the figure but lying inside and approximately conformable to
the solvus) is crossed can spontaneous perthite formation take place. On
the solvus the solid solutions and the exsolved products have equal free
energy: solvus = $\partial\Delta F/\partial x = 0$; the spinodal curve is the locus of the
second derivative with respect to composition: spinode = $\partial^2\Delta F/\partial x^2 = 0$.
Furthermore, the unmixing reactions: anorthoclase → antiperthite; soda
sanidine → mesoperthite; sanidine → perthite are extremely slow at low
temperatures, and the sanidines, etc., if once brought down to ordinary
temperature, remain in the homogeneous state, metastably, for geological
periods

The physical properties of these alkali feldspars are unusual, and not paralleled in other mineral groups; they are specially considered in section 3.23.

1.412 Perthites and antiperthites

At lower temperatures, an exsolution takes place in the solid state, and characteristic intergrowths known as perthites are formed.

Perthites have a very wide distribution, indeed the great majority of the alkali feldspars are more or less perthitic, and, as new knowledge accumulates about the plagioclases, it becomes increasingly clear that antiperthites are common in plagioclases of all compositions, see, e.g. Rimsaite and Lachance (1966). Thus, perthitic intergrowths represent the most common mineral combinations in nature and merit special attention.

Since the early investigations by Breithaupt, Gerhard and Tschermak (see figure 1.15) mineralogists have been fascinated by this peculiar mineral intergrowth, and sundry guesses and theories have been offered to explain its development.

During recent years it has been shown that the formation of perthite is governed by extremely complex combinations of different processes of great consequence in paragenetic studies (see caption to figure 1.14). These processes explain a variety of growth patterns and mineral associations which used to be regarded as unrelated phenomena.

A description and classification of typical perthites will be given, followed by a discussion of the processes responsible for their development and evolution.

Compositionally, a distinction may be made between common *perthite*, *mesoperthite* and *antiperthite*. They are made up, respectively, of (1) a host crystal of K-feldspar with inclusions of albite, (2) an intimate mixture of about equal amounts of K-feldspar and albite (sometimes oligoclasic), and (3) a host crystal of albite (or plagioclase) with inclusions of K-feldspar. (Similar phenomena are the peristerites and the labradorizing plagioclases composed of sub x-ray intergrowths of two plagioclases, see sections 1.422 and 1.423.)

Morphologically, the exsolved phase typically forms small strings, or lamellae, or blebs of some shape making up a characteristic pattern (figures 1.15–1.19). Usually there is crystallographic continuity between the exsolved phase and the host crystal.

Sometimes, however, the unmixing of plagioclase proceeds in a manner which results in the formation of a fine, myrmekite-like intergrowth of potassium feldspar and reoriented plagioclase. Apparently similar structures have been described as myrmekitic antiperthite by Geier and Sederholm (Drescher-Kaden, 1948).

Again, the unmixing of potassium-rich ternary feldspars may result in the formation of an intergrowth of plagioclase and quartz which may be very difficult to distinguish from true myrmekite. Indeed, often recrystallization takes place during and after the unmixing; both the potassium and sodium feldspars may invert diffusively and become reoriented, or the

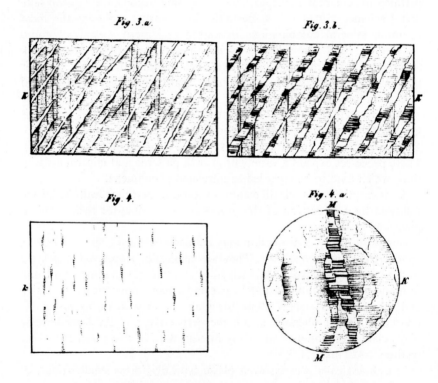

FIGURE 1.15 Tschermak's (1864) original drawings of perthites
Figures 3(a) and 3(b) give natural scale and three times magnification, respectively. Perthite from Chester, Pa., U.S.A. On (001) are lamellae parallel to (110) and (100), those parallel to (110) show albite twins. Figures 4 and 4(a) give natural scale and 80 times magnification, respectively. Green perthite from Sungangarsok, Greenland, shows lamellae parallel to (100) with albite twins

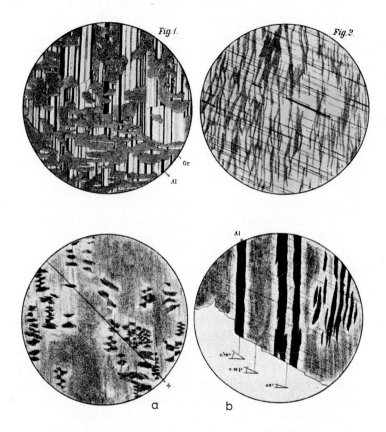

FIGURE 1.16 Brögger's (1890) drawings of iridescent cryptoperthite and of microperthite, composition Or_{40},Ab_{60}, Frederiksvaern (= Stavern), Norway

Figures a and b show thin sections parallel to (010) and (001) respectively with coarse albite lamellae (black), and cryptoperthitic areas in between (grey); the albite lamellae are surrounded by light rims (white on the figures). On (010) albite exhibits an extinction angle of $19°$; the white rims show only $5°$, but this value gradually increases toward the grey crypto-perthitic areas in which it attains $12°$ (this is graphically indicated in the drawing). Brögger's conclusion was that the original homogeneous alkali feldspar (Or_{40}, Ab_{60}) had 'split' (= exsolved) into the two components (pure Or in the white rims, and pure Ab in the black lamellae). The grey areas represent submicroscopic 'splitting', for which he introduced the name cryptoperthite. Figures 1 and 2 show two sections of a microperthite, 70 times magnified and represent thin sections parallel to (001) and (010), respectively. Orthoclase is grey, albite with its twin lamellae is white and black

exsolved albite may dissolve and pass into solution with the plagioclase present to form one homogeneous phase. Eventually, the original unmixing pattern will be completely obliterated (Ramberg, 1962). The evolution of granite texture by processes of this kind was convincingly demonstrated by Tuttle (1952).

The mechanism of the unmixing will be treated presently, after a short review of the mineralogical (morphological) classification of the types of perthite.

Classification of perthites

I. According to the size of the lamellae (Tuttle, 1952) the following exsolution series emerges:

1. Sub x-ray perthite 15 Å 2. X-ray perthite $< 1\,\mu$ 3. Cryptoperthite 1–$5\,\mu$ (Becke, 1880) 4. Microperthite 5–100 μ (Brögger, 1890) 5. (Macro) Perthite 100–1000 μ ($= 1$ mm)

II. Based on textural features (first considered by Olaf Andersen, 1928) a similar genetic series is obtained:

1. String perthite. The strings are rounded, often elliptic, shading into lenticular forms. They lie parallel to (010), forming an angle of $-73°$ with (001). The diameter is 1–10 μ or less.
2. Film perthite. The films never exceed 10 μ and are usually much thinner; they lie normal to (010) and at an angle of $-73°$ to (001).
3. Vein perthite. The veins are about 0·1 mm thick, often running parallel to (001), but frequently in other directions.
4. Patch perthite. The patches are short lamellae of Carlsbad–albite twins arranged in the peculiar way that has given rise to the term chess-board albite. They are frequently elongated in the direction of the b axis when seen in sections parallel to (001), and elongated roughly parallel to the c axis in sections $\|$(010).
5. Interlocking perthite. The two feldspars penetrate each other in bodies with sinuous and slightly interlocking contact faces.

Additional varieties are:

6. Guttate perthite. The drops are about 0·02 mm in diameter; some of them resolve under high magnification into a multitude of very thin disc-like plates or films, one behind the other like the leaves in a book. These leaves are roughly parallel to (100) (Barth, 1930).
7. Braid perthite. The braids consist of thin, intertwined ribbons or lenses oriented parallel to ($1\bar{1}0$) and (110); named by Goldich and

Kinser (1939), they were first described by Tschermak (1864), see figure 1.15.

8. Plate perthite. The plates lie in the zone [010] forming an angle of 20° with the base (001) (Laves and Soldatos, 1962, 1963).

Perthite lamellae of various orientation, of various morphology and of various chemical composition and structural state may all be present in the same host crystal of potassium feldspar (see, for example, Ito and Sadanaga, 1952; Laves, 1952; Mawdsley, 1927; de Saénz, 1965).

MacKenzie and Smith (1962) have arranged the perthites in what they loosely called a 'cooling sequence' from 1 to 5

	Host K-feldspar	Lamellae	Host rock
1	Monoclinic	Anorthoclase	Lavas
2	Monoclinic	Anorthoclase and plagioclase	Dikes
3	Monoclinic	Two plagioclases	Granites, syenites
4	Monoclinic	One plagioclase	Various granitoids
5	Triclinic	One plagioclase	Granitoids and gneisses

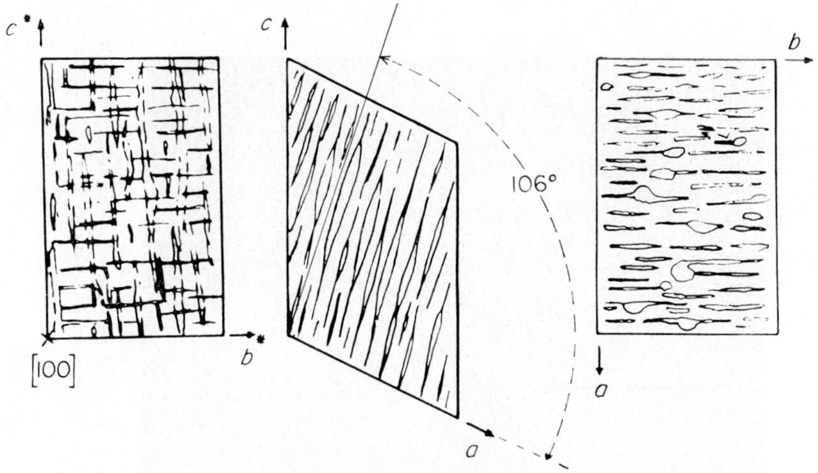

FIGURE 1.17 Aspect of film and string microperthite in different directions, Valentines, Uruguay. (From Saénz, 1965.) The bulk composition is Or_{42}, Ab_{44}, An_{14}. The unmixed phase is oligoclase (An_{18-20}) in a host of microcline. The films lie on ($\bar{h}$ 0 l) faces inclined about 106° to (001). The strings lie along [l 0 h] contained in the (h 0 l) plane; these directions coincide approximately with ($\bar{6}$01) and [106]. On (001) the strings appear as spots and the films as thin straight lines

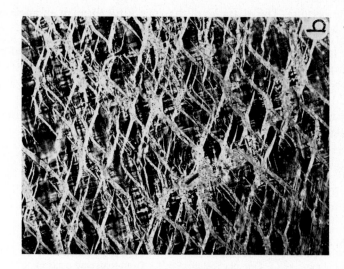

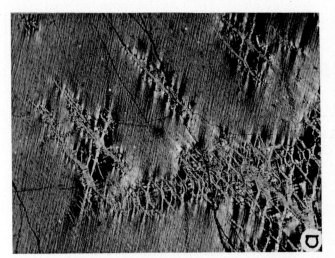

FIGURE 1.18 Film perthite which in places form braid perthite. Cross twins of microcline are seen between the perthite lamellae. Section parallel to (001). Linear magnification. (*a*) × 10, (*b*) × 16. From larvikite, Stavern, Norway

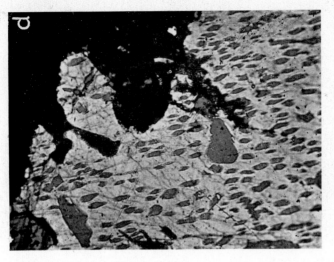

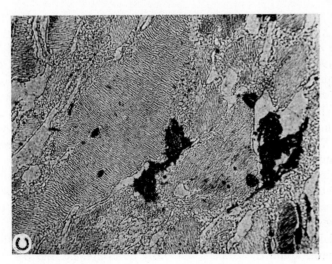

FIGURE 1.18 Film perthite passing into guttate perthite. Such drop perthites are characteristic of calcic rocks. The exsolved phase is usually oligoclasic and even andesinic in composition. The drop shape is obviously related to this composition. Linear Magnification (c) × 10, (d) × 18. From jotunnorite, Jotunheimen, Norway

FIGURE 1.18 (*e*) Very coarse vein perthite pattern in amazonite. The albitic perthite lamellae (grey and black) are up to 5 mm wide and exhibit polysynthetic albite twins. The white, cross-hatched pattern in the microcline is typical M-twinning. From pegmatite, Tördal, Norway

Sanidine with monalbitic cryptoperthite lamellae was described by Soldatos (1965) and by Jung (1965); it should be placed at the top of the cooling sequence.

Mechanism of the perthite formation. The pioneering x-ray work of Kozu and Endo (1921) on perthites showed that the separate phases could be homogenized and partially unmixed again by suitable heat treatment. This shows unequivocally that the principal genetic processes are: solution, exsolution, resolution.

In principle, the formation of perthite is explained by the physico-chemical fact that feldspars form extended series of solid solutions at elevated temperatures; at lower temperatures the solutions become unstable and exsolve into the constituent components.

The initial stage is the nucleation of the exsolving phase. For perthite blebs to form, uphill diffusion is obviously necessary, i.e. the Na ions must migrate against the concentration gradient. The solvus (figure 1.14) indicates where the unmixed phase has lower free energy than the mixed crystal, the spinodal (a curve situated on the inner, concave side of the solvus) indicates where the uphill diffusion becomes possible. The nucleation is followed by either a continuous precipitation or a discontinuous (or cellular) precipitation.

During *continuous* precipitation the precipitate is drawn from the surroundings, resulting in concentration gradients which decrease with increasing distance from the nucleus. This is the normal process during the exsolution of alkali feldspar, in which the exsolution relations are simple. The Al–Si–oxygen chains are not affected, only K and Na are relocated in the crystal lattice (Schwarcs, 1966). The nuclei of albite (or of K-feldspar) are forced to grow along special crystallographic directions that are determined by the host feldspar. This arises from a strong tendency to eliminate excess strains by forming *coherent* interfaces. The close similarity of the two crystal lattices, those of the K-feldspar and

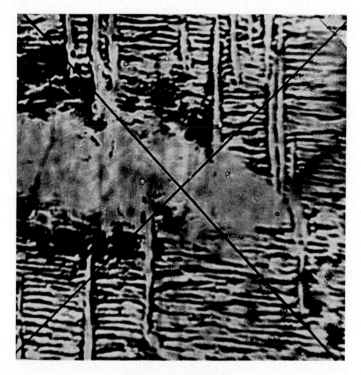

FIGURE 1.19 Antiperthite

Section parallel to (001). Black is orthoclase, white is albite. Neither orthoclase nor albite shows twin lamellae; both phases exhibit monoclinic optics, the extinction on (001) is straight, see text p. 124

albite, allows coherent interfaces to form only if the two lattices are oriented in parallel.

Examples of the strong dominance of the host crystal over the precipitate are afforded *inter alia* by Aberdam and others (1964, see figure 1.20),

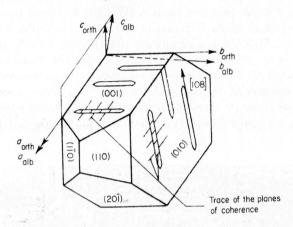

FIGURE 1.20 Schematic drawing of an orthoclase cryptoperthite from a pegmatite of the valley of l'Ardèche. The albite lamellae are parallel to $(\bar{8}01)$ and have a width of 0.5μ. a^* in orthoclase is parallel to a^* in albite; the faces (010) of orthoclase, and particularly of albite, are deformed on an x-ray scale so as to become mutually parallel. (After Aberdam and others, 1964)

and by Soldatos (1962) who found cryptoperthite lamellae displaying two types of orientation:

Type I:
    1. In microclines showing albite twinning:
       b^* in albite is parallel to b^* in microcline.
    2. In microclines showing pericline twinning:
       b^* in albite is parallel to b in microcline.

Type II:
    a^* in cryptoalbite is parallel to a^* in microcline.

He concluded that cryptoperthites exsolving at elevated temperatures, when the potassium feldspar still is monoclinic, are of type I; coherency to the host is preserved in the c direction and the composition face is therefore approximately parallel to the c axis. Cryptoperthites exsolving at lower temperatures from a triclinic potassium feldspar are affected by the triclinic symmetry and will be of type II, see figure 1.20.

In very coarsely twinned microclines, or in single microclines, plate perthite develops because the Al/Si distribution in microcline and in albite tends to be coherent.

The *discontinuous* precipitation process is fundamentally different. This kind of exsolution is identical to phase transformations in alloys. Nucleation takes place along microscopically small fissures, around small inclusions and at grain boundaries; growth of the precipitate of, say, albitic composition will proceed into an adjacent K-feldspar with which the albite has no crystallographic relation. An incoherent interface is thus formed; this interface, in contrast to coherent interfaces, rapidly moves into the host crystal, the growth rate is high because of the uncoupled, rapid transfer of atoms across the boundary.

There is an interesting statistical correlation between locale of nucleation and type of precipitate: intragranular perthite, nucleated within the host crystal and dominated by it, grows by continuous precipitation. Intergranular perthite nucleated at grain boundaries may grow by discontinuous precipitation (Carstens, 1967).

A comparison of the continuous and the discontinuous processes of precipitation shows that perthites formed by continuous precipitation exhibit coherent interfaces and parallel orientation with respect to the host crystal; the rate of growth is low, and the direction of growth is determined by the host crystal. Carstens (1967) contended that the restrictions thus imposed on the precipitate may prevent attainment of physicochemical equilibrium during growth. Perthites formed by discontinuous precipitation have incoherent interfaces, and are free to grow in any direction; the supply of atoms is copious and the growth rate is high. Chemical equilibrium is attained.

In the plagioclases and in the ternary feldspars, the kinetics of the exsolution reactions are complicated; for not only are the K, Na and Ca ions affected, but the Al and Si ions also have to move during the exsolution process. The attainment of equilibrium is therefore seriously obstructed; the consequences are important, for, in addition to the crystallographic orientation and the texture, the sorts of phases in the precipitate are also influenced by the sites of nucleation and growth.

There is strong evidence that during cooling under equilibrium conditions an alkali feldspar containing calcium in solid solution will precipitate a fine intergrowth of plagioclase and quartz. This is not a classical perthite, but, nevertheless, a precipitate formed by exsolution in the same manner as perthite is formed.

It is highly significant that such mixtures of plagioclase–quartz are never found inside a host feldspar, but nucleate and burgeon inter-granularly or along incoherent boundaries. In contrast, intragranular (non-equilibrium) precipitation invariably results in coherent growths and perthitic structures, see Spencer (1945), Voll (1960), Ramberg (1962), Hubbart (1966).

The substitution of alkalis by calcium in the alkali feldspars is best explained by the relation

$$2(\mathrm{Na,K}) \rightarrow \mathrm{Ca}\square$$

where $\square$ stands for vacant sites. Quartz is liberated by decomposition of the supersaturated alkali feldspar (Phillips, 1964).

In this connexion, it should be noted that recent experimental work of Carman and Tuttle (1963, 1967) indicates an appreciable amount of Schwantke's (1909) silica-rich 'anorthite' molecule in plagioclases, see section 1.31.

The following molecules form series of solid solutions:

$$\mathrm{NaAlSi_3O_8} - \mathrm{Ca_{\frac{1}{2}}AlSi_3O_8}$$

$$\mathrm{KAlSi_3O_8} \ - \mathrm{Ca_{\frac{1}{2}}AlSi_3O_8}$$

Wyart and Sabatier (1965) demonstrated that by keeping albite (or adul-aria) in contact with a solution of $CaCl_2$ in an autoclave at 300–600°c, mixed crystals of this series are formed containing up to 30% of the calcium end member. If higher concentrations are attempted, SiO_2 is precipitated (as cristobalite), the end products being anorthite and silica.

Temperature of the perthite formation. (Hubbart, 1965) investigated antiperthite from charnockites and found by microprobe analysis that almost pure orthoclase substance had exsolved from a ternary feldspar of bulk composition $Or_{13}Ab_{46}An_{41}$. This composition indicates that the exsolution started just above 900°c and continued to temperatures under 500°c, see figure 5.45.

An interesting feature of many perthite lamellae is that they are zoned. Barth (1956a) found that, among some 200 thin sections of pegmatite K-feldspars, 18 exhibited zoning of the perthite lamellae. Typically, the central part is in the range An_{10}–An_{25}, and the rim almost pure albite. By using the principle of the two-feldspar thermometer, Barth concluded that in these pegmatites the exsolution process started immediately after the formation of the alkali feldspars, around 600°c, and continued down to 400°c, where it stopped, probably because the energy barrier prevents further diffusion.

The perthite lamellae in the pegmatite feldspars are often very coarse and widely spaced; this indicates large diffusion distances for the alkali ions, which again indicates a great mobility of the lattice constituents at moderate temperatures (see also Wyart and Sabatier, 1956a, 1960). Orthoclase or M-twinned microcline may under these conditions transform into the microcline single crystals that are found sporadically in most pegmatites.

It is worthy of mention that if the feldspars become subjected to external pressure the strain energy will activate the sodium atoms, and exsolution will continue at still lower temperatures until practically complete unmixing is attained.

Wyart and Sabatier (1962), Gabis and Turon (1964), made synthetic cryptoperthite intergrowths by diffusion at around 500°c and 650 bar vapour pressure in the presence of alkali chloride. The orientation and crystallography of the resulting intergrowths are similar to those of natural perthites.

Cathodoluminescence, the emission of light during electron bombardment, is a new tool in the study of perthites. Smith and Stenstrom (1965) showed that separate phases in feldspar perthites can be distinguished by colour and intensity variations. The luminescence emitted by microcline is a function of the orientation of the crystal lattice, and the cross-hatched twinning can be seen. Occurrence of mottled luminescence indicates that microcline nucleates at the boundary between orthoclase and albite. Other phenomena have supported the suggestion, already made by Spencer (1930, 1935) on account of his observations on 'shadow' perthite crossed by a microperthite, that earlier stages of exsolution may be effaced by homogenization; they may correspond to certain intensity variations in the luminescence.

Thus, the study of perthites by this method offers exciting possibilities of bringing to light new details of the complex history of their formation and evolution.

Not treated in this section are the inadequately known exsolution phenomena exhibited by the peristerites and the labradorizing plagioclases. For their investigation and for the investigation of moonstone, the electron microscope has proved to be of great value. They are discussed in sections 1.422 and 1.423.

In a general way, the interplay of temperature, stress, locale of nucleation, rate of nucleation, rate of diffusion, catalytic action of volatile and other elements explains the great variety observed in size, orientation and structure of the perthite intergrowths, and connects perthites with more myrmekite-like intergrowths of two feldspars and of plagioclase–quartz.

A good example of the type of information pertinent to rock genesis which can be extracted from careful feldspar studies is to be found in a paper by Parsons (1965), in which it is deduced that the feldspars of the syenite of Loch Ailsh (Assynt, Scotland) crystallized as homogeneous, sodium-rich sanidines (of the bulk composition now observed) in the range 1060–750°c, and between zero and 3000 bar vapour pressure. Cooling produced (*a*) varying degrees of Al/Si order and (*b*) unmixing into a two-sanidine perthite (very top of the 'cooling sequence', p. 21) which inverted to a sanidine–anorthoclase perthite above 615°c, yielding M-twinned Na-rich phases (number 1 in the cooling sequence). Further cooling then produced low-albite–microcline perthite (number 5 in the cooling sequence); late-stage fluids partly in conjunction with stress lead to local development of ultra-coarse perthite, and partly, to ultra-high triclinicity of the microcline (see section 3.213).

These results suggest that detailed and meticulous work is necessary and that generalized studies of K-feldspar as petrogenetic indicators have little value.

1.42 Sodium–Calcium feldspars or plagioclases

1.421 General

The continuous mixed-crystal series from albite to anorthite is sub-divided as follows (Calkins, 1917):

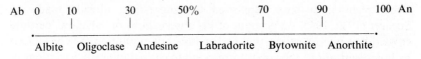

A few years after the discovery of isomorphism by Mitscherlich in 1820, J. F. Hessel (1826) proposed that the feldspars represent isomorphous series of sodium–potassium aluminotrisilicate with calcium aluminoorthosilicate. Tschermak (1864) declared the plagioclases to represent 'isomorphic mixtures' of $NaAlSi_3O_8$ and $CaAl_2Si_2O_8$. But this was met with vigorous opposition: the formulae were not analogous, and according to the accepted Mitscherlich idea of isomorphic substitution the bivalent Ca should not substitute for the univalent Na. As a puzzling contrast the isomorphic mixtures of Ab and Or are less perfect, although they only involve a simple substitution of Na for K in analogous formulae.

Many mineralogists and chemists at the time preferred to regard the plagioclases as made up of a number of discrete chemical compounds, or double salts, at fixed compositional intervals between Ab and An. The minerals oligoclase, andesine or labradorite were then regarded as having a constant chemical composition. Fouqué (1894), concluding his great work on feldspars of volcanic rocks (p. 604) wrote: 'Au point de vue pratique la loi de Tschermak présente une utilité incontestable . . . mais . . . la simplicité, la beauté des conclusions ne doit pas faire oublier l'imperfection des prémisses. . . . Il ne faut donc pas attribuer aux consequences qui s'en déduisent une rigueur qui en dépasse la portée initiale.'

Not until Day and Allen in 1905 by melting and recrystallization experiments demonstrated the formation of crystals of all compositions was the solid solution theory firmly established. For further historical data see chapter 6.

Here it is important to add that although the plagioclases at elevated temperatures form a series of nearly ideal solid solutions, the conditions at lower temperatures are much more complicated.

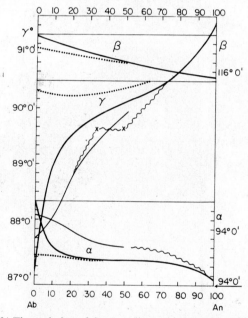

FIGURE 1.21 The variation of the crystallographic constants with the composition in plagioclases. Full curves: Natural plagioclases; average values from goniometer measurements by Schmidt (1915). Thin curves: natural plagioclases, a series of 9 samples, x-ray measurements by Smith (1956). Wavy lines: natural plagioclases, x-ray measurements by Bambauer and others (1965, 1967); observe the breaks in angle γ at about An_{30} and An_{50}. Dotted curves: high-temperature plagioclases after Smith (1956). Compare figure 4.24 which gives the variations in the reciprocal axes at 1000°c

All plagioclase feldspars exhibit triclinic symmetry. The crystallographic elements and the physical properties vary throughout the series from albite to anorthite and are intermediate between the two end members; but the high-temperature plagioclases that approach the conditions of an ideal mixed-crystal series, exhibit properties that are different from those of the low-temperature plagioclases that do not mix in all proportions, see figure 1.21.

The principal crystal faces are the same as those of the other feldspars, and the habits are similar (the small obliquity of the triclinic cell makes this possible). Cleavage (001) is perfect, but (010) varies, and is apparently better the more pronounced the lamellar structure of the albite twins. The murchisonite parting, so common in orthoclases, seems absent in plagioclases. Skeleton crystals and microlites develop in many lavas and are also found in artificial preparations.

FIGURE 1.22 Zoned plagioclase in quartz microdiorite, Estérel, France. The crystal is 2 mm long. The core has An_{50} except for the two irregular white areas representing strongly corroded relics of an early plagioclase of An_{70}. The outermost zones approach An_{40}. There are two rod-shaped inclusions of green hornblende. (After Quin, 1962)

Twinning is frequent; characteristic of all plagioclases is the regularly repeated twinning according to the 'albite law' (section 2.2) resulting in a fine striation on the (001) cleavage plane. It can be used as a diagnostic feature to distinguish the plagioclases from all other feldspars. (In the other triclinic feldspars, microcline and anorthoclase, which are also twinned according to the albite law, the twin lamellae are microscopically thin and cannot be recognized even with a magnifying glass.) Twinning is also common after the pericline law; if polysynthetic, this gives another series of fine striations seen on (010), see section 2.4. Carlsbad, Baveno and Manebach twins are also common.

Zoning is common in the plagioclases and often covers a large compositional range, particularly in crystals of effusive rocks. The equilibrium diagram by Bowen (1913) of the system albite–anorthite (figure 5.17) explains the development of normally zoned crystals of plagioclase (calcic core, sodic shell) in a cooling magma. In certain lavas, intricately zoned feldspars with sodic centres, or with alternating zones as shown in figures 1.22–1.25 are observed. In order to explain this it has been postulated that lava pulsations are brought about by discharge of mineralizers, or by incomplete decantations in restricted magma parts of different

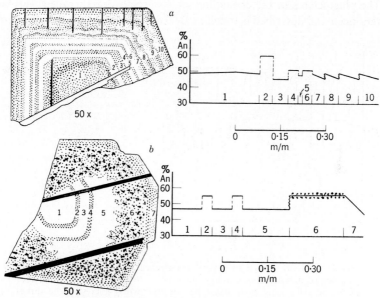

FIGURE 1.23 Examples of zoned plagioclase crystals. The curves represent the anorthite contents of the consecutive zones. Ordinate = anorthite content, abscissa = distance from core. (After Paliuc, *Schweiz. Mineral. Petrog. Mitt.*, **12**, 1932)

temperatures and viscosities or else that the feldspars did not crystallize from a magma of the composition of the rock in which they are found.

Zoning patterns of igneous plagioclases have been discussed by many authors, for example, Emmons and Mann (1953), Hills (1936), Homma (1932), Larsen and Irving (1938), Leedal (1952), Pittman (1963), Vance (1962). Figure 1.24 shows the pattern of oscillatory normal zoning (Phemister, 1934) with the range of values reported for the zone width and the amplitude of the compositional oscillations; Harloff (1927) had explained the oscillations as a result of an interplay between the rate of diffusion in a magma and the rate of growth of plagioclase crystals; he is supported by Bottinga and others (1966). Wiebe (1967) interpreted the pre-intrusive history of a granite stock by plagioclase zoning.

Vance (1965, 1966) described so-called patchy zoning (see figure 1.25) and explained it as the result of a two-stage replacement process involving resorption (related to a decrease in pressure) followed by crystallization of a more sodic feldspar at lower pressure. He believes that zoning of this type is a diagnostic igneous textural feature indicating that the magma contained a crystalline phase and was neither superheated nor saturated in its volatile components.

The plagioclases of the crystalline schists are also often zoned; this was first noticed and described in detail by Becke (1903), who also demonstrated

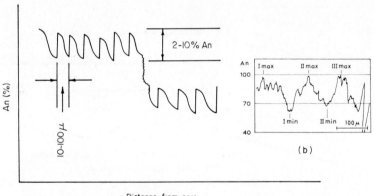

FIGURE 1.24 (*a*) Sketch of typical occurrence of oscillatory zoning in plagioclase phenocrysts. (Bottinga and others, 1966); (*b*) The fine structure of the actual zoning as revealed by electron probe analysis. The three maxima correspond to 98, 100 and 97% An, and the two minima to 66 and 69% An respectively. Plagioclase from a gabbro dike, Alatornio, Northern Finland. (Härme and Siivola, *Compt. Rend. Soc. Geol. Finlande*, **38**, 1966)

that in these rocks regular inverse zoning (sodic core, calcic shell) is common, but the range is never as large as that found in magmatic plagioclases. The inverse zoning indicates a response to increasing temperature (Barth, 1956b), i.e. it developed during progressive metamorphism.

Cannon (1966) demonstrated that careful studies of zoning in metamorphic plagioclase, with its implication of disequilibrium conditions, are of great help in unravelling metamorphic/metasomatic episodes.

Zoned plagioclases in anatectic rocks are discussed on p. 50.

Clouded plagioclases are found in various types of rocks, igneous and metamorphic. Clouding may also be encountered in K-feldspar, apatite, spinel, olivine, pyroxenes, amphiboles, micas, quartz, garnet, calcite, but is most characteristic in plagioclase. The particles which produce clouding generally consist of opaque ore, but other minerals, such as spinel, garnet, rutile and others, may be present both in the plagioclases and in the surrounding rock. Powder diffraction patterns of concentrates of dust-like particles from zones of bronze iridescence and blue iridescence in labradorite phenocrysts in the Adirondack anorthosite revealed magnetite as the only apparent oxide phase in the bronze zones, and coexisting magnetite and brookite in the blue zones (Boone and others, 1967).

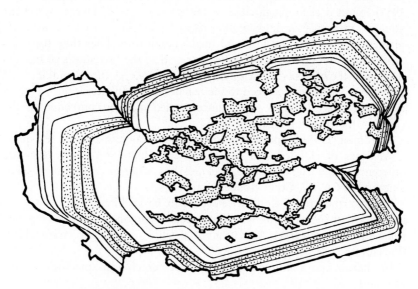

FIGURE 1.25 Patchy zoning. Two plagioclase grains in parallel synneusis relationship. Rim and included plagioclase *stippled:* $An_{13} \rightarrow An_{17}$. Core *without stippling:* $An_{24} \rightarrow An_{27}$. Section parallel to (010). The patches are elongate parallel to (001). (Vance, 1965)

The 'stuffed' plagioclases (*plagioclases farcis, gefüllte Plagioklase*) differ by containing predominantly particles of clinozoisite and muscovite, minerals that are not otherwise encountered in the encasing rock, but may be explained as occurring diaphtoretically in the feldspars (Cornelius, 1935).

Poldervaart and Gilkey (1954) gave a review on clouded plagioclases: slight clouding may be the result of an exsolution of iron which was dissolved in the plagioclase crystal at the time of its formation. More intense clouding may have been produced by diffusion of extraneous material into the crystal after its formation.

Cloudy zones are frequent, particularly in zoned plagioclase phenocrysts from volcanic rocks. In trachybasalts and trachyandesites from Chaîne de Puys, France, the plagioclases exhibit clear cores of andesine and shells of labradorite between which a continuous cloudy zone is situated (Bentor, 1951).

The pattern of the distribution of the clouding is variegated. Strong clouding is only observed in intermediate plagioclases. In gabbroic rocks, plagioclase may be clouded in the phenocrysts but clear in the groundmass. Herz (1951) observed that in the Baltimore gabbro the clouding increased with increasing An content of the plagioclases. Carstens (1955, 1957) found a clear plagioclase in the main norite of Dyröy, while the younger, transgressive gabbro dikes carried plagioclases that are distinctly pigmented. In coronites he found the clouding to be later than the polysynthetic twinning, and temporally restricted to the first stages of the formation of the coronas; the clouding exists as long as the development of the corona garnets is confined to the reaction rims. In later stages, as soon as garnets start to grow in an uncontrolled manner, unrelated to the coronas, the clouding disappears.

Friedman (1955) found that coronites always contain clouded feldspars.

Analyses of clouded and non-clouded feldspars show no systematic difference in the iron contents. Nockolds and Mitchell (1948) found small amounts of Cu, Ni, Co in clouded plagioclases.

The distribution of clouded feldspars in basic dikes in Mysore State indicates that the clouding was introduced in conjunction with the palingenic (or rheomorphic) formation of a suite of younger charnockites (Pichamuthu, 1959).

In charnockite and in charnockite aureoles clouded plagioclases are common.

The cause of the clouding is obscure. In addition to exsolution, advocated by MacGregor (1931), Anderson (1937), and others, the idea of a later introduction of iron has been discussed, for example, during thermal metamorphism. But Wager and Deer (1939) argued that the clouding of the plagioclases in the Skaergaard intrusives cannot be due to subsequent thermal metamorphism because it occurs only in the middle part of the layered series, and is absent in the uppermost layered rocks.

Bentor's (1951) and Carstens' (1955, 1957) observations are in favour of a magmatic origin of the clouding.

Stern (1964) suggested that the preferential clouding of the inter-mediate plagioclases could be explained by the inhomogeneous structures (schillerization of labradorite, peristerites) which permit easy diffusion of foreign matter.

Rao (1964) thinks that clouding in some plagioclases is neither of exsolution origin nor of extraneous source, but represents a by-product in the metamorphic replacement of biotite and hornblende by plagio-clase.

1.422 High- and low-temperature variants

In the more detailed mineralogy of the plagioclase feldspars, the differ-ence between high- and low-temperature modifications plays a significant role (Köhler, 1942).

Within specific ranges of composition and temperature there are at least seven distinct crystalline lattices corresponding to variants in the plagioclase structure (see section 3.4).

The effect of temperature is most pronounced in the sodic part of the plagioclase series. The crystalline lattice of high albite takes a liberal amount of calcium into solid solution, but low albite accepts only traces of calcium (or potassium). In contrast to the continuous high-temperature series of mixed crystals, the plagioclases at room temperature thus exhibit a compositional break: between albite (An_1) and calcic oligoclase (An_{24}) there is a hiatus, no mixed crystals exist. Plagioclases of this range are inhomogeneous and are called *peristerites*.

Until quite recently this fact was unknown to mineralogists. The diffi-culties in detecting the hiatus lie chiefly in the very slow rates of the inter-crystalline ionic diffusion; a homogeneous high-temperature oligoclase of composition, say, An_{15} will, upon slow cooling, break up into two phases: albite and calcic oligoclase. But these phases are always submicroscopi-cally small, and only by investigations into rather complicated x-ray reflections has it been possible in recent years to arrive at the right interpretation. By the use of an optical microscope, even with the highest magnification, any oligoclase looks homogeneous, and its optical pro-perties, actually produced by the superposition of small crystalline lamellae, correspond to those of a mixed crystal. However, plagioclase crystallizing primarily at low temperatures can never assume any composition between An_1 and An_{24} (see figure 1.26).

It is now clear that two coexisting 'primary' plagioclases of different composition, albite and oligoclase, are present in some relatively low-grade metamorphic rocks (lower than the almandine or staurolite isograds). It

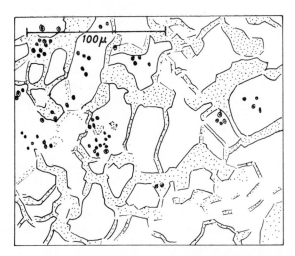

FIGURE 1.26 Albite–oligoclase relations in schists from Haast River, New Zealand. Thin grains of oligoclase (dotted) between albite grains. (Drawn from photo in Crawford, 1966)

is worthy of note that in such rocks the oligoclase has approximately twice as much potassium as the albite (see also, Brown, 1962; Christie, 1959, 1962; De Waard, 1959; Evans, 1964; Karl, 1954; Laves, 1954; Noble, 1962; Rutland, 1961, 1962; Wenk, 1958).

Peristerite was used by Böggild (1924) to designate oligoclase emitting a characteristic blue or bluish white lustre. The name was first used by Thomson (1843) for a perthite, see chapter 6. This material is often (falsely) called moonstone by jewellers. Laves (1954) demonstrated by x-ray studies that the lustre is a consequence of unmixing; Ribbe and van Cott (1962) observed the unmixed phases in dark-field and in phase-contrast microscopy.

Brown (1960) proposed that the more calcic oligoclases (An_{18-25}), as they exsolve, become unstable and react with other minerals in the rock, thus changing the bulk composition of the plagioclase toward albite. This process continues until the composition becomes such that the calcic phase is completely surrounded by albite and this can no longer react. Brown's hypothesis is supported by the ratio of albite to oligoclase in peristerites which is never less than 1:1 although it can be as great as 50:1, suggesting that any excess oligoclase is always removed by some mechanism.

Brown (1962) in a comprehensive review discussed the shape and position of the solvus and concluded that plagioclases in the compositional range An_2 to An_{17} are unmixed into two phases of about An_2 and An_{26}; the top of the solvus being at about 550°c. No plagioclase in the bulk composition range An_{17} to An_{26} has so far been found to be unmixed. According to Christie (1968) the explanation is that no uphill diffusion can take place in the composition range An_{17}–An_{26}, which lies between the solvus and the spinode (see figure 1.14 and caption).

Iiyama and others (1963), Iiyama (1966) determined experimentally that the peristerite solvus was unsymmetric with the top close to the albite side at 730°c.

Tsuji (1965) suggested that the solvus closes at the upper part of the amphibolite facies.

Crawford (1966) contended from her studies of two suites of regionally metamorphosed semi-pelitic schists that the albite limb of the curve is vertical in contrast to the sloping oligoclase limb, producing a skewed solvus. The crest of the solvus lies at a temperature between the almandine and staurolite isograds, perhaps 450 to 500°c. At low temperatures the area of unmixing extends from An_1 to An_{24}.

Fleet and Ribbe (1965) investigated peristerites in the range An_2–An_{17} by transmission electron microscopy and electron diffraction and found them to be unmixed in albite and oligoclase lamellae between a few hundred and several thousand angstrom units thick and approximately parallel to (0$\bar{8}$1).

Monroe and Sass (1967) observed lamellae in oligoclase (An_{15}) that were parallel to (0$\bar{8}$1), 1000 Å thick, and persisted for several microns before pinching out.

Nissen and Bollmann (1966) found the lattice constants of the exsolved oligoclase lamellae to correspond to An_{30}, but measurements on replicas indicated An_{18}. Consequently, the oligoclase lattice is deformed by the host albite, see pp. 26 and 74. This fact calls for great caution in the determination of the composition of the peristerite lamellae from published x-ray data (see Brown, 1960).

The peristerite lustre—as distinct from the diffuse scatter of moonstones—is characterized by sharp reflections. It is probably due to differences in refractive index between the two exsolved phases.

The lustre does not disappear at higher temperatures; dry heating produces lattice disorder *within* the lamellae, but not *between* them. But by prolonged heating under water pressure peristerites eventually homogenize.

Aventurine or *sunstone* is an interesting variety of plagioclase; it may be albitic, but is usually in the range oligoclase–labradorite. It shows a reddish–golden lustre or flitter caused by thin flakes oriented parallel to various structurally defined planes; they are usually scales of hematite, sometimes goethite or ilmenite (?); flakes of native copper (as in pottery, see p. 244) have been observed in a calcic labradorite from Modoc Co., Calif. (Andersen, 1917).

Similar aventurine flitter is known from other minerals, e.g. quartz, alkali feldspar, cordierite, cancrinite, carnallite.

Andersen's (1915) careful investigations show that the oriented hematite flakes lie parallel to planes that do not correspond to the growth planes of feldspar. Consequently, hematite is not formed during the growth of the feldspar.

If hematite is an exsolution product it should disappear upon heating. At temperatures above $1235°c$ the hematite inclusions do rapidly disappear, but, if subsequently kept at lower temperatures (e.g. at $1000°c$), they rapidly reappear at exactly the same spots. Andersen's explanation is that by intense heating a eutectic melt develops around the inclusions and congeals to a glass upon rapid cooling—the feldspar then looks homogeneous. By reheating at lower temperatures the glass devitrifies and hematite reappears.

Neumann and Christie (1962) found no correlation between the iron content of the plagioclase and the aventurine effect. But they found a marked difference in the structural state between the red aventurine core and the white dull mantle of twenty plagioclase samples from Bjordammen, Norway: the red cores represent the lowest thermal state, the white mantles a higher thermal state.

Various references are scattered in the literature which are likely to confuse the issue of the origin of aventurine. It seems that no final conclusions can be drawn from Andersen's experiments; the hematite inclusions (1) are not oriented parallel to growth planes of the feldspar, and (2) are not resorbed by the feldspar lattice upon heating.

It might also be added that the most probable exsolution product should be not hematite but iron feldspar, and subsequent alteration of iron feldspar into hematite is unlikely.

The origin of aventurine is still an open question. In the most recent paper on the subject, Neumann and Christie (1962, p. 134) state: 'we admit that, even with the aid of modern experimental and diagnostic equipment, we cannot add anything new to the excellent treatise on aventurine feldspars given more than 45 years ago by Olaf Andersen.'

1.423 Intermediate plagioclases

Plagioclases more calcic than oligoclase are possibly homogeneous at all temperatures, but indications of compositional hiatuses in the labradorite and bytownite ranges are found (see section 3.4). The difference between high- and low-temperature modifications becomes smaller with increasing calcium content, and although easily detectable optically or by x-rays, it loses some of its mineralogical significance. However, it remains an excellent tool in exploring the genetic relationships of rock complexes, see Table 1.1.

TABLE 1.1

Plagioclases from a vertical profile through the layered series of the Skaergaard intrusion. (From Gay, 1961)

Sample name	Height (m)	Composition[a] (% An)	Optics: state[b]	X-ray: state[b]
Unlaminated layered series	2500	32	L–LT	TH
	2500	27	TH	TH–H
Ferrogabbros	2450	27	H	H
	2450	32	TH	H
	2450	34	LT	L
	2400	32	T	TH
	2375	35	LT	LT
	2300	35	TH	H
	2200	38	TH	H
	2100	35	TH	H
	2050	39	T	T
	2000	37	LT	L–LT
	1800	39	T	T
	1700	42	LT	LT
Middle gabbros	1500	45	L–LT	L
	1200	46	L	L
	1050	52	L	L
Hypersthene–olivine gabbros	850	53	L	L
	500	55	L	—
	350	66	L	L
Transitional layered series	0	68	L	L

[a] The compositions could not be determined very accurately due to the marked zoning which occurs in many of the plagioclases. Average values are given.

[b] The structural states were determined both optically and by x-rays, and are classified as follows:

L = low; T = transitional; H = high, with combinations.

An interesting rock type is anorthosite, a plagioclasite, frequently forming very large 'batholiths' covering, in places, tens of thousands of square kilometres. Anorthosite is a monomineralic rock consisting almost exclusively of plagioclase whose composition usually corresponds to andesine or labradorite (but oligoclasic and bytownitic bodies are also known) almost always containing small amounts of alkali feldspar as antiperthitic intergrowths, see Carstens (1967). The anorthosite plagioclases are the low-temperature variants. High-temperature andesines and labradorites are found in lavas—they may be glassy as, for example, those from Etna, Vesuvius, Kilauea.

A particularly beautiful labradorite, An_{66}, in perfectly homogeneous transparent, large crystals is known from the newly formed volcanic island, Surtsey, off the southern coast of Iceland. Another transparent, labradorite phenocryst, $An_{67}Ab_{32}Or_1$ is found in basalt in Lake County, Oregon. The excellent quality of the crystals made it possible to determine the physical properties with great accuracy.

TABLE 1.2

Lattice parameters for high-temperature labradorite

	Surtsey[a]	Lake Co.[b]
$a:b:c$	0·6360:1:0·5523	0·6355:1:0·5520
a_0 (Å)	8·186	8·176
b_0 (Å)	12·871	12·865
c_0 (Å)	$2 \times 7·109$	$2 \times 7·102$
α	93° 34′	93° 27′
β	116° 02′	116° 03′
γ	90° 22′	90° 31′
V (Å³)	671	669·5

[a] Wenk and others (1965), Wenk (1966).
[b] Stewart and others (1966).

It is worthy of note that large non-zoned plagioclase crystals (An_{66-67}) are common in basaltic rocks whose normative anorthite content usually corresponds to a much more sodic plagioclase; the intratelluric formation of such crystals does not fully explain the high frequency of this composition.

Labradorite schiller is characteristic of plagioclases of intermediate composition. It was first noticed on pieces brought by a missionary, Mr.

Wolff, from the Isle of St. Paul, on the coast of Labrador (about 1770). In contrast to the peristerite lustre which is always bluish and restricted to faces near (010), the labradorite schiller is emitted in all colours and from faces of different orientation, but almost always visible through faces parallel to (010). Böggild's (1924) very careful measurements on a great number of crystals gave as result that there is no definite plane of schiller; it does not correspond to a crystallographic direction. Therefore it is probably irrelevant that Schröder (1964) found ($\bar{2}$ 10.1) as the actual plane of schiller in one labradorite of An_{55} (see also Baier and Pense, 1957).

In addition to the peristerite break from An_2 to about An_{26}, Doman and others (1965) found, in the andesine–labradorite range, two discontinuities indicating exsolution and consequential appearance of labradorization. Supporting evidence comes from electron-transmission micrographs of labradorite with schiller showing two kinds of alternating lamellae about $0.09\,\mu$ broad. However, x-ray and electron diffraction photographs of such material do not show any sign of exsolution lamellae or of twinning.

Laves and others (1965) tried to reconcile these facts by suggesting that true mixed crystals of intermediate plagioclase become unstable at low temperature (ca. 500°c?) and unmixing starts as lamellar 'fluctuation domains' with different Na/Ca and Si/Al ratios. As the cell volumes of Na-rich and Ca-rich plagioclases are not very different, the domains will influence each other to minimize any strain of their boundary regions (as is manifest in many cryptoperthites, cf. quasi-homogeneous perthites, see p. 74); a minimum strain may result from an 'unstable' Si/Al distribution which, however, is not detectable by the diffraction techniques.

Mellis and Nilsson (1965) demonstrated that the colour of the schiller depends on (1) the composition of the labradorite and (2) the amount of the needle-shaped opaque inclusions (magnetite with ilmenite lamellae).

Nissen and Bollmann (1966) found that, in plagioclase with a few per cent potassium feldspar, the schiller is produced by regular lamellae, 1000–2000 Å thick in labradorite, narrower in andesine. The crystals are uniform with regard to x-rays.

1.43 Ternary feldspars (anorthoclases, sanidines)

Any feldspar containing more than 5% of the third component may be called ternary.

Ternary mixed crystals are known from lavas (= high-temperature rocks). Anorthoclase is albite containing up to one-third K-feldspar (and some Ca-feldspar). Such feldspars were first described by Förstner (1877) and named *Natronorthoklas* from the lavas of the island of Pantellaria.

Potassian oligoclase is well known, and *potassian andesine* with a K-feldspar content attaining 10% is also known (Muir, 1962). The term *lime anorthoclase* was used by Aoki (1959) and by Muir (1962); it covers part of the field of potassian oligoclase of figure 1.27. Some *soda sanidines* are also ternary feldspars. The *anemousite* of Washington and Wright (1910) from the island of Linosa in the Mediterranean was considered to be deficient in silica. According to Ernst and Nieland (1934), it is chemically normal andesine of varying composition and with deviating optical properties. Muir (1955) showed it to exhibit high-temperature optics (see p. 13).

Anorthoclases and related feldspars are most widespread as groundmass constituents of slightly alkalic lavas. Some of the Hawaiian alkalic rocks bear a characteristic interstitial alkali feldspar with a small positive optic angle and a refractive index, $\beta = 1\cdot54$–$1\cdot55$. This material was

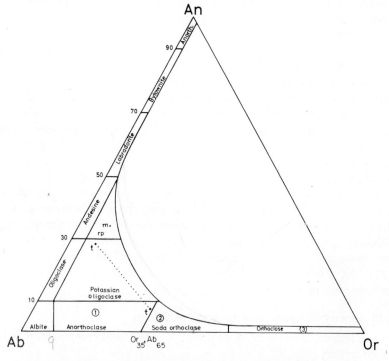

FIGURE 1.27 Nomenclature of ternary feldspars: (1), (2), (3) correspond in bulk composition to antiperthite, mesoperthite and perthite, respectively; t–t are the projection points of two coexisting feldspars in trachyte; m and rp represent potassian andesines from mugearite, and from rhomb porphyry respectively, see text

identified by Barth (1930) as 'anemousite' and by Macdonald (1942, 1964) as 'potash oligoclase'. Phenocrysts of anorthoclasic composition are also known (e.g. Shimizu and Kuno, 1960). Optically positive feldspars ($+2V = 45\text{--}75°$) of similar composition were reported by Antun (1964) from composite dike rocks of the Oslo region, and by Sugi (1940) from olivine dolerite from Fu-shun, Manchuria. In the latter case, the anomalous optics may be due to superposition of (submicroscopic) twin lamellae.

Crystallographic constants of a typical ternary feldspar are listed in table 1.3.

The possibility of different structural states among anorthoclases has not been investigated in detail. The correspondence between lattice parameters of synthetic alkali feldspars and those of homogeneous natural calcium-poor anorthoclases suggests that the natural feldspars are structurally very similar to their synthetic counterparts.

TABLE 1.3

Lattice parameters of homogeneous potassian oligoclase, $Or_{17}Ab_{65}An_{18}$, from recent alkaline trachyte, Ross Island, Antarctica. (Boudette and Ford, 1966)

	a	b	c	α	β	γ
Direct values	8·228	12·915	7·127	92° 36′	116° 18′	90° 17′
Reciprocal values	0·1356	0·0775	0·1567	86° 58′	63° 39′	88° 24′

The so-called rhomb feldspars from trachyandesitic lavas with typical face development of only (110) and ($\bar{2}01$), sometimes with ($\bar{1}01$) giving a rhomb-shaped cross-section (see figure 1.5), are usually perthitic, representing stages in the unmixing of an originally homogeneous ternary feldspar. The composition of a potassian andesine from a rhomb porphyry in Oslo plots at rp in figure 1.27. Similar rhomb porphyry feldspars are known from Mt. Erebus, Antarctica, and Mt. Kenya, Africa. An analysed feldspar fraction from mugearite (Muir and Tilley, 1961) is plotted onto figure 1.27 (point m).

Two different ternary feldspars may coexist in a rock. Examples are phenocrysts of soda sanidine and potassian oligoclase (or potassian andesine) in pitchstones from Sgurr of Eigg, Scotland, and in trachytes from Jan Mayen, North Atlantic (Carmichael, 1965) (see figure 1.27, projection points t–t).

In addition to multiple M-twins (albite–pericline combinations)— which are most clearly seen in sections normal to the a axis, as the rhombic section lies close to (001)—Manebach and, more commonly, Carlsbad twins are found. In the lavas, the Carlsbad twins occasionally have (100) as composition face; threelings, fourlings and sixlings occur.

For a historical survey of the use of the name anorthoclase, see Brousse (1959), Laves (1952).

1.5 SUMMARY OF OCCURRENCE AND FORMATION

Feldspars are the chief constituents of many types of crystalline schists, of migmatites, gneisses and granites, and of most magmatic rocks.

If feldspars are potentially present in a rock magma, and if micas are prevented from crystallizing (say by lack of H_2O), and if, furthermore, the bulk composition of the potential feldspars lies in the ternary solubility gap of figure 1.27, then two feldspar types will crystallize simultaneously. Such are the conditions in most calc–alkalic granitoid rocks. Gabbroic rocks are frequently too low in potassium to form alkali feldspar, and only plagioclases develop. On the other hand, magmas of alkalic rocks are usually too low in calcium to form plagioclase and only a solid solution of alkali feldspar results. Upon slow cooling, such alkali feldspar exsolves

TABLE 1.4

Distribution of feldspars in igneous rocks (weight per cent). (Handbook of Physical Constants. *Geol. Soc. Am.*, *Spec. Papers*, **36**, 3, 1942)

	Granite	Syenite	Grano-diorite	Quartz diorite	Diorite	Gabbro	Olivine gabbro	Dia-base
Alkali feldspars	40	72	15	6	3			
Plagioclase	26	12	46	56	64	65	63	62
All feldspars	66	84	61	62	67	65	63	62

TABLE 1.5

Areal distribution of feldspars (percentage). (Barth, *J. Geol.*, **57**, 59, 1949)

	Oslo igneous province	Pacific islands	Earth's crust
Alkali feldspars	62	18	31
Plagioclase	16	30	29
All feldspars	78	48	60

into perthite. However, in many granites, the rather low temperature of (re)crystallization of the feldspars virtually restricts the formation of mixed crystals to the Na–Ca plagioclase series. Thus, two primary feldspar phases develop: almost pure plagioclase and a potassium feldspar with only small amounts of soda in solid solution. This soda exsolves upon cooling, and produces sparse perthite lamellae in a host crystal of almost pure orthoclase or microcline.

Mehnert (1962) gave an account of the composition and distribution of feldspars in magmatic, metamorphic and anatectic rocks. He pointed out that modern methods of rapid analysis, permit a statistical study of the composition of feldspars. Some problems can be approximated by mathematical models and with the aid of computers.

A number of igneous rock bodies have been investigated in this way, and 'isopleths' for frequency and composition of the feldspars have been constructed. It appears that in many granitic bodies an original plagioclase and many other minerals were replaced by a porphyric K-feldspar which must have been introduced in solution, the source of which could be the magma itself. Normally, cooling begins at the borders and proceeds inwards. Consequently, the outer parts of the rock body are usually rather low in K-feldspar and rich in plagioclase with a higher An content, while the inner parts are enriched in K-feldspar at the expense of plagioclase, which here displays a low An content.

Metamorphic rocks are more difficult to investigate; they usually have a complicated history of evolution and may be strongly heterogeneous.

The formation of K-feldspar, mostly in the form of crystalloblasts, is a metasomatic process. All minerals can be either partially or completely replaced by K-feldspar, the end product being a 'syenite' in which pure K-feldspar predominates—not a 'granite' as often asserted. Feldspathization advances as a front even on a microscopic scale, leaving behind numerous small particles of unaltered plagioclase. This indicates that not much diffusive exchange of alkalis can take place. The phenocrysts (often 'augen') are identical in magmatic and metamorphic rocks; a temperature series can thus be established in both kinds of rock according to the triclinicity values of the K-feldspar.

K-feldspar occurs as adularia in hydrothermal veins, similarly Na-feldspar is found as pericline.

Albitization takes place regionally in a great variety of rocks through various kinds of metasomatic processes, chiefly by the formation of fenite, spilite, or adinole.

Fenitization: Strong sodium-bearing solutions emitted from carbonate–silicate magmas react with, and albitize, the potassium feldspars and the plagioclases of the wall rock, quartz is also replaced. The end product is an albite fenite.

Spilitization: early orogenic basalts, generally of submarine eruption, have a tendency to become albite basalts, or spilites. The sodium probably derives from sea water. The general reaction is:

$$CaAl_2Si_2O_8 + 4SiO_2 + 2Na^+ \rightleftharpoons 2NaAlSi_3O_8 + Ca^{2+}$$

At moderately elevated temperatures, sodium-rich feldspars are more stable than calcium-rich feldspars. In the laboratory, a mixture of anorthite, sodium carbonate and silica under vapour pressure at $300°C$ yields albite and calcium carbonate. The reaction is reversible and shifts to the left with higher temperatures.

Adinolization: in the contact aureoles of orogenic diabases and basalts, quartz–albite rocks—formed by albitization and generally called adinoles—frequently develop. Special names are soda hornfels, spilosite (spotted), desmosite (banded). Donnelly (1963) gave an account of the formation of albite in early orogenic volcanic rocks.

Albitites of bulk feldspar composition $An_2–An_{13} \pm$ microcline may contain two plagioclases, one albitic, another oligoclasic (see under peristerite, section 1.422). Elliott (1966) suggested that they owe their origin to the partial fusion of their enclosing amphibolites under conditions of high water vapour pressure, because experiments show that under these pressure and temperature ($P–T$) conditions amphibole begins to melt and that the first liquid is of the composition of albite. This is supported by the association of amphibolites with albite veins in the upper almandine–amphibolite facies.

Albite pegmatites are not uncommon. The usual geological association is twofold. (1) With albitites: the mineralogy of the pegmatites closely resembles that of the albitites, into which they often pass by transition; the grain size is rather small, few crystals exceed 1–3 cm. (2) With carbonatites: albite–calcite pegmatites with transitions into true ringite pegmatites (containing albite, calcite, biotite, tourmaline, apatite) with albite crystals attaining a length of $\frac{1}{2}$ m (e.g. on Seiland, Norway). This albite is always antiperthitic.

Plagioclase of low $P–T$ formation is nearly always pure albite (see p. 10), but plagioclase of higher $P–T$ formation varies with the bulk composition of the rock; so clear is this correlation that a closed system must be assumed (with regard to the plagioclase formation). Thus plagioclase composition may serve as a geothermometer only in rocks of similar bulk composition.

The series of plagioclases in low-grade metamorphic rocks is discontinuous (see section 1.422). Frequency diagrams show high values of albite, 0–5% An, but low values of oligoclase, 5–20% An (De Waard, 1959; Lyons, 1955; Compton, 1955; Wenk, 1958). An interesting distribution pattern in calcareous phyllite from the western Alps (Tessin) was published by Wenk (1962): An-rich plagioclases in the centre, An-poor plagioclases at the borders of the rock body. Assuming that this sequence

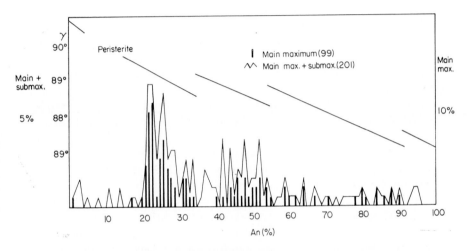

FIGURE 1.28 Relation between frequency and composition in the plagio-clases. (From Ohta, personal communication; see Hunahashi and others, 1968)

corresponds to decreasing *P–T* conditions, the highest temperatures will be in the centre of the rock mass. But, in detail, the isopleths of equal An content are independent of the tectonic structure and do not coincide with the geologic and tectonic units. The inference is that the isopleths delineate an uprise of magma from greater depths. Figure 1.28 gives a graphical survey of the frequency relations of the various plagioclases.

In anatectic rocks, differential melting takes place; the first liquid to form is the 'metatect'. According to theoretical and experimental results, the plagioclases of the metatect should be poorer in An than are those of the solid rock. But this has not been confirmed; plagioclases of anatectic rocks exhibit the same An content whether they come from the metatect or the restite, thus indicating a closed rock system with the same plagioclase crystallizing from all parts of the rock when the system cools. However, at higher *P–T* conditions the system becomes more open, the metatect moves, the plagioclases assume complicated structures, irregular and patchy zoning develops, often due to inclusions of older plagioclases more or less corroded. The main part of the crystal is unzoned; a transitional zone is slightly enriched in An and exhibits idiomorphic outlines; beyond this zone there extends a xenomorphic rim of decreasing An, down to pure albite. Composition and zoning of metamorphic plagioclases of non-anatectic origin were recently discussed by Misch (1968).

Thus the mineralogy and paragenesis of feldspars in rocks are useful indicators of temperature, and other conditions of formation.

Authigenic feldspars form *in situ* at low pressures and temperatures on the earth's surface or at moderate depth. They may form contemporaneously with sedimentary deposition, or at any one time during diagenesis or epigenesis.

It is of interest that hydrothermal synthesis of well-developed crystals of orthoclase has been achieved in the range 195–200°c (Barrer and Hinds, 1950).

Baskin (1956), in a survey on identification, nature and origin of authigenic feldspars, showed that idiomorphic outlines, the chemical composition (non-perthitic character) and the checker-board pattern (roc tourné twinning) distinguish authigenic from detrital feldspars in sediments. Mineralogically they are orthoclase (adularia habit) or 'sanidine' according to Saénz (1963), microcline and albite. Alkali feldspar mixed crystals (anorthoclase, etc.) are not formed authigenically. Plagioclase (labradorite) has been recorded from one locality only (barite concretions in Cuba, see Králík and Mišík, 1966).

The amount of authigenic feldspar rarely exceeds 1–2% of the total sediment, but may occasionally attain 70% (Degens, 1965; Weiss, 1954). Microcline of high triclinicity seems to be typically present in the clay-sized residues of carbonate rocks (Reynolds, 1963). Albite is restricted to carbonates and crystals are usually larger than those of potassium feldspar, but the size rarely exceeds 1 mm in diameter; potassium feldspars may also occur in sandstone and shale. Authigenic feldspars are commonly found as rims around detrital feldspars. Heald (1950) observed that rims on albite and orthoclase are of the same variety as the core, whereas growths on microcline can be either adularia or microcline. On clastic grains of orthoclase and microcline, Glover and Hosemann (1967) found composite overgrowths of high sanidine on (001) faces, and orthoclase and low sanidine on (010) faces, and all three varieties on (110) and (1$\bar{1}$0) faces.

REFERENCES

Aberdam, D., Kern, R., Leymarie, P. and Pierrot, M. (1964). Etude cristallographique détaillée d'une orthose cryptoperthitique. *Compt. Rend.*, **258**, 1268.

Andersen, O. (1915). On aventurine feldspars. *Am. J. Sci.*, **40**, 351. [*Transl. Z. Krist.*, **56**, 553 (1922).]

Andersen, O. (1917). Aventurine labradorite from California. *Am. Mineralogist*, **2**, 91.

Andersen, O. (1928). The genesis of some types of feldspars from granite pegmatites. *Norsk Geol. Tidsskr.*, **10**, 116.

Anderson, G. H. (1937). Granitization, albitization and related phenomena in the northern Inyo Range. *Bull. Geol. Soc. Am.*, **48**, 1.

Anderson, G. H. and Maclelland, D. D. (1937). An unusual feldspar from the northern Inyo Range. *Am. Mineralogist*, **22**, 208.

Antun, P. (1964). Zur Genese der gemischten Gänge im Oslogebiet (erläutert an einem neuen Granitporphyr-Doleritgang vom Frognerpark). *Norsk. Geol. Tidsskr.*, **44**, 43.

Aoki, K. (1959). Petrology of alkali rocks of the Iki islands and Higashi-matsuura district, Japan. *Sci. Rept. Tohoku Univ.*, *Third Ser.*, **6**, 261.

Baier, E. and Pense, J. (1957). Elektronmikroskopische Untersuchungen an Labradoren. *Naturwissenschaften*, **44**, 110.

Bambauer, H. U., Corlett, M., Eberhard, E., Gubser, R., Laves, F., Nissen, H. U. and Viswanathan, K. (1965). Variations in x-ray powder patterns of low structural state plagioclases. *Schweiz. Mineral. Petrog. Mitt.*, **45**, 327.

Bambauer, H. U., Corlett, M., Eberhard, E. and Viswanathan, K. (1967). Diagrams for the determination of plagioclases using x-ray powder methods. *Schweiz. Mineral. Petrog. Mitt.*, **47**, 333.

Barrer, R. M. and Hinds, L. (1950). Hydrothermal synthesis of well developed crystals of orthoclase. *Nature*, **166**, 562.

Barth, T. F. W. (1930). Pacificite, an anemousite basalt. *J. Wash. Acad. Sci.*, **20**, 60.

Barth, T. F. W. (1933). An occurrence of iso-orthoclase in Virginia. *Am. Mineralogist*, **18**, 478.

Barth, T. F. W. (1956a). Studies in gneiss and granite II: The feldspar equilibrium temperature in granitic rocks of the pre-Cambrian of Southern Norway. *Norske Videnskap.-Akad. Skrifter, Oslo*, No. **1**.

Barth, T. F. W. (1956b). Zonal structure in feldspars of crystalline schists. *Third Reun. Intern. Reactiv., Solid State, Madrid, 1956, Sect.*, **III**, 363.

Baskin, Y. (1956). A study of authigenic feldspars. *J. Geol.*, **64**, 132.

Becke, F. (1880). Die Gneissformation des niederösterreichischen Waldviertels. *Tschermaks Mitt., N. F.*, **4**, 199.

Becke, F. (1903). Über Mineralbestand und Struktur der kristallinen Schiefer. *Akad. Wiss. Wien, Denkschr.*, **75**.

Bentor, Y. K. (1951). On the formation of cloudy zones in plagioclases. *Schweiz. Mineral. Petrog. Mitt.*, **31**, 535.

Berzelius, J. and Gahn, J. G. (1815). Undersökning af några i grannskapet af Fahlun funna Fossilier. *Afhandl. Fys. Kemi, Mineral.*, **4**, 180.

Bloss, F. D. (1964). Optical extinction of anorthite at high temperature. *Am. Mineralogist*, **49**, 1125.

Böggild, O. B. (1924). On the labradorization of feldspars. *Kgl. Danske Videnskab. Selskab, Medd.*, **6**, No. 3.

Boone, C. M., Romey, W. D. and Thompson, D. S. (1967). Oscillatory zoning in calcic andesine—sodic labradorite phenocrysts in the anorthosite of North Creek dome, Adirondack Mountains (Abstract). *Anorthosite Symp., State Univ. Coll., Plattsburgh, N.Y., Oct. 6–8, 1966.*

Bottinga, Y., Kudo, A. and Weill, D. (1966). Some observations on oscillatory zoning and crystallization of magmatic plagioclase. *Am. Mineralogist*, **51**, 792.

Boudette, E. L. and Ford, A. B. (1966). Physical properties of anorthoclase from Antarctica. *Am. Mineralogist*, **51**, 1374.

Bowen, N. L. (1913). The melting phenomena of the plagioclase feldspars. *Am. J. Sci.* (4), **35**, 583.

Breithaupt, A. (1830). Über die Felsite und einige neue Specien ihres Geschlechtes. *Schweigger J. Chem. Phys.* **55**, 246.

Breithaupt, A. (1823), (1832). *Vollständige Charakteristik des Mineralsystems.* Arnoldi, Dresden (3rd ed., 1832).

Brögger, W. C. (1890). Die Mineralien der Syenitepegmatitgänge der südnorwegischen Augit- und Nephelinsyenite. *Z. Krist.*, **16**, 560.

Brousse, R. (1959). Remarques sur l'emploi en pétrographie des termes d'anorthose et de microcline–anorthose. *Bull. Soc. Franc. Mineral. Crist.*, **82**, 384.

Brown, W. L. (1960). The crystallographic and petrologic significance of peristerite unmixing in the acid plagioclases. *Z. Krist.*, **113**, 330.

Brown, W. L. (1962). Peristerite unmixing in the plagioclases and metamorphic facies series. *Norsk Geol. Tidsskr.*, **42**, II (Feldspar Vol.), 354.

Bunch, T. E. and Olsen, E. (1967). Meteoritic alkali feldspar. *Program Ann. Meeting Geol. Soc. Am., 1967*, 27.

Calkins, F. C. (1917). A decimal grouping of the plagioclases. *J. Geol.*, **25**, 157.

Cannon, R. T. (1966). Plagioclase zoning and twinning in relation to the metamorphic history of some amphibolites and granulites. *Am. J. Sci.*, **264**, 526.

Carman, J. H. and Tuttle, O. F. (1963). Experimental study bearing on the origin of myrmekite (Abstract). *Ann. Meeting Geol. Soc. Am.*, 29A.

Carman, J. H. and Tuttle, O. F. (1967). Experimental verification of solid solution of excess silica in sanidine from rhyolites (Abstract). *Ann. Meeting Geol. Soc. Am.*, 33.

Carmichael, J. S. E. (1965). Trachytes and their feldspar phenocrysts. *Mineral. Mag.*, **34** (Tilley Vol.), 107.

Carstens, H. (1955). On the clouding of plagioclase in coronited meta-dolerites. *Norsk. Geol. Tidsskr.*, **35**, 129.

Carstens, H. (1957). Investigations of titaniferous iron ore deposits. *Kgl. Norsk Videnskab. Selskabs, Skrifter*, No. 3, 37.

Carstens, H. (1967). Exsolution in ternary feldspars. I, II. *Contrib. Mineral. Petrolog.*, **14**, 27.

Catanzaro, E. J. and Gast, P. W. (1960). Isotopic composition of lead in pegmatitic feldspars. *Geochim. Cosmochim. Acta*, **19**, 113.

Chaisson, U. (1950). The optics of triclinic adularia. *J. Geol.*, **58**, 537.

Christie, O. H. J. (1959). Note on the equilibrium between plagioclase and epidote. *Norsk Geol. Tidsskr.*, **39**, 268.

Christie, O. H. J. (1962). Feldspar structure and the equilibrium between plagioclase and epidote. *Am. J. Sci.*, **260**, 149.

Christie, O. H. J. (1968). Spinodal precipitation in silicates. I. *Lithos*, **1**, 187.

Compton, R. R. (1955). Trondhjemite batholith near Bidwell Bar, California. *Bull. Geol. Soc. Am.*, **66**, 9.

Cornelius, H. P. (1935). Zur Deutung gefüllter Feldspäte. *Schweiz. Mineral. Petrog. Mitt.*, **15**, 4.

Crawford, M. L. (1966). Composition of plagioclase and associated minerals in some schists from Vermont, USA, and South Westland, New Zealand, with inferences about the peristerite solvus. *Beitr. Mineral. Petrolog.*, **13**, 269.

Day, A. L. and Allen, E. T. (1905). The isomorphism and thermal properties of the feldspars. *Carnegie Inst. Wash. Publ.*, **31**.

Degens, E. T. (1965). Authigenic feldspars. In *Geochemistry of Sediments*, Prentice Hall, Englewood Cliffs, New Jersey, pp. 47–51.

Des Cloizeaux, A. (1874). *Manuel de Minéral*, II. p. 36.

Des Cloizeaux, A. (1876). Mémoire sur l'existence, les propriétés optiques et cristallographiques, et la composition chimique du microcline, nouvelle espèce de feldspath triclinique à base de potasse, suivi de remarques sur l'examen microscopique de l'orthose et des divers feldspaths tricliniques. *Ann. Chim. Phys.* [5], **9**, 433; *Compt. Rend.*, **82**, 885.

De Waard, D. (1959). Anorthite content in plagioclase in basic and pelitic crystalline schists as related to metamorphic zoning in the Usu massif, Timor. *Am. J. Sci.*, **257**, 553.

Doman, R. C., Cinnamon, C. G. and Bailey, S. W. (1965). Structural discontinuities in the plagioclase feldspar series. *Am. Mineralogist*, **50**, 724.

Donnelly, T. W. (1963). Genesis of albite in early orogenic volcanic rocks. *Am. J. Sci.*, **261**, 957.

Drescher-Kaden, F. K. (1948). Die Feldspat–Quartz Reaktionsgefüge der Granite und Gneise und ihre genetische Bedeutung. Springer, Berlin/Heidelberg.

Duffin, W. J. (1964). Plagioclase reactions. *Mineral. Mag.*, **33**, 812.

Duparc, L. (1904). Sur une nouvelle variété d'orthose. *Compt. Rend.*, **138**, 714.

Elliott, R. B. (1966). The association of amphibolite and albitite, Kragerø, South Norway. *Geol. Mag.*, **103**, 1.

Elliston, J. (1966). The genesis of the Peko Ore body. *Australasian Inst. Mining Met. Proc.*, **218**, 9.

Emerson, D. O. (1964). Absence of optically positive potash feldspar in the Inyo Mountains. *Am. Mineralogist*, **49**, 194.

Emmons, R. C. and Mann, V. (1953). A twin–zone relationship in plagioclase feldspars. In Selected Petrogenic Relationship of Plagioclase. *Geol. Soc. Am.*, *Mem.*, **52**, 41.

Ernst, E. and Nieland, H. (1934). Plagioklase von Linosa, ein Beitrag zur Anemousitfrage. *Mineral. Petrog. Mitt.*, **46**, 93.

Evans, B. W. (1964). Co-existing albite and oligoclase in some schists from New Zealand. *Am. Mineralogist*, **49**, 173.

Fleet, S. G. and Ribbe, P. H. (1963). An electron-microscope investigation of a moonstone. *Phil. Mag.*, **8**, No. 91, 1179.

Fleet, S. G. and Ribbe, P. H. (1965). An electroscope study of peristerite plagioclases. *Mineral. Mag.*, **35**, 165.

Förstner, H. (1877). Über Natronorthoklas von Pantellaria. *Z. Krist.*, **1**, 547; **8**, 125 (1883).

Fouqué, F. (1894). Contribution à l'étude des feldspaths des roches volcaniques. *Bull. Soc. Mineral. France*, **17**, 306.

Friedman, G. M. (1955). Petrology of the Memesagamesing Lake norite mass, Ontario. *Am. J. Sci.*, **253**, 590.

Füchtbauer, H. (1948). Einige Betrachtungen an authigenen Albiten. *Schweiz. Mineral. Petrog. Mitt.*, **28**, 709.

Füchtbauer, H. (1956). Zur Entstehung und Optik authigener Feldspäte. *Neues Jahrb., Monatsh.*, **1**, 9.

Gabis, V. and Turon, M. (1964). Orientation de l'orthose et de l'albite dans des cryptoperthites de substitution obtenues par synthèse. *Compt. Rend.*, **259**, 1159.

Gay, P. (1961). Some recent work on the plagioclase feldspar. *Inst. "Lucas Mallada," Curs. Conf.*, **VIII**, 159.

Glover, J. E. and Hosemann, P. (1967). Authigenic high sanidine from Western Australia. *Nature*, **214**, 262.

Goldich, S. and Kinser, J. H. (1939). Perthite from Tory Hill, Ontario. *Am. Mineralogist*, **24**, 407.

Goldsmith, J. R. and Ehlers, E. G. (1952). The stability relations of anorthite and its hexagonal polymorph in the system $CaAl_2Si_2O_8$. *J. Geol.*, **60**, 386.

Gysin, M. (1948). Les feldspaths potassiques des granites de Gastern et de quelques granites de l'Aar. *Schweiz. Mineral. Petrog. Mitt.*, **28**, 230.

Harloff, C. (1927). Zonal structure in plagioclases. *Leidsche Geol. Mededeel.*, **2**, 99.

Heald, M. T. (1950). Authigenesis in West Virginia sandstones. *J. Geol.*, **58**, 624.

Herz, N. (1951). Baltimore gabbro, Maryland. *Bull. Geol. Soc. Am.*, **62**, 979.

Hessel, J. F. (1826). Über die Familie Feldspath. Taschenb. gesammt. Mineralogie, *Z. Mineral.*, **1**, 289.

Hills, E. S. (1936). Reverse and oscillatory zoning in plagioclase feldspars. *Geol. Mag.*, **73**, 49.

Homma, F. (1932). Über das Ergebnis von Messungen an zonaren Plagioklasen aus Andesiten mit Hilfe des Universaldrehtisches. *Schweiz. Mineral. Petrog. Mitt.*, **12**, 345–352.

Hubbart, F. H. (1965). Antiperthite and mantled feldspar textures in charnockite from S.W. Nigeria. *Am. Mineralogist*, **50**, 2040.

Hubbart, F. H. (1966). Myrmekite in charnockite from S.W. Nigeria. *Am. Mineralogist*, **51**, 762.

Hunahashi, M., Kim, C. W., Ohta, Y. and Tsuchiva, T. (1968). Co-existence of plagioclases of different compositions in some plutonic and metamorphic rocks. *Lithos*, **1**, 311.

Iiyama, J. T. (1966). Contribution à l'étude des equilibres sub-solidus du systeme ternaire orthose–albite–anorthite à l'aide des réactions d'échange d'ions Na–K au contact d'une solution hydrothermale. *Bull. Soc. Franc. Mineral. Crist.*, **89**, 442.

Iiyama, J. T., Wyart, J. and Sabatier, G. (1963). Equilibre des feldspaths alcalins et des plagioclases à 500, 600 et 800°c sous une pression d'eau de 1000 bars. *Compt. Rend.*, **256**, 5016.

Ito, T. and Sadanaga, R. (1952). The lamellar structure of certain microcline and anorthoclases. *Acta Cryst.*, **5**, 441.

Jung, D. (1965). Ein natürliches Vorkommen von Monalbit? *Z. Krist.*, **121**, 425.

Kano, H. (1956). High-temperature optics of natural sodic plagioclases. *Mineral. J. (Tokyo)*, 1–255.

Karl, F. (1954). Über Hoch- und Tieftemperaturoptik von Plagioklasen und deren petrographische und geologische Auswertung am Beispiel einiger alpiner Ergussgesteine. *Tschermaks Mineral. Petrog. Mitt.*, **4**, 320.

Kazakov, A. N. (1956). On the occurrence of positive microclines. *Mem. Soc. Russe. Mineral.*, **85**, 433; *Proc. Ud. SSR Mineral. Soc. (Russ.)*; *Abstr. Zentr. Mineral.*, **1**, 240.

Köhler, A. (1942). Drehtischmessungen an Plagioclaszwillingen von Tief- und Hochtemperaturoptik. *Mineral. Petrog. Mitt.*, **53**, 159.

Kozu, S. and Endo, Y. (1921). X-ray analyses of adularia and moonstone, and the influence of temperature on the atomic arrangement of these minerals. *Sci. Rept. Tohoku Univ., Third Ser.*, **1**, 1.

Králík, J. and Mišík, M. (1966). Authigenic feldspars from the baryte concretion from the Tertiary of Cuba. *Geol. Carpathica Geol. Sbor. Akad. Vied. Bratislava*, **17**, 105.

Krebs, B. (1921). Der Albit von Rischuna in morphologischer Bedeutung. *Z. Krist.*, **56**, 386.

Lacroix, A. (1927). Constitution lithologique de la Polynesie Australe. *Mem. Acad. Sci.*, **59**, 17.

Larsen, E. S. and Irving, J. (1938). Petrologic results of a study of the minerals from the Tertiary volcanic rocks of the San Juan region. *Am. Mineralogist*, **23**, 227.

Laves, F. (1950). The lattice and twinning of microcline and other potash feldspars. *J. Geol.*, **58**, 560.

Laves, F. (1951). A revised orientation of microcline and its geometrical relations to albite and cryptoperthites. *J. Geol.*, **59**, 510.

Laves, F. (1952). Phase relations in the alkali feldspars II: The stable and pseudostable phase relations in the alkali feldspar system. *J. Geol.*, **60**, 567.

Laves, F. (1954). The coexistence of two plagioclases in the oligoclase composition range. *J. Geol.*, **62**, 409.

Laves, F. (1965). The correlation of optics and lattice geometry of microcline. *Am. Mineralogist*, **50**, 509.

Laves, F. and Goldsmith, J. R. (1955). The effect of temperature and composition on the Al–Si distribution in anorthite. *Z. Krist.*, **106**, 227.

Laves, F., Nissen, H.-U. and Bollmann, W. (1965). On schiller and submicroscopical lamellae of labradorite. *Naturwissenschaften*, **52**, 427.

Laves, F. and Schneider, T. (1956). Über den rhombischen Schnitt in sauren Plagioklasen. *Schweiz. Mineral. Petrog. Mitt.*, **36**, 622.

Laves, F. and Soldatos, K. (1962). Plate perthite, a new perthitic intergrowth in microcline single crystals, a recrystallization product. *Z. Krist.*, **117**, 218.

Laves, F. and Soldatos, K. (1963). Die Albit/Mikroklin-Orientierungsbeziehungen in Mikroklinperthiten und deren genetische Deutung. *Z. Krist.*, **118**, 69.

Leedal, G. P. (1952). The Cluanie igneous intrusion, Inverness-shire and Ross-shire. *Quart. J. Geol. Soc. London*, **108**, 35.

Luczizky, W. (1905). Der Granit von Kössein im Fichtelgebirge und seine Einschlüsse. *Tschermaks Mineral. Petrog. Mitt.*, **24**, 347.

Lyons, J. B. (1955). Geology of the Hanover quadrangle, New Hampshire–Vermont. *Bull. Geol. Soc. Am.*, **66**, 105.

Macdonald, G. A. (1942). Potash-oligoclase in Hawaiian lavas. *Am. Mineralogist*, **27**, 793.

Macdonald, G. A. and Katsura, G. A. (1964). Chemical composition of Hawaiian lavas. *J. Petrol.*, **5**, 82.

MacGregor, G. A. (1931). Clouded feldspars and thermal metamorphism. *Mineral. Mag.*, **22**, 524.

MacKenzie, W. S. and Smith, J. V. (1962). Single crystal x-ray studies of crypto- and microperthites. *Norsk Geol. Tidsskr.*, **42**, II (Feldspar Vol.), 72.

Makart, H. and Preisinger, A. (1965). Determination of feldspars in rocks. *Tschermaks Mineral. Petrog. Mitt.* [3], **9**, 315.

Mallard, F. (1876), (1881), (1884). Explications des phénomènes optiques anomaux que présentent un grand nombre de substances cristallisées. *Ann. Mines*, **10**, 187; *Bull. Soc. Mineral. France*, **4** (1881); *Traité de Cristallographie*, II, Paris, 1884, p. 263.

Mason, B. (1965). Feldspar in chondrites. *Science*, **148**, 943.

Mawdsley, J. B. (1927). St. Urbain Area, Charleroix District, Quebec. *Can. Geol. Surv. Mem.*, **152**.

Mehnert, K. R. (1962). Composition and distribution of feldspars in magmatic and metamorphic rocks. *Norsk Geol. Tidsskr.*, **42**, II (Feldspar Vol.), 455.

Mellis, O. and Nilsson, C. A. (1965). Der Labrador von Ylämaa, Finland, 43. Jahrstag (Abstract). *Deut. Mineral. Ges.*, 39.

Michel-Lévy, A. (1879). Identité probable du microcline et de l'orthose. *Bull. Soc. Mineral. France*, **2**, 135.

Misch, P. (1968). Plagioclase composition and non-anatectic origin of migmatite gneisses in Northern Cascade Mountains of Washington State. *Contrib. Mineral. Petrol.*, **17**, 1.

Monroe, E. A. and Sass, D. B. (1967). Electron microscope study of exsolution and schiller in peristerite feldspars (Abstract). *Ann. Meeting Geol. Soc. Am. Program*, 153.

Muir, I. D. (1955). Transitional optics of some andesines and labradorites. *Mineral. Mag.*, **30**, 545.

Muir, I. D. (1962). The paragenesis and optical properties of some ternary feldspars. *Norsk Geol. Tidsskr.*, **42**, II (Feldspar Vol.), 477.

Muir, I. D. and Tilley, C. E. (1961). Mugearites and their place in alkalic igneous rock series. *J. Geol.*, **69**, 186.

Neumann, H. and Christie, O. H. J. (1962). Observations on plagioclase aventurines from Southern Norway. *Norsk Geol. Tidsskr.*, **42**, II (Feldspar Vol.), 389.

Niggli, P., Königsberger, J. and Parker, R. L. (1940). *Mineralien der Schweizeralpen*. Wepf, Basel.

Nissen, H.-U. and Bollmann, W. (1966). Submicroscopic fabrics in feldspars. *Intern. Congr. Electron Microscopy, 6th, Kyoto*, 591.

Noble, D. C. (1962). Plagioclase unmixing and the lower boundary of the amphibolite facies. *J. Geol.*, **70**, 234.

Nockolds, S. R. and Mitchell, R. L. (1948). The geochemistry of some Caledonian plutonic rocks. *Trans. Roy. Soc. Edinburgh*, **56**, 2, 533.

Oftedal, I. (1957). Heating experiments on amazonite. *Mineral. Mag.*, **31**, 417.

Parker, R. B., King, J. S. and World, R. G. (1963). Rubidium in alkali feldspar perthites. *Contrib. Geol. Univ. Wyoming*, **2**, 59.

Parsons, I. (1965). The feldspathic syenites of the Loch Ailsh Intrusion, Assynt, Scotland. *J. Petrol.*, **6**, 365.

Perry, K., Jr. (1966). Representation of feldspar chemical analyses (Abstract). *Ann. Meeting Geol. Soc. Am.*, 160.

Perry, K., Jr. (1968). Representation of mineral chemical analyses in 11-dimensional space: I. Feldspars. *Lithos*, **1**, 201.

Phemister, J. (1934). Zoning in plagioclase feldspar. *Mineral. Mag.*, **23**, 541.

Phillips, E. R. (1964). Myrmekite and albite in some granites of the New England Batholith, New South Wales. *J. Geol. Soc. Australia*, **11**, 49.

Pichamuthu, C. S. (1959). The significance of clouded plagioclase in the basic dykes of Mysore State, India. *J. Geol. Soc. India*, **1**, 68.

Pittman, E. D. (1963). Use of zoned plagioclase as an indicator of provenance. *J. Sediment. Petrol.*, **33**, 380.

Poldervaart, A. and Gilkey, A. K. (1954). On clouded plagioclase. *Am. Mineralogist*, **39**, 75.

Przibram, K. (1956). Über Farbe und Luminiszenz der Feldspate. *Sitzber. Oesterr. Akad. Wiss. Math. Naturw. Kl.*, **165**, 281.

Quin, J. P. (1962). Le zonage des plagioclases dans les estérellites du massif de l'Estérel. *Bull. Soc. Franc. Mineral. Crist.*, **85**, 245.

Raman, C. V., Tayaraman, A. and Srinivasan, T. K. (1950). The structure and optical behaviour of the Ceylon moonstones. *Proc. Indian Acad. Sci.*, **A32**, 123.

Ramberg, H. (1962). Intergranular precipitation of albite formed by unmixing of alkali feldspar. *Neues Jahrb. Mineral., Abhand.*, **98**, 14.

Rao, Y. J. (1964). Clouding in some plagioclase feldspars. *Intern. Geol. Congr., 22nd, India, Rept. Sect.*, **16**, 233.

Reinhard, M. (1964). Über das Grundgebirge des Sottoceneri im Süd-Tessin. *Beitr. Geol. Karte Schweiz.*, **117**, 5.

Reynolds, R. C. (1963). Potassium–rubidium ratios and polymorphism in illites and microclines from the clay size fraction of proterozoic carbonate rocks. *Geochim. Cosmochim. Acta*, **27**, 1097.

Ribbe, P. H. and Cott, H. C. van. (1962). Unmixing in peristerite plagioclases observed by dark-field and phase-contrast microscopy. *Can. Mineralogist*, **7**, 278.

Rimsaite, J. and Lachance, G. R. (1966). Illustrations of heterogeneity in phlogopite, feldspar, euxenite and associated minerals. *Mineral. Soc. India, IMA Vol.*, 209.

Rose, G. (1823). Über den Feldspath Albit, Labrador und Anorthit. *Ann. Phys. L. W. Gilbert*, **73**, 173.

Rutland, R. W. R. (1961). The control of anorthite content of plagioclase in metamorphic crystallization. *Am. J. Sci.*, **259**, 76.

Rutland, R. W. R. (1962). Feldspar structure and the equilibrium between plagioclase and epidote. *Am. J. Sci.*, **260**, 153.

de Saénz, I. M. (1963). Authigener Sanidin. Optische und röntgenopraphische Untersuchungen. *Schweiz. Mineral. Petrog. Mitt.*, **43**, 485.

de Saénz, I. M. (1965). Origin of ternary film and string perthites from a Uruguayan migmatite. *Schweiz. Mineral. Petrog. Mitt.*, **45**, 103.

Schmidt, E. (1915). Die Winkel der kristallographischen Achsen der Plagioklase. *Chem. Erde* **1**, 351.

Schröder, A. (1964). Die Schillerfläche am Labradorit. *Naturwissenschaften*, **51**, 507.

Schwantke, A. (1909). Die Beimischung von Ca in Kalifeldspat und die Myrme-kitbildung. *Centralbl. Mineral.*, 311.

Schwarcs, H. P. (1966). Oxygen isotope fractionation between host and exsolved phases in perthite. *Bull. Geol. Soc. Am.*, **77**, 879.

Sen, K. S. (1959). Potassium content of natural plagioclases, and the origin of antiperthites. *J. Geol.*, **67**, 479.

Sen, K. S. (1963). Some consequences of ordering and unmixing in sodic plagio-clases on epidote–plagioclase equilibrium in regionally metamorphosed rocks. *Am. J. Sci.*, **261**, 786.

Shimizu, J. and Kuno, H. (1960). Notes on rock-forming minerals: (14) Anortho-clase phenocrysts in trachyte from Puu Anahulu, Hawaii Island. *J. Geol. Soc. Japan*, **66**, 547.

Smith, J. V. (1956). The powder patterns and lattice parameters of plagioclase feldspars I. *Mineral. Mag.*, **31**, 47.

Smith, J. V. and Stenstrom, R. C. (1965). Electron-excited luminescence as a petrologic tool. *J. Geol.*, **73**, 627.

Soldatos, K. (1962). Über die kryptoperthitische Albit-Ausscheidung in Mikro-klinperthiten. *Norsk Geol. Tidsskr.*, **42**, II (Feldspar Vol.), 180.

Soldatos, K. (1965). Über eine monokline kryptoperthitische Natronfeldspat-Modifikation. *Z. Krist.*, **121**, 317.

Spencer, E. (1930). A contribution to the study of moonstone from Ceylon and other areas, and of the stability relations of the alkali feldspars. *Mineral. Mag.*, **22**, 291.

Spencer, E. (1935). The potash–soda feldspars, I. Thermal stability. *Mineral. Mag.*, **24**, 453.

Spencer, E. (194?). Myrmekite in graphic granite and in vein perthite. *Mineral. Mag.*, **27**, 79

Stern, P. (1964). Zur Petrographie von Nordhoeks Bjerg und Nörlunds Alper, Hudson Land. *Medd. Grønland*, **168**, No. 5.

Stewart, D. B., Walker, G. W., Wright, T. L. and Fahey, J. J. (1966). Physical properties of calcic labradorite from Lake County, Oregon. *Am. Mineralogist*, **51**, 177.

Sugi, K. (1940). On the nature of some plagioclases apparently with small optical angles, etc. *Mem. Fac. Sci., Kyushu Univ., Ser. D*, 1.

Tane, J. T. (1962). A propos des feldspaths potassiques observés dans des laves spilitiques du massif du Palvoux. *Compt. Rend.*, **254**, 3715.

Thomson, T. (1843). Notice of some new minerals. *Phil. Mag.*, **22**, 188.

Thorez, J. and Michot, J. (1964). L'orthose ferrifère de Vedrin. *Ann. Soc. Geol. Belg., Bull.*, **86**, No. 10, 543.

Tschermak, G. (1864). Chemisch–mineralogische Studien I: Die Feldspath-gruppe. *Akad. Wiss. Wien., Sitzber.*, **50**, 566.

Tsuboi, S. (1936). Petrological notes. *Jap. J. Geol. Geogr.*, **13**, 333.

Tsuji, S. (1965). Possible effect of peristerite solvus in plagioclase of the Higo metamorphics, Kyusyu, Japan. *J. Geol. Soc. Japan*, **72**, 63.

Tuttle, O. F. (1952). Origin of contrasting mineralogy of extrusive and plutonic salic rocks. *J. Geol.*, **60**, 107.

Ueda, T. and Tatekawa, M. (1966). On the anorthite found in lava flow. *Mem. Coll. Sci., Univ. Kyoto, Ser. B*, **32**, 285.

Vance, J. A. (1962). Zoning in igneous plagioclase: Normal and oscillating zoning. *Am. J. Sci.*, **260**, 746.

Vance, J. A. (1965). Zoning in igneous plagioclase: Patchy zoning. *J. Geol.*, **73**, 636.

Vance, J. A. (1966). Patchy zoning in plagioclase: A reply. *J. Geol.*, **74**, 518.

Voll, G. (1960). New work on petrofabrics. *Liverpool Manchester Geol. J.*, **2**, 503.

Wager, L. R. and Deer, W. A. (1939). The petrology of Skaergaard intrusion, Kangerdlugssuaq, E. Greenland. *Medd. Grønland*, **105**, No. 4.

Washington, H. S. and Wright, F. (1910). A feldspar from Linosa and the existence of soda anorthite (carnegieite). *Am. J. Sci.*, **29**, 52.

Weiss, M. P. (1954). Feldspathized shales from Minnesota. *J. Sediment. Petrol.*, **24**, 270.

Wenk, E. (1958). Über Diskontinuitäten in Plagioklasserien metamorphen Ursprungs. *Schweiz. Mineral. Petrog. Mitt.*, **38**, 494.

Wenk, E. (1962). Plagioclas als Indexmineral in den Zentralalpen: Die Paragenese Calcit-Plagioclas. *Schweiz. Mineral. Petrog. Mitt.*, **42**, 139.

Wenk, E., Schwander, H. and Wenk, H. R. (1965). Labradorit von Surtsey. *Acta Natur. Islandica*, **2**, No. 5.

Wenk, H. R. (1966). Labradorite from Surtsey, Iceland. *Schweiz. Mineral. Petrog. Mitt.*, **46**, 81.

Wiebe, R. (1967). Plagioclase stratigraphy and preintrusive history of a granite stock (Abstract). *Ann. Meeting Geol. Soc. Am. Program*, 237.

Wyart, J. and Sabatier, G. (1956a). Mobilité des iones alcalins et alcalino-terreux dans les feldspaths. *Bull. Soc. Franc. Mineral. Crist.*, **79**, 444.

Wyart, J. and Sabatier, G. (1956b). Transformation mutuelles des feldspaths alcalins reproduction du microcline et de l'albite. *Bull. Soc. Franc. Mineral. Crist.*, **79**, 574.

Wyart, J. and Sabatier, G. (1960). Sur la mobilité des ions Si et Al dans les feldspaths en présence d'eau. *Bull. Soc. Franc. Mineral. Crist.*, **83**, 141.

Wyart, J. and Sabatier, G. (1962). L'équilibre des feldspaths et des feldspathoides en présence de solutions sodi-potassiques. *Norsk Geol. Tidsskr.*, **42**, II (Feldspar Vol.), 319.

Wyart, J. and Sabatier, G. (1965). Réaction des feldspaths alcalins avec des solutions hydrothermales de $CaCl_2$. *Compt. Rend.*, **260**, 1681.

Zavaritsky, A. N. (1943). On amazonite. *Zap. Vses. Mineralog. Obshchestva*, **72**, 29.

Zhirov, K. K., Stishov, S. M. (1965). Geochemistry of amazonization. *Geochem. Intern.* **2**, 16.

2

Survey of Pseudosymmetry
and Twinning

2.1 PSEUDOSYMMETRY

A *tetragonal* pseudosymmetry is clearly seen in crystals dominated by c (001) and b (010), which are also the directions of the two perfect cleavages (inclined approximately at 90°). The a axis of the feldspar is the pseudo-tetragonal c axis.

A *hexagonal* pseudosymmetry becomes apparent by orienting the b axis vertically; it corresponds to the main hexagonal c axis. The feldspar axes a [100], c [001], and [$\bar{1}$01] which lie nearly in a horizontal plane, and intersect at angles close to 60°, correspond to the three horizontal a axes in the hexagonal system.

A *cubic* pseudosymmetry is shown by the following resetting (Fedorow, 1902):

> the feldspar c axis becomes [111]
>
> the feldspar a axis becomes [00$\bar{2}$]
>
> the feldspar b axis becomes [$\bar{2}$20]

The relation between the optical orientation and the pseudocubic symmetry was discussed by Glauser (1960).

A *monoclinic* pseudosymmetry is very pronounced in all triclinic members of the feldspar group; the crystallographic axes, α and γ, deviate at maximum a few degrees from 90°.

The frequent occurrence of twinning in feldspars is related to these pseudosymmetries. In particular, the ubiquitous polysynthetic twinnings in microcline and plagioclase produce compound crystals that are mimetically monoclinic.

The physical condition for the formation of twins is that the crystal lattice is almost continuous across a twin boundary. Consequently, if the

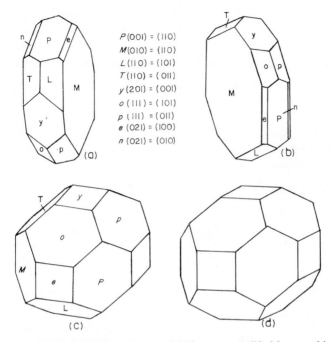

$P(001) = (110)$
$M(010) = (110)$
$L(110) = (101)$
$T(110) = (011)$
$y(201) = (001)$
$o(111) = (101)$
$p(111) = (011)$
$e(021) = (100)$
$n(021) = (010)$

FIGURE 2.1 Pseudocubic symmetry of feldspars exemplified by anorthite. (*a*) Anorthite crystal, conventional setting; (*b*) Same crystal in pseudocubic setting; (*c*) Same crystal again, drawn with equal central distances for pseudocubically corresponding faces, the pseudohexahedron and pseudo-rhombic dodecahedron clearly standing out; (*d*) Cubic crystal with (100) and (110), for comparison. (Burri, 1962)

lattice has planes or axes that are pseudosymmetry elements, they may serve as planes or axes of twins, see figure 3.5.

2.2 TWINNING LAWS

Twinning laws can be described by stating the twin axis. The twin plane is, by definition, normal to the twin axis, but the composition plane, i.e. the plane along which the two twin individuals are in contact, may be either normal to the axis (and thus identical to the twin plane) or parallel to the axis. Accordingly, one may distinguish:

1. Normal twins: The twin axis normal to the composition face which is also a crystallographic face.
2. Parallel twins: The twin axis parallel to the composition face (or to a crystal edge).

3. Complex twins can be described as the result of two operations: that of a normal twin plus that of a parallel twin. However, the same operations may also be described by a rotation about one twin axis that is normal to a crystal edge and at the same time parallel to a crystal face.

A remarkably complete paper on the twin laws of the feldspars was written as early as 1835 by G. E. Kayser. Today a copious literature exists. The salient points have been systematized and summarized by Burri (1962). The various cases are displayed in the following tables. They refer to triclinic symmetry, in the monoclinic system the number of cases reduce (see below).

2.21 Normal twins
(See figures 1.3*a,b*, 1.11.)

Name	Twin plane	Remarks
X	(100)	Identical to Carlsbad B in monoclinic feldspar
Albite	(010)	Usually polysynthetic
Manebach	(001)	Called *Four-la-Brouque* by Gonnard (1883)
Baveno	(021) or (0$\bar{2}$1)	Usually two individuals[a]
Prism	(110) or (1$\bar{1}$0)	Rare. For triclinic feldspars the designation 'prism' would not be correct

[a] The so-called *Banater Verwachsungen* are cross-shaped intergrowths of plagioclases with mutually parallel (001) and (010) faces. They are probably Baveno twins (Tschermak, 1874); Streckeisen, 1932; Burri, 1963).

In addition there are a number of very rare normal twins, whose twin planes are: (111), (1$\bar{1}$1), (130), (1$\bar{3}$0), ($\bar{2}$01), ($\bar{1}$11), ($\bar{1}$12). The four first have no special names, the three last ones are called Cunnersdorf, Breithaupt law and Goodsprings, respectively. The planes (320) and (3$\bar{2}$0) were mentioned by Gates (1953, p. 65) but have not been confirmed.

2.22 Parallel twins
(See also figures 1.3*c*, 2.8, 2.9.)

Name	Twin axis	Composition plane	Remarks
Ala A	[100] = *a* axis	(001)	Called *Estérel* by Lacroix (1897)
Pericline	[010] = *b* axis	Rhombic section	Usually polysynthetic
Carlsbad	[001] = *c* axis	*A*(010) or *B*(100) or irregular	Usually two individuals

There are two rare cases: *Petschau* with twin axis $[1\bar{1}0]$, i.e. the edge between c (001) and m (110) ('Kantengesetz' of Tschermak, 1887) and *Nevada* with twin axis $[\bar{1}12]$, i.e. edge between α $(1\bar{1}1)$ and m (110) (Drugman, 1938).

2.23 Complex twins
(See also figures 1.10, 1.12, 2.4.)

Name	Twin axis	Composition plane	Remarks
Albite–Carlsbad	⊥ [001]	(010)	Called *Roc Tourné* by Lacroix (1897)
Manebach–Ala	⊥ [100]	(001)	Nearly identical to a special case of the pericline law[a]
Albite–Ala	⊥ [100]	(010)	Albite–Estérel
Manebach–pericline	⊥ [010]	(001)	Called Scopi by Viola (1900)
X–Carlsbad	⊥ [001]	(100)	Nearly identical to a special case of the pericline law[a]
X–pericline	⊥ [010]	(100)	Rare. (= Carlsbad B in monoclinic feldspars)

[a] Manebach–Ala, X–Carlsbad and X–pericline are supposed to be the true interpretations respectively of the so-called Acline A, Acline B and Carlsbad B twin of Duparc and Reinhard (1923).

A rapid survey of the feldspar twin system was formulated by Burri (1964, 1965). The axes of the parallel twins, Ala, pericline and Carlsbad, correspond to the direct crystallographic axes a, b, c, whereas the axes of the three normal twins, X, albite, Manebach, correspond to the reciprocal axes, a^*, b^*, c^*. The twin axes of the six complex twins are each normal to two other twin axes, of which one is a normal twin axis, the other a parallel twin axis. They may therefore be obtained by vectorial multiplication. The twin axes of Baveno and 'Prism' are normal to faces of simple indices belonging to the zones [100] and [001] and result from vectorial addition in the reciprocal system.

Each of the direct axes a, b, c is normal to the two opposite reciprocal axes a^*, b^*, c^*, and vice versa; thus the vectorial products are:

$$a\,b \;=c^*, \quad b\,c \;=a^*, \quad c\,a \;=b^*$$
$$a^*b^* =c\,, \quad b^*c^* =a\; =c^*a^*=b$$

and consequently

$$(b^*a) = (c^*a) = (a^*b) = (c^*b) = (b^*c) = (a^*c) = 0$$

The twin axis of each of the six complex twins listed above derives by the multiplications shown in column (2). In the monoclinic system, $b = b^*$, and the complex twin laws reduce as shown in columns (3) and (4). Note that the monoclinic symmetry permits two different formulations for both Carlsbad and Manebach twins.

Triclinic system		Monoclinic system	
(1) Twin law	(2) Twin axis	(3) Twin axis	(4) Twin law
Albite–Carlsbad	b^*c	$b\ c\ = a^* = \perp (100)$	Carlsbad
Manebach–Ala	c^*a	$c^*a\ = b\ =\quad [010]$	No twin
Albite–Ala	b^*a	$b\ a\ = c^* = \perp (001)$	Manebach
Manebach–pericline	c^*b	$c^*b^* = a\ =\quad [100]$	Manebach
X–Carlsbad	a^*c	$a^*c\ = b\ =\quad [010]$	No twin
X–pericline	a^*b	$a^*b^* = c\ =\quad [001]$	Carlsbad

Thus the introduction of monoclinic symmetry reduces the six complex twins to two simple twins: in two cases, b becomes twin axis and, as it is a digyre, no twins result; of the remaining four cases, two lead to the two possible monoclinic formulations of the Carlsbad law and the other two to the corresponding formulation of the Manebach law.

Gottardi (1962) has described rare and complex twinning in albite from Elba. An example is a combination of Baveno and Manebach twinning in pure albite. The Baveno brings (001) into near, but not exact coincidence

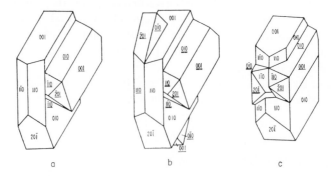

FIGURE 2.2 Rare and imperfect twins (Gottardi, 1962)

with (010); the Manebach twinning permits the corresponding parts of the Baveno twins to continue almost undisturbed as albite twins. But the composition face is then slightly out of step, see figure 2.2.

There also exist regular aggregations of crystal units that are not ideal twins but exhibit mutual crystallographic relations of various kinds such that the composite aggregate exhibits a high symmetry (*übergeordnete Symmetrie* of Glauser, 1963, 1964).

2.3 TWIN BOUNDARIES

Figure 3.5 gives an example of the homogeneous continuation of the crystal lattice across the boundary of two twins. All true twin boundaries show similar lattice relations, but they will not be treated in detail here.

FIGURE 2.3 Plagioclase with wedge-shaped albite twin lamellae. (Manolescu, *Schweiz. Mineral. Petrog. Mitt.*, **14**, 452, 1934)

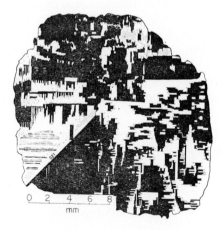

FIGURE 2.4 High-temperature basaltic plagioclase (An$_{48}$) showing Baveno–pericline–albite combination twinning. (Oftedahl, *Norsk Geol. Tidsskr.*, **46**, 1946)

A noteworthy feature of many actual twin boundaries is that they are not straight. Vernon (1965) thinks that plagioclases with lamellar twins which gradually change thickness across a grain or form lenticular terminations are mechanical twins, whereas simple and lamellar twins which show angular steps in the twin interface or form abrupt, planar terminations are formed by grain growth in the solid state (in accordance with experiments by Starkey and Brown, 1964), see figures 2.3 and 2.4. Furthermore, even in normal twins the twin boundary, or composition face, often does not correspond to a crystallographic face but represents vicinal forms. Other 'defects' in twins are: different width and different optical behaviour in two conjugate sets of twin lamellae (J. D. MacKenzie, 1923; Berek, 1925; Köhler and Raaz, 1945); crossed twin axes (Tertsch, 1941), or incomplete rotation around the twin axis (up to 12° misfit has been reported) (Barth, 1930; Emmons and others, 1960; Wang, 1933). Berek (1925) definitely speaks of a 'Fehlbildung' at which two individuals of different chemical composition aspire to achieve a twinned position. These observations indicate a discontinuity in the space lattice at the composition plane, which is contrary to our ideas of twin formation. The inference is that the discontinuity is secondary. Along the twin boundary there is often a zone of turbidity or clouding, perhaps indicating metasomatic alteration, see also p. 80.

The so-called internal optical scatter in plagioclase was defined by Vogel (1964) as the scatter of projection plots of adjacent twin lamellae within a single crystal. Tobi (1965) pointed out that whether or not such internal scatter is susceptible to demonstration depends on a fundamental choice of the procedure of measurement. If the measurements are based on the assumptions that the composition plane of a twin corresponds to its ideal crystallographic orientation, then the logical interpretation may be imperfect twinning or different composition of contiguous twin lamellae. But if it is assumed that the adjoining lamellae have the same composition and are correctly rotated, then the measurements indicate

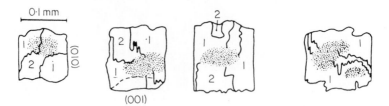

FIGURE 2.5 Growth twins in authigenic microcline from Pontiskalk. (Perrenoud, *Schweiz. Mineral. Petrog. Mitt.*, **32**, 1952)

that the composition plane is irregular, that it is curved, or composed of a number of vicinal planes, or non-parallel with the ideal crystallographic direction.

Within the next few years, the electron probe will greatly augment our knowledge of the relation between chemical composition and optical properties of plagioclase, and the problem of internal scatter and of defect twins will be solved.

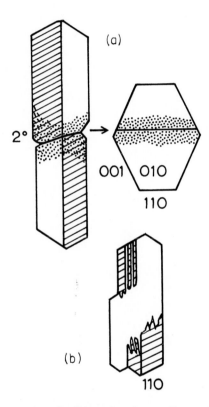

FIGURE 2.6 (*a*) Authigenic albite twinned according to the complex X–Carlsbad law. Crystal to the left is oriented with vertical *c* axis; the transverse twin boundary is roughly parallel to (100). The crystal to the right shows this boundary on (010) as a straight line strictly parallel to the *c* axis. The two parts separated by the boundary are displaced 1–2° (corresponding to the angle (100)/(010) deviating about 0·5° from 90°).

(*b*) In other crystals, the transverse twin boundary is incomplete. The trace of the boundary (= composition plane) is jagged and irregular with a main direction roughly parallel to (100). The twin individuals are here strictly parallel and represent true albite twins. (After Füchtbauer, 1948)

The peculiar relations of twin plane and orientation in the albite–pericline combinations called M-twins in cross-hatched microcline are described on p. 73.

The pericline twins merit special comment. Their composition plane is the so-called rhombic section.

2.4 RHOMBIC SECTION

In the triclinic system, a crystal edge Ob of figure 2.7 is not normal to a crystal face, f. The plane that passes through Ob and through the line RR' that is normal to the projection OP of Ob is called a *rhombic section* with regard to Ob and f. Obviously, the position of this section depends on the interaxial angles α, β, γ. The conventional setting of triclinic feldspars makes Ob the b axis and f (010).

G. vom Rath (1876) found that, in the pericline twins of feldspars of Alpine veins, b was the twin axis and the composition plane was a non-crystallonomic face which he called the rhombic section.

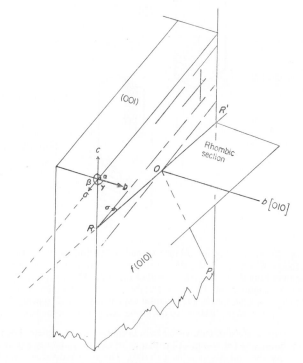

FIGURE 2.7 Definition of a rhombic section

The function of this composition plane is to make the discontinuity in the crystalline lattice across the twin plane as small as possible. Again, in the plane of the rhombic section the rates of growth of the faces (110) and (1$\bar{1}$0) are equal (Goldsztaub and Saucier, 1959). The study of the rhombic

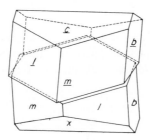

FIGURE 2.8 The pericline law in plagioclase. Schematic drawing by vom Rath (1876)

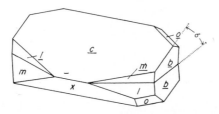

FIGURE 2.9 Typical habit of pericline from the Swiss Alps

section has played an interesting part in the study of the feldspars. The history of the pericline law has been treated by Schmidt (1915).

The angle σ is the angle between the a axis [= the trace of the basal cleavage on (010)] and the trace of the rhombic section on (010). The angle s between the basal cleavage and the rhombic section differs only slightly from the angle σ.

As pointed out by Tunell (1952), incorrect formulae for the calculation of these angles are found in the literature. The correct relations are:

$$\cot \sigma = \frac{\cos \alpha^*}{\cot \gamma} = \frac{\cos (001 \wedge 010)}{\cot \gamma} = \cot \beta - \frac{\cos \alpha}{\cos \gamma \sin \beta}$$

$$\cot s = \frac{\cot \alpha^*}{\cos \gamma}$$

As the crystallographic angles change in the plagioclase series, so the rhombic section changes. This is graphically illustrated in figure 2.10.

In the plagioclases, the position of the composition plane is revealed by a series of fine striations on (010). By measuring the angle between the basal cleavage and the striations, the chemical composition of the crystal is indicated, see figure 2.9.

However, it was soon noticed that the composition plane of the pericline twins, particularly in sodic plagioclases, did not generally coincide with the rhombic section calculated from the usually accepted mineralogical data. Many authors have claimed that from measurements of the

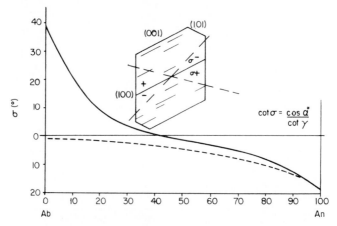

FIGURE 2.10 The relation between the position of the rhombic section (expressed by σ) and the composition of the plagioclases. The full curve is calculated from measurements of the interaxial angles of natural plagioclases compiled by Wulfing (1915). The dashed curve refers to measurements on heated plagioclases and on synthetic materials

position of this plane no accurate conclusion can be drawn as to the chemical composition of the feldspar (Duparc and Reinhard, 1924; Barth, 1928).

The explanation of the discrepancies became evident with the knowledge of the permanent disorder of the Al–Si distribution induced in plagioclases exposed to heat. The interaxial angles of a high-temperature plagioclase are different from the angles of a low-temperature plagioclase of the same composition; intermediate stages are also known (see fig. 1.21). Such differences in the axial angles obviously affect the position of the rhombic section, and, as seen from figure 2.10, the effect is particularly large for sodic plagioclases (J. V. Smith, 1958b, 1962; Barth and Thoresen, 1965).

Baskin (1956) measured authigenic albite that was heated around 1100°c for 28 days; his data are given in figure 2.11: α* varies only slightly, γ increases rapidly, passes 90° and keeps on changing for 10 days. After 10 days the curve flattens, and the change in γ is apparently completed. σ

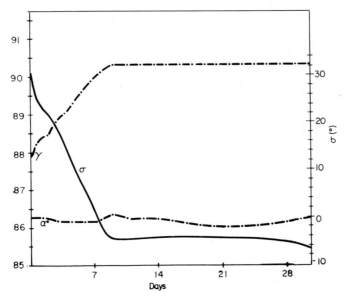

FIGURE 2.11 Variation in α*, γ and σ of authigenic albite heated at 1065–1120°c (by Baskin, 1956) for 28 days (measured at room temperature). The curves indicate that after 10 days equilibrium was established

decreases from 30°, unheated, to −4°, heated. Baskin's experiments strongly indicate that after 10 days complete disorder was reached, consequently the σ value in high-temperature albite should be about minus four degrees.

In microcline the 'triclinicity' varies from a maximum value, designated by 1, to zero (= monoclinic symmetry). This variation affects the position of the rhombic section. By observations on natural microcline, Reinhard and Bächlin (1936) found variations of the composition plane of the pericline twins from −75° to −90° (figure 2.12).

Baskin (1956) investigated the changes of the crystallographic elements of authigenic microcline during heating at 1120°c. From his data the corresponding changes in the position of the rhombic section were calculated. They are displayed in figure 2.13.

Feldspars

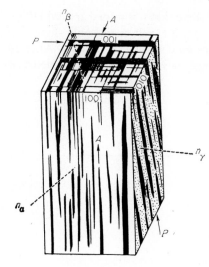

FIGURE 2.12 Microcline showing poly-synthetic twinning on a microscopic scale, thus simulating monoclinic symmetry. $A-A$ = albite twins parallel to (010). $P-P$ = pericline twins parallel to the rhombic section. (Reinhard and Bächlin, 1936)

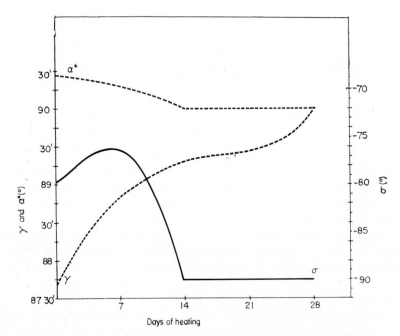

FIGURE 2.13 Variation in α^*, γ and σ of authigenic microcline heated at 1120°C (by Baskin). Again equilibrium was established within about 28 days

In anorthoclases, which are high-temperature minerals, the σ values vary with the composition as shown by figure 2.14 (Barth and Thoresen, 1965). For practically all compositions, σ is in the range $-2°$ to $-3°$.

The simple thermal effect (thermal homogeneous expansion) also affects the position of the rhombic section which, therefore, reflects the temperature at which the twinning took place, see figure 2.15.

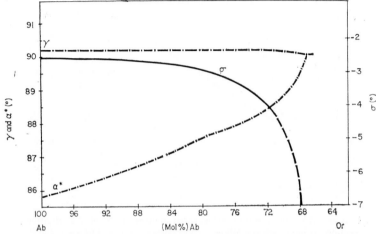

FIGURE 2.14 Variation in α^*, γ and σ in the anorthoclase series. The angles change regularly with composition. α^* and γ reach 90° at the same time, σ goes toward $-45°$

This was used by Mügge (1930) in an effort to determine the temperature of the formation of anorthite showing primary pericline twinning. Anorthite crystals from Vesuvius, composition $An_{97.1}$, with known interaxial angles, were used. The theoretical value of σ is $-17·15°$. Mügge consistently found a smaller numerical value, $\sigma = -14°$ on average. This difference should reflect the difference between the temperature of formation and the temperature at which the measurements were made. The validity of the argument was confirmed by subsequently producing in the same crystals artificial pericline twins by shearing at room temperature. The composition plane then gave $\sigma \simeq -18·7°$ (Mügge and Heide, 1931).

M-twins typical of microcline and anorthoclase used to be regarded as simple combinations of albite and pericline twins. However, Laves (1950) found that cross-hatched microcline always revealed a special orientation between the two albite twin components, A_1A_2, and the two pericline twin components, P_1P_2, such that the (010) twin plane of the albite twins was perpendicular to the [010] twin axis of the pericline twins. This combination was later called an M-twin by Smith and MacKenzie (1958).

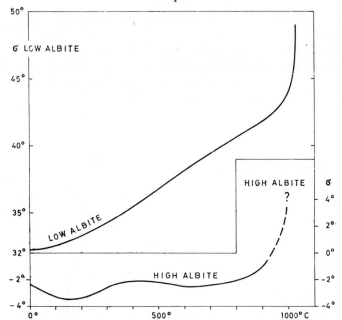

FIGURE 2.15 The position at elevated temperatures of the rhombic section in high and low albite. (After Stewart and v. Limbach, 1967)

Since (010) is not perpendicular to [010] in triclinic material, it is necessary for M-twinned triclinic microcline to inherit this crystallographic relation from a monoclinic phase. A variety of M-twin is the *diagonal association* described by MacKenzie and Smith (1955, 1962), and Smith and Mac-Kenzie (1954, 1959). Of the four twin lamellae, $A_1A_2P_1P_2$, two are eliminated, such that only A_1 and P_2 (or A_2 and P_1) are left. At the same time, the two lamellae adjust themselves to an angular position intermediate between that of the albite and that of the pericline twins of the M-association.

Small deviations from the M-law were found by Laves and Soldatos (1962) in certain microcline perthites. Angles of up to 20′ between the axis perpendicular to (010) and [010] (between b^* and b) were measured. But in such cases both the exsolved albite blebs and the contiguous parts of the encasing K-feldspar were distorted.

The reciprocal angles were:

K-feldspar: $\alpha^* = 90°\,40'$, $\gamma^* = 90°\,10'$ Na-feldspar: $\alpha^* = 86°\,49'$, $\gamma^* = 90°\,10'$

In particular, the distortion of the K-feldspar is large; normal microclines always show $(\gamma^* - 90°) \gg (\alpha^* - 90°)$. Here it is the opposite: $(\gamma^* - 90°) \ll (\alpha^* - 90°)$, Laves refers to this as distorted M-twinning (*verzerrte Mikroklin-Verzwillingung*).

It should be noted that Na-feldspar in the form of cryptoperthitic inclusions quite generally may suffer this kind of distortion. In a great many microcline cryptoperthites, Laves and Soldatos (1963) found γ^* values of the Na-feldspar very close to that given above, see also figure 1.20.

In exsolved anorthoclases, Ito and Sadanaga (1952) found that the Na-rich triclinic perthitic phase is twinned after the albite and/or the pericline law. When K-feldspar makes up more than 70% of the bulk, the exsolved Na-feldspar regularly exhibits polysynthetic albite twinning. If K-feldspar is less than 70%, the pericline-twinned Na-feldspar appears, and the ratio of pericline/albite twins increases as the K-feldspar/Na-feldspar decreases. When K-feldspar makes up only 40% (60% Na-feldspar) the albite twins disappear leaving only pericline twins.

The (100) faces are left unchanged by the pericline twinning because $\gamma^* \simeq 90°$. Indeed, in the pericline twins the direct angle γ, and in the albite twins the reciprocal angle γ^* persistently equal $90°$, irrespective of the nature of the mother feldspar from which they have been produced by exsolution; for the pericline twins have the direct b axis, and the albite twins have the reciprocal b^* axis as twin axis. The ease with which poly-symmetry synthesis takes place in a triclinic crystal when one of its direct interaxial angles is $90°$ is known, from the wollastonite group (Ito, 1950).

Obviously, the angle σ is a one-valued function of the interaxial crystal angles, α, β, γ. Again the interaxial angles are functions of (1) the chemical composition, (2) the structural state, (3) the absolute temperature, (4) the stress–strain pattern in crystals of polysynthetic twinning or of perthitic or other lamellar structures, see figures 2.10–2.14. Thus there are exciting possibilities of demonstrating changes in the feldspars subsequent to the formation of the pericline twins. Further study of the pericline compos-sition plane, using x-rays to determine crystallographic data from which the angle σ can be calculated, would seem to be desirable, and should yield results of great significance in petrology, see also p. 81.

2.5 GENESIS OF TWINS

According to the theory of twinning of the French school of crystallo-graphers, the fact conditioning the occurrence of twins is that there exists in the space lattice a cell, simple or multiple, exhibiting either rigorously or approximately more symmetry than the crystal. The following defini-tions are used by Donnay (1940, 1943):

1. *The twin lattice* is the lattice having the edges of that cell for its primitive translations.
2. *The twin elements* are the elements of symmetry (or pseudosymmetry) which this particular cell possesses but which the crystal itself does not

have as elements of symmetry. The twin elements are reticular, i.e. a twin plane is a lattice plane, a twin axis is a lattice row.
3. *The index of the twin* is the ratio of the total number of lattice nodes to the number of lattice nodes restored by twinning.
4. *The obliquity of the twin* is the angle between the true normal to the twin plane and the lattice row nearly normal to it.

Donnay (1940) first proposed that the reticular conditions (low index, small obliquity) which make it possible for twinning to occur at all, also account for the relative frequencies (or width of lamellae) of polysynthetic albite twinning in feldspars.

In triclinic feldspar, albite twins and pericline twins have the same obliquity, viz. the angle between [010] and $\perp$ (010); they also have the same index ($= 1$). Other things being equal, the two sets of twinning, albite twins and pericline twins, should have the same frequency and the same width of the lamellae. This is obviously true in ordinary microcline and in M-twins of other triclinic feldspars. But in plagioclases this is not so evident.

However, in plagioclases (and anorthoclases) another interesting phenomenon is worth discussing. The obliquity of the twins changes rapidly with the chemical composition. Donnay (1940) first computed the obliquity, ϕ, for various compositions of the plagioclases.

The relation is:

$$\sin^2 \phi = (\cos^2 \alpha + \cos^2 \gamma - 2 \cos \alpha \cos \beta \cos \gamma)/\sin^2 \beta$$

where α, β, γ are the interaxial angles for the direct cell. If the reciprocal cell angles are known, the expression becomes:

$$\cos \phi = \sin \alpha^* \sin \gamma = \sin \alpha \sin \gamma^*$$

Gay (1956) was able to extend Donnay's work using more reliable crystallographic data and also taking into consideration the high-temperature states of the plagioclases, a phenomenon which was not fully recognized before. Eventually, J. V. Smith (1958a) showed that the obliquity is affected more by temperature than by composition, see figure 2.15.

Table 2.1 (from Stewart and von Limbach, 1967) demonstrates the effect of heating on the obliquity. The authors comment that the small variation of ϕ of low albite with temperature makes it improbable that any correlations of the frequency of twinning with temperature can be established, and, indeed, the low albite of metamorphic rocks occurs either as single crystals or as very coarse albite twins throughout the temperature range of its occurrence. The variation of ϕ in high albite is also small but two and a half times greater than that observed in low albite.

TABLE 2.1

Effect of heating low and high albite on the obliquity, ϕ, and on the rhombic section, σ

Low albite

T°C	26	141	245	364	488	628	759	883	1010	1127
ϕ	4° 17·5'	4° 13·5'	4° 15·0'	4° 4·5'	4° 0·5'	3° 48·0'	3° 44·0'	3° 35·0'	3° 28·5'	3° 1·0'
σ	32° 14·7'	32° 47·5'	33° 48·8'	34° 53·6'	36° 32·3'	36° 29·0'	40° 43·3'	41° 36·1'	44° 28·0'	49° 4·1'

High albite

T°C	26	154	318	605	902	931	980	1026	1062
ϕ	−4° 3·0'	−3° 49·0'	−3° 24·5'	−2° 46·0'	−1° 36·0'	−1° 23·0'	−1° 5·0'	−0° 46'	0°
σ	−2° 41·5'	−3° 30·1'	−2° 24·8'	−0° 32·7'	−0° 28·5'	−6° 54·7'	2° 34·9'	9° 0·4'	0°

The twin lamellae in pure albite and pure anorthite are broader than in intermediate plagioclases; particularly oligoclase of small twin obliquity exhibits narrow twin lamellae. And in anorthoclase, which has the smallest twin obliquity of all triclinic feldspars, the lamellae are exceedingly narrow. However, Vance (1961) correctly pointed out that much of the evidence is inadmissible because the observed twins are probably secondary glide twins.

The petrologic significance of twinning in feldspars and its relation to external habit, zoning, etc., was treated in an early pioneering work by Köhler (1949b).

The genetic aspects of twinning were discussed by J. V. Smith (1962); Vance (1961) reviewed the literature and established criteria for distinguishing primary from secondary twinning.

Forces external to the crystal lattice may 'trigger' the twinning. That is to say, certain environmental conditions may be favourable for twinning while others may not. A favourable environment is often called the cause of twinning, although this is not a very happy way of phrasing it. Obviously,

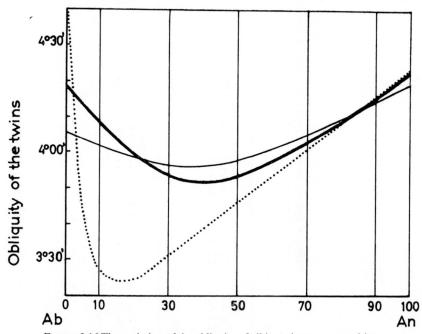

FIGURE 2.16 The variation of the obliquity of albite twins vs. composition. Dotted curve = natural plagioclases after Donnay (1940). Thick curve = natural plagioclases. Thin curve = heated and synthetic plagioclases. (After J. V. Smith, 1958a)

the conditions that make twinning possible must prevail continuously over the time interval during which the twins are formed.

Specifically, twins may be produced (1) during the *growth* of the crystals, (2) by *transformation* of the crystals into another modification, and (3) by *mechanical shear*. The growth twins are primary, the others are usually secondary.

(1) Primary twins frequently grow in magmatic rocks (growth twinning of Buerger, 1945). High temperature, generally speaking, favours the formation of twins. They may be polysynthetic, for example, in albite twinning, but they are often simple twins, Carlsbad, Manebach, etc., or complex twins or other combination twins.

Reference to the literature indicates that there is some controversy as to the primary nature of polysynthetic twinning.

Many workers maintain that most and perhaps all polysynthetic twinning in plagioclase is secondary (Baier, 1930; Emmons and Gates, 1943; Emmons and Mann, 1953; Köhler, 1949a; Köhler and Raaz, 1945); others express the opposite view (Barber, 1936; Gorai, 1951; Turner, 1951), see Vance (1961). The 'combination twins' of Ross (1957) are formed by the drifting together and joining of crystals in a magma according to a twin law (= synneusis twins, see figure 1.25).

Primary twins are also frequent in metamorphic rocks (although low-grade metamorphic rocks are remarkable for their large proportion of untwinned feldspar); the mechanism of growth may be similar to that of twins in magmatic rocks, or it may be directed by an early, pre-existing crystal. Thus it appears that if albite crystals undergo microclinization in a rock, then the microcline produced will inherit the framework of the albite. If the original albite was untwinned, the microcline will become untwinned; if the albite was twinned, the microcline should inherit the twin laws of the albite. The same principle applies to the artificial preparation of microcline as described by Laves (1951), see Euler and Hellner (1961).

(2) Secondary twinning by inversion has been mentioned on p. 7. It takes place with the formation of M-twins by the diffusive transformation of orthoclase (or sanidine) into microcline. And it takes place by the displacive transformation of soda sanidine into anorthoclase (see p. 126). In sodic plagioclases similar inversion twins may form. This has been staunchly advocated by Austrian petrologists (Köhler and Raaz, 1945; Köhler, 1949b); and eventually proved by heating experiments; see section 3.23.

(3) Secondary twinning by mechanical deformation: Laves (1952) pointed out that the ease of production of glide twinning is completely controlled by the Al/Si distribution in the feldspar framework. If a thin

cleavage flake of disordered albite is watched under the microscope and pressed by a needle, twin lamellae are seen to develop. On release of the pressure the lamellae disappear. This operation can be repeated. Ordered albite, however, is not susceptible and will not twin in response to pressure; for, in the ordered lattice, the twinning would have to break strong chemical bonds and cause a considerable moving of the Si and Al ions. If twinning occurred at a state of partial order, the Si/Al pattern would be different at either side of the twin boundary. This misfit would have a tendency to adjust itself with time. Nevertheless, in a polysynthetically twinned crystal of this sort the one set of lamellae must behave optically different from the other set. This may explain the inference often reported that two lamellae in twin position are of different composition (because they are optically different), see p. 66.

In Ca-rich plagioclase, glide twinning is again possible, for the Si–Al–oxygen framework here exhibits monoclinic symmetry. In fact, as early as 1883 van Werveke produced glide twinning in anorthite, This has later been confirmed by many petrographers (see p. 73). It is an interesting research project to find the exact relation between crystallographic order and twinning.

Vance (1962) made interesting observations on the rhombic section of a zoned igneous plagioclase crystal showing two generations of pericline

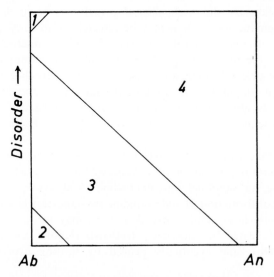

FIGURE 2.17 Development of glide twins in plagioclases. Area 1 represents the possible field of monalbite, twinning is precluded by the monoclinic symmetry. In area 2 twinning is precluded on structural grounds. In area 3 twinning is possible but not easy. In area 4 twinning is easy

twinning: one growth twinning, the other glide twinning. Plotting the angle of the rhombic section against composition for each set of twins gives curves indicative of an intermediate structural state. The curve for the growth twins is closer to the high structural state than that for the glide twins and supports the primary origin of the former and the partial inversion of the crystal prior to formation of the glide lamellae. Both rhombic sections are probably relict with respect to the present structural state.

Cannon (1966) found in some amphibolites and granites that the pericline twins do not reflect the present rhombic sections of the plagioclases; they were possibly formed when the plagioclases were in a higher structural state. Starkey (1967) studied the development of glide twins and demonstrated that the history of a plagioclase crystal may be interpreted by measuring the orientation of the composition planes of secondary pericline twins. He postulated a relation between the structural state (and composition) of plagioclases and the ease of formation of pericline–albite twins by gliding, see figure 2.17.

Kind and frequency of plagioclase twinning in various rock types have been statistically studied by many investigators (for example, Gorai, 1951; Tobi, 1961, 1962; Turner, 1951). Such studies are subject to the possibility of misinterpretation because a correlation may be either primary, secondary or the result of several factors.

Gorai (1951) has divided the plagioclase twins, from a petrological point of view, into the following groups:

C-twins, characteristic of volcanic and plutonic rocks: Carlsbad, albite–Carlsbad, Manebach, Manebach–acline, Baveno, Ala B, albite–Ala.
A-twins, characteristic of igneous as well as metamorphic rocks: albite and pericline twins.

Gorai's (1965) observations on artificial plagioclases are worthy of mention. Plagioclases (An_{0-30}) from melts exhibit 85% of albite and albite–Carlsbad twins (= C-twins). Plagioclases (An_{30-50}) by devitrification at $1000-1200°c$ (i.e. $100-200°$ below melting) show no twins at all. Gorai's conclusion is that formation of Carlsbad and albite–Carlsbad twins is very difficult by crystallization in solid media.

Tobi (1961) thinks that the various twin patterns will emerge more clearly if not only the relative amounts of C-twins, but also the relative amounts of twins with (010) as composition plane be taken into consideration. This '(010) twin ratio' should be $1·00$ for albite grown in the greenschist facies, $1·00-0·75$ for plagioclase of magmatic rocks and hornfelses, and smaller than 0·50 for plagioclase grown in the almandine–amphibolite facies.

The problem seems to be quite complicated. Thus Suwa (1956) observed that the chemical composition of the plagioclase greatly affected the type of twinning, and this may be related to discontinuities in the plagioclase structure at An_{32} and An_{72}. Suwa also found that, for example, the albite–Carlsbad twinning (roc tourné, see below) gradually disappeared with progressive recrystallization. Porphyroblasts may be twinned differently from the groundmass feldspar. Sarbadhikari (1965) similarly found differences in the twinning pattern between phenocrysts and groundmass feldspars in basalt.

Very little is known about the elimination of twinning. A twin is thermodynamically unstable, for the twin plane (composition plane) is a section of high free energy. In the course of time a twin should, therefore, convert into a single crystal.

Usually it takes some sort of external energy, mechanical energy, stress or heat, to eliminate the twin structure. Observations by Prasad (1966) indicate that effacing of plagioclase twinning may be effected in various ways, and usually during a post-tectonic deformation period.

Chess-board albite affords an interesting example. It is twinned according to the roc tourné laws, and is morphologically characterized by dense arrays of narrow discontinuous albite lamellae. The twin boundaries are usually stepped or lenticular and commonly terminate abruptly. The composite crystal is therefore distinguished by an unusually large area of incoherent twin boundary surfaces. It has been studied by Carstens (1966) in relation to recrystallization. Such albites are often present in regional metamorphic rocks, and mechanical twinning has been suggested (Starkey, 1959). But the origin is in dispute. Chess-board twinning seems to be confined to rather pure albite (Battey, 1955), and it is probable that the difficulties involved in the twinning of ordered low albite (see p. 80–81) are of importance in controlling the peculiar twin pattern.

Whatever the origin, there is a strong tendency in chess-board albite to recrystallize during post-tectonic annealing conditions. This behaviour is alien to all other feldspars which manifestly—in contrast to, for example, calcite or quartz—recrystallize only with great difficulty.

It is natural to view this behaviour in relation to the chess-board twin pattern. The internal energy is considerably higher than that of the untwinned albite, or albite having normally spaced and coherent twin lamellae. Strain energy is stored along the twin boundaries, especially along those which are incoherent. It has been shown (Startsev, 1963), by an investigation of the mechanism of formation of mechanical twins in calcite, that the twinning is accompanied by point defects, stacking faults and positioned dislocations in addition to the twinning dislocations. Thus very large strains may be introduced in minerals during the act of twinning. It is this excess energy that Carstens believes is the driving force of recrystallization in the chess-board albite.

REFERENCES

Baier, E. (1930). Lamellenbau und Entmischungsstruktur der Feldspäte. *Z. Krist.*, **73**, 465.

Barber, C. T. (1936). The effect of heat on the optical orientation of plagioclase feldspars. *Mineral. Mag.*, **24**, 343.

Barth, T. F. W. (1928). Die Lage des rhombischen Schnittes bei sauren Plagioklasen. *Z. Krist.*, **68**, 616.

Barth, T. F. W. (1930). Mineralogy of the Adirondack feldspars. *Am. Mineralogist*, **15**, 129.

Barth, T. F. W. and Thoresen, K. (1965). The attitude of the rhombic section in triclinic feldspars, with a note on 'diclinic' crystals. *Norsk Geol. Tidsskr.*, **45**, 83.

Baskin, Y. (1956). Observations on heat-treated authigenic microcline and albite crystals. *J. Geol.*, **64**, 219.

Battey, M. H. (1955). Alkali metasomatism and petrology of some keratophyres. *Geol. Mag.*, **92**, 104.

Berek, M. (1925). Zwillings-Fehlbildung an Plagioklasen und ihre Bedeutung für die Anwendung der Ossowschen Diagramme. *Z. Krist.*, **61**, 177.

Brown, W. L. (1960). The crystallographic and petrologic significance of peristerite unmixing in the acid plagioclases. *Z. Krist.*, **113**, 330.

Buerger, M. J. (1945). The genesis of twin crystals. *Am. Mineralogist*, **30**, 469.

Burri, C. (1962). A survey of feldspar-twinning. *Norsk Geol. Tidsskr.*, **42**, II (Feldspar Vol.).

Burri, C. (1963). Bemerkungen zur sog. 'Banater Verwachsung' der Plagioklase. *Schweiz. Mineral. Petrog. Mitt.*, **43**, 71.

Burri, C. (1964). Versuch einer einfachen Systematik der wichtigsten Plagioklas-Zwillingsgesetze. *Schweiz. Mineral. Petrog. Mitt.*, **44**, 421.

Burri, C. (1965). Bemerkungen zur Formulierung der Zwillingsgesetze monokliner Feldspäte. *Schweiz. Mineral. Petrog. Mitt.*, **45**, 457.

Cannon, R. T. (1966). Plagioclase zoning and twinning in relation to the metamorphic history of some amphibolites and granulites. *Am. J. Sci.*, **264**, 526.

Carstens, H. (1966). The effect of twinning on the recrystallization of albite. *Norsk Geol. Tidsskr.*, **46**, 358.

Donnay, J. D. H. (1940). Width of albite-twinning lamellae. *Am. Mineralogist*, **25**, 578.

Donnay, J. D. H. (1943). Plagioclase twinning. *Bull. Geol. Soc. Am.*, **54**, 1645.

Drugman, J. (1938). On some unusual twinning laws observed in the orthoclase crystals from Goodsprings, Nevada. *Mineral. Mag.*, **25**, 1.

Duparc, L. and Reinhard, M. (1923). Les méthodes de Fedorof et leur application à la détermination des plagioclases. *Bull. Suisse Mineral. Petrog. Mitt.*, **3**, 1.

Duparc, L. and Reinhard, M. (1924). La détermination des plagioclases dans les coupes minces. *Mem. Soc. Phys. Hist. Nat., Geneve*, **40**, 1, 150.

Emmons, R. C., Crump, R. M. and Ketner, K. B. (1960). High- and low-temperature plagioclase. *Bull. Geol. Soc. Am.*, **71**, 1417.

Emmons, R. C. and Gates, R. M. (1943). Plagioclase twinning. *Bull. Geol. Soc. Am.*, **54**, 287.

Emmons, R. C. and Mann, V. (1953). A twin-zone relationship in plagioclase feldspars. In Selected Petrogenic Relationships of Plagioclase. *Geol. Soc. Am., Mem.*, **52**, 41–54.

Euler, R. and Hellner, E. (1961). Hydrothermale und röntgenographische Untersuchungen an gesteinsbildenden Mineralen VI, Über hydrothermal hergestellten triklinen K-Feldspat. *Z. Krist.*, **115**, 433.

Fedorow, E. V. (1902). Beiträge zur zonalen Krystallographie. V. Complicationsgesetze und richtige Aufstellung der Krystalle. *Z. Krist.*, **35**, 23.

Füchtbauer, H. (1948). Einige Beobachtungen an authigenen Albiten. *Schweiz. Mineral. Petrog. Mitt.*, **28**, 707.

Gates, R. M. (1953). Petrogenic significance of perthite. *Geol. Soc. Am., Mem.*, **52**, 55.

Gay, P. (1956). A note on albite twinning in plagioclase feldspars. *Mineral. Mag.*, **31**, 301.

Glauser, A. (1960). Beziehungen zwischen der optischen Orientierung und der hypokubischen Aufstellung natürlicher basischer Plagioklase. *Schweiz. Mineral. Petrog. Mitt.*, **40**, 323.

Glauser, A. (1963). Über die optische Orientierung einiger Plagioklas-Zwillinge aus Linosa. *Schweiz. Mineral. Petrog. Mitt.*, **43**, 81.

Glauser, A. (1964). Zur optischen Orientierung einer komplexen hochtemperatur-Andesin-Zwillingsgruppe aus Island. *Schweiz. Mineral. Petrog. Mitt.*, **44**, 429.

Goldsztaub, S. and Saucier, H. (1959). Sur la section rhombique dans la macle du péricline. *Bull. Soc. Franc. Mineral. Christ.*, **82**, 99.

Gonnard, M. (1883). Note sur orthose du porphyre quartzifère de Four-la-Brouque près Issoire. *Bull. Soc. Mineral. France*, **6**, 265.

Gorai, M. (1951). Petrological studies on plagioclase twins. *Am. Mineralogist*, **36**, 884.

Gorai, M. (1965). Twinning in some artificial plagioclases. *Indian Mineralogist*, **6**, 51.

Gottardi, G. (1962). Studio cristallografico di rare e complesse geminazione nell'albite di uno roccia elbana. *Atti Soc. Toscan. Sci. Nat. Pisa, Proc. Verbali Mem., Ser. A*, **1962**.

Ito, T. (1950). *X-ray Studies on Polymorphism*. Maruzen, Tokyo.

Ito, T. and Sadanaga, R. (1952). The lamellar structure of certain microclines and anorthoclases. *Acta Cryst.*, **5**, 441.

Kayser, G. E. (1835). Über einen Cyclus von zwölf Zwillingsgesetzen, nach welchen die Kristalle der ein- und eingliedrigen Feldspathgattungen verwachsen sind. *Pogg. Ann. Phys. Chem.*, **34**, 109.

Köhler, A. (1949a). Recent results of the investigation of the feldspars. *J. Geol.*, **57**, 592.

Köhler, A. (1949b). Erscheinungen an Feldspaten in ihrer Bedeutung der Gesteinsgenesis. *Tschermaks Mineral. Petrog. Mitt.*, (3), **1**, 51.

Köhler, A. and Raaz, F. (1945). Gedanken über die Bildung von Feldspat-Zwillingen in Gesteinen. *Verhandl. Geol. Bundesanstalt*, **1945**, 163.

Lacroix, A. (1897). *Mineralogie de la France et de ses Colonies*, Vol. 2. Baudry, Paris.

Laves, F. (1950). The lattice and twinning of microcline and other potash feldspars. *J. Geol.*, **58**, 548.

Laves, F. (1951). Artificial preparation of microcline. *J. Geol.*, **59**, 511.

Laves, F. (1952). Mechanische Zwillingsbildung in Feldspaten in Abhängigkeit von Ordnung–Unordnung der Si/Al Verteilung innerhalb des (Si, Al)$_4$O$_8$-Gerüstes. *Naturwissenschaften*, **39**, 546.

Laves, F. and Soldatos, K. (1962). Plate perthite, a new perthitic intergrowth in microcline single crystals, a recrystallization product. *Z. Krist.*, **117**, 218.

Laves, F. and Soldatos, K. (1963). Die Albit/Mikroklin-Orientierungsbeziehungen in Mikroklinperthiten und deren genetische Deutung. *Z. Krist.*, **118**, 69.

MacKenzie, J. D. (1923). A study of feldspar crystals from Norway, Maine. *Am. Mineralogist*, **8**, 193.

MacKenzie, W. S. (1956). The orientation of the pericline twin lamellae in triclinic alkali feldspars. *Mineral. Mag.*, **31**, 41.

MacKenzie, W. S. and Smith, J. V. (1955). The alkali feldspars I: Orthoclase microperthites. *Am. Mineralogist*, **40**, 707.

MacKenzie, W. S. and Smith, J. V. (1962). Single crystal x-ray studies of crypto- and microperthites. *Norsk Geol. Tidsskr.*, **42**, II (Feldspar Vol.), 72.

Mügge, O. (1930). Über die Lage des rhombischen Schnittes im Anorthit und seine Bedeutung als geologisches Thermometer. *Z. Krist.*, **75**, 337.

Mügge, O. and Heide, F. (1931). Einfache Schiebung am Anorthit. *Neues Jahrb.*, *Beilage Bd.*, **64**, Abt. A (Brauns Vol.), 163.

Prasad, E. A. V. (1966). On the elimination of plagioclase twinning. *Indian Acad. Sci.*, **64B**, 296.

Rath, G. vom. (1876). Die Zwillingsverwachsung der triklinen Feldspathe nach dem sog. Periklin-gesetz und über eine darauf gegründete Unterscheidung derselben. *Sitzber. Kgl. Preuss. Akad. Wiss.*, *Berlin*, **147**; *Neues Jahrb.*, etc., **689**.

Reinhard, M. and Bächlin, R. (1936). Über die gitterartige Verzwillingung beim Mikroklin. *Schweiz. Mineral. Petrog. Mitt.*, **16**, 215.

Ross, J. V. (1957). Combination twinning in plagioclase feldspars. *Am. J. Sci.*, **255**, 650.

Sarbadhikari, T. R. (1965). On the difference in twinning between phenocrysts and groundmass plagioclase of basalt. *Am. Mineralogist*, **50**, 1466.

Schmidt, E. (1915). Die Winkel der kristallographischen Achsen der Plagioklase. *Chem. Erde*, **1** (1919), 351.

Schneider, T. R. (1957). Röntgenographische und optische Untersuchungen der Umwandlung Albit–Analbit–Monalbit. *Z. Krist.*, **109**, 245.

Smith, J. V. (1958a). The effect of temperature, structural state and composition of the albite, pericline and acline-A twins of plagioclase feldspars. *Am. Mineralogist*, **43**, 546.

Smith, J. V. (1958b). The effect of composition and structural state on the rhombic section and pericline twins of plagioclase feldspars. *Mineral. Mag.*, **31**, 914.

Smith, J. V. (1962). Genetic aspects of twinning in feldspars. *Norsk Geol. Tidsskr.*, **42**, II (Feldspar Vol.), 243.

Smith, J. V. and MacKenzie, W. S. (1954). Further complexities in the lamellar structure of alkali feldspars. *Acta Cryst.*, **7**, 380.

Smith, J. V. and MacKenzie, W. S. (1958). The alkali feldspars IV: The cooling history of high-temperature, sodium-rich feldspars. *Am. Mineralogist*, **43**, 872.

Smith, J. V. and MacKenzie, W. S. (1959). The alkali feldspars V: The nature of orthoclase and microcline perthites and observations concerning the polymorphism of potassium feldspar. *Am. Mineralogist*, **44**, 1169.

Soldatos, K. (1962). Über die kryptoperthitische Albit–Ausscheidung in Mikroklinperthiten. *Norsk Geol. Tidsskr.*, **42**, II (Feldspar Vol.), 180.

Starkey, J. (1959). Chess-board albite from New Brunswick. *Can. Geol. Mag.*, **96**, 141.

Starkey, J. (1967). On the relationship of pericline and albite twinning to the composition and structural state of plagioclase feldspar. *Schweiz. Mineral. Petrogr. Mitt.*, **47**, 257.

Starkey, J. and Brown, W. L. (1964). Künstliche Erzeugung mechanischer Zwillinge in Anorthit, $CaAl_2Si_2O_8$. *Z. Krist.*, **120**, 388.

Startsev, V. J. (1963). The formation of defects in crystal lattice by twinning. *Proc. Intern. Conf. Crystal Lattice Defects. Phys. Soc. Japan*, **18**, Suppl., III, 16.

Stewart, D. B. and von Limbach, D. (1967). Thermal expansion of low and high albite. *Am. Mineralogist*, **52**, 389.

Streckeisen, A. (1932). Junge Eruptivgesteine im östlichen Banat mit besonderer Berücksichtigung ihrer Feldspäte. *Bull. Soc. Romania Geol. Bukurest*, **1**, 18.

Suwa, K. (1956). Plagioclase twinning in Ryoke metamorphic rocks from the Mitsue-mura area, Kii peninsula, Central Japan. *J. Earth Sci., Nagoya Univ.*, **4**, 91.

Tertsch, H. (1941). Zur Hochtemperaturoptik der Plagioklase. *Zentralbl. Mineral.* (A), 137; *Tschermaks Mineral. Petrog. Mitt.*, **54**, 193 (1942).

Tobi, A. C. (1961). Pattern of plagioclase twinning as a significant rock property. *Koninkl. Ned. Akad. Wetenschap., Proc. Ser. B.*, **64**, 576.

Tobi, A. C. (1962). Characteristic patterns of plagioclase twinning. *Norsk Geol. Tidsskr.*, **42**, II (Feldspar Vol.), 264.

Tobi, A. C. (1965). The cause of internal optical scatter in plagioclase, and the occurrence of lamellar albite–ala B twinning. *Am. J. Sci.*, **263**, 712.

Tschermak, G. (1874). Die Formen und die Verwachsungen des Labradorites von Verespatak. *Tschermaks Mineral. Mitt.*, 269.

Tschermak, G. (1887). Zwillingsartige Verwachsungen von Orthoklas. *Tschermaks Mineral. Petrog. Mitt.*, **8**, 414.

Tunell, G. (1952). The angle between the *a*-axis and the trace of the rhombic section on the (010)-pinacoid in the plagioclases. *Am. J. Sci.* (Bowen Vol.), 547.

Turner, F. J. (1951). Observations on twinning of plagioclase in metamorphic rocks. *Am. Mineralogist*, **36**, 581.

Vance, J. A. (1961). Polysynthetic twinning in plagioclase. *Am. Mineralogist*, **46**, 1097.

Vance, J. A. (1962). Observations on the rhombic section of a zoned plagioclase crystal. *Mineral. Mag.*, **33**.

Vance, J. A. (1965). Zoning in igneous plagioclase: patchy zoning. *J. Geol.*, **73**, 636.

Vernon, R. H. (1965). Plagioclase twins in some mafic gneisses from Broken Hill. *Mineral. Mag.*, **35**, 488.

Viola, C. (1900). Feldspatstudien. *Z. Krist.*, **32**, 305.

Vogel, T. A. (1964). Optical–crystallographic scatter in plagioclase. *Am. Mineralogist*, **49**, 456.

Wang, S. W. (1933). A study on the orthoclase crystals and twins of Chiaocheng, Shansi. *Bull. Geol. Soc. China*, **12**, 456.

Werveke, L. van. (1883). Eigentümliche Zwillingsbildung an Feldspath und Diallag. *Neues Jahrb. etc.*, **2**, 97.

Wülfing, E. A. (1915). Lassen siche die kristallographischen Fundamentalwinkel der Plagioklase mit der Zusammensetzung in gesetzmässige Beziehung bringen? *Sitzber. Heidelberg. Akad. Wiss. Math.-Naturw. Kl.*, *A*, No. 13.

3

The Structures of the Feldspars

3.1 SURVEY OF THE CRYSTAL STRUCTURE

3.11 Introduction

The fundamental unit of structure in crystalline silica and in all silicates is the positive silicon atom surrounded by four oxygen atoms in tetrahedral coordination. In the silica minerals (quartz, tridymite, etc.), these tetrahedra are linked together by sharing corners to form interlocking oxygen–silicon chains building up a continuous three-dimensional framework, see figure 3.1.

Machatschki (1928) pointed out that the feldspar minerals are characterized by a silica framework in which from one-quarter to one-half of the tetravalent Si atoms are replaced by trivalent Al. The two feldspar anions representing the ultimate ratios of substitution are:

$$[AlSi_3O_8]^- \quad \text{in which every fourth Si is replaced by Al}$$

$$[Al_2Si_2O_8]^{2-} \text{ in which every second Si is replaced by Al}$$

Thus, positive cations, like Na^+, K^+ or Ca^{2+}, are induced to enter into the framework to ensure electroneutrality. Loewenstein (1954) showed that Al can replace a maximum of 50% of the silicons in the three-dimensional frameworks. For 50% substitution, rigorous alternation between Si and Al tetrahedra becomes necessary: the unit cell of anorthite has double the size of that of albite (see below).

Schiebold (1928, 1931) proposed a crystal structure for orthoclase, but he did not pay sufficient attention to the ideas of Machatschki. The correct detailed sanidine structure, based on a unit cell containing $4(KAlSi_3O_8)$ was first determined by Taylor (1933). In 1934 Taylor, Darbyshire and Strunz worked out the rough structures of all the principal feldspars.

The unit cell of orthoclase contains four units of the formula $KAlSi_3O_8$, i.e. there are in the cell:

4 K atoms

4 Al atoms

12 Si atoms

32 O atoms

Taylor thought that his structure had to be either triclinic or isomorphous to one of the hemihedral groups of the monoclinic system, for there are no suitable fourfold sites for the Al atoms in a unit cell of holohedral monoclinic symmetry. However, there are no other indications of

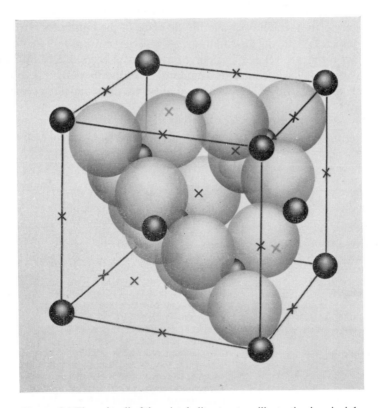

FIGURE 3.1 The unit cell of the cristobalite structure illustrating in principle how the oxygen tetrahedra form interlocking chains with open interstices in between. Crosses indicate the centres of the interstices into which large ions (like Na or Ca) may enter. To balance the valences Al must then in part replace Si in the centres of the tetrahedra

hemihedry in the monoclinic feldspars and Taylor's proposal seemed, therefore, rather unsatisfactory to mineralogists. The true explanation, which was later adopted by Taylor, emerges by application of the principle of the variate atom equipoints of Barth and Posnjak (1931), according to which Al and Si *together* occupy sixteen equivalent atomic sites. Because of the similar scattering power of Al and Si it was not possible, however, to prove this arrangement from intensity measurements of x-ray reflections.

Barth (1934) further proposed that the triclinic and monoclinic form of potassium feldspars differ from each other in the pattern of the distribution of silicon and aluminium atoms. In triclinic microcline, representing the low-temperature form, Al and Si are *ordered*, occupying crystallographically distinct positions. In the truly monoclinic forms of K-feldspar, which were divided into sanidine (with the plane of the optic axes in the symmetry plane), and adularia (with the plane of the optic axes normal to the symmetry plane) the distribution of Al and Si is more or less disordered. The two forms are related by 'polytropy', and pass gradually into each other. Sanidine has a completely random Al/Si distribution, and adularia a partly ordered distribution which still preserves the monoclinic symmetry

TABLE 3.1

Accurate structural analyses of the rock-forming feldspars, 1949–1964

Feldspar	Reference
Sanidine	Cole, Sörum and Kennard (1949)
	Onorato, Penta and Sgarlata (1963)
	Ribbe (1963)
Orthoclase	Jones and Taylor (1961)
Intermediate microcline	Bailey and Taylor (1955)
Low (maximum) microcline	Brown and Bailey (1964)
	Finney and Bailey (1964)
High albite	Ferguson, Traill and Taylor (1958)
	Williams and Megaw (1964)
Low albite	Ferguson, Traill and Taylor (1958)
	Ribbe, Ferguson and Taylor (1962)
	Williams and Megaw (1964)
Anorthite	Cole, Sörum and Taylor (1951)
	Kempster, Megaw and Radoslovich (1962)
	Megaw, Kempster and Radoslovich (1962)
	Ribbe and Megaw (1962)
Plagioclase	Cole, Sörum and Taylor (1951)
	Sörum (1951, 1953)
	A number of unpublished Ph.D. Theses at Cambridge, England
	Fleet, Chandrasekhar and Megaw (1966)

'this is geometrically possible, but no data are available through which to suggest any actual arrangement'.

Chao, Hargreaves and Taylor (1940), apparently unaware of Barth's work, concluded that sanidine has a random Al/Si distribution and that orthoclase has (4Al + 4Si) in one of the eightfold sets and 8Si in another (see below). Cole, Sörum and Kennard (1949) did not support the conclusion, but admitted that this might be the difference between orthoclase and sanidine.

Laves (1950) listed the six main Al/Si distributions theoretically possible within the framework of Taylor's structure determination and remarked that the two main monoclinic cases (1) with maximum disorder: (2Al + 6Si) + (2Al + 6Si) and (2) with maximum order: (4Al + 4Si) + (4Si + 4Si) could have continuous variation between them and would not need different names. He proposed a distinction between sanidine (high) and sanidine (low) with a continuous sequence of intermediate members.

Order or disorder in the Al + Si distribution in feldspars is directly reflected in the nuclear resonance spectrum which in the ordered structure

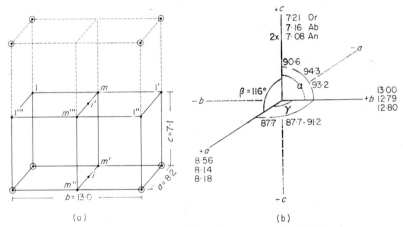

FIGURE 3.2 The relations of the unit cells of the various feldspars
(a) Full lines denote the semi-unit cell in all feldspars. In the true 14 Å structures the c axis is doubled (dotted lines) and the following positions vanish: 1, 1′, 1″, 1‴; m, m′, m″, m‴ and i; in the body-centred anorthite i′ remains, but in the primitive anorthite i′ disappears. In sanidine and orthoclase the unit cell is truly monoclinic. The other feldspars exhibit triclinic unit cells in which the angles α and γ differ from 90°; see (b)

(b) Interaxial angles. The values of the angles α and γ (β remains very close to 116° in all feldspars) together with the values of the lengths of the edges of the unit cells are presented for the various triclinic feldspars always in the same sequence: microcline–albite–anorthite

has sharp satellites that gradually disappear as the structure becomes more disordered. Thus the direct proof of disorder in feldspars was given.

Laves (1960) gave a historical survey of the development of the feldspar structures and, in 1962 and 1965, Taylor gave a summary account of the structures of the principal feldspars.

In table 3.1, recent structural works are listed.

3.12 Types of structure

The unit cell or semi-unit cell of all feldspars is a parallelepiped with a volume around 700 Å³, and of the following approximate dimensions:

$$
\begin{array}{llll}
a & 8\cdot2 \text{ Å} & \alpha & 90° \\
b & 13\cdot0 \text{ Å} & \beta & 116° \\
c & 7\cdot1 \text{ Å} & \gamma & 90°
\end{array}
$$

It contains four units of the formulae given in table 3.2.

TABLE 3.2

Unit cells and space groups for feldspars. (From Taylor, 1962)

Ideal composition	Material	$a(Å)$	$b(Å)$	$c(Å)$	$\alpha(°)$	$\beta(°)$	$\gamma(°)$	Space group
KAlSi$_3$O$_8$	Sanidine	8·564	13·030	7·175	90	115·99	90	$C2/m$
	Orthoclase	8·562	12·996	7·193	90	116·01$_5$	90	$C2/m$
	Intermediate microcline	8·578	12·960	7·211	90·30	115·97	89·13	$C\bar{1}$
	Maximum microcline	8·561	12·966	7·216	90·65	115·83	87·70	$C\bar{1}$
NaAlSi$_3$O$_8$	Low albite	8·138	12·789	7·156	94·33	116·57	87·65	$C\bar{1}$
	High albite	8·149	12·880	7·106	93·37	116·30	90·28	$C\bar{1}$
CaAl$_2$Si$_2$O$_8$	Anorthite (low temperature)	8·177	12·877	14·169	93·17	115·85	91·22	$P\bar{1}$
Ab$_{74}$An$_{22}$	Oligoclase	8·169	12·836	7·134	93·83	116·45	88·99	$C\bar{1}$
Ab$_{52}$An$_{48}$	Andesine (high temperature)	8·176	13·879	7·107	93·40	116·17	90·40	$C\bar{1}$
Ab$_{20}$An$_{80}$	Bytownite	8·171	12·869	14·181	93·37	115·97	90·53	$I\bar{1}$

The relations between the direct and reciprocal lattice values are for triclinic feldspars,

$$a^* = \frac{bc \sin \alpha}{V}, \quad b^* = \frac{ac \sin \beta}{V}, \quad c^* = \frac{ab \sin \gamma}{V}$$

where V is the volume of the unit cell;

$$\cos \alpha^* = \frac{\cos \beta \cos \gamma - \cos \alpha}{\sin \beta \sin \gamma}, \quad \cos \beta^* = \frac{\cos \alpha \cos \gamma - \cos \beta}{\sin \alpha \sin \gamma},$$

$$\cos \gamma^* = \frac{\cos \alpha \cos \beta - \cos \gamma}{\sin \alpha \sin \beta};$$

$d_{(hkl)} = [h^2a^{*2} + k^2b^{*2} + l^2c^{*2} + 2klb^*c^* \cos \alpha^* + 2lhc^*a^* \cos \beta + 2hka^*b^* \cos \gamma^*]^{-\frac{1}{2}}$

For monoclinic feldspar they reduce to,

$$a^* = \frac{1}{\sin \beta}, \; b^* = \frac{1}{b}, \; c^* = \frac{1}{c \sin \beta}; \; d_{(hkl)} = [h^2a^{*2} + k^2b^{*2} + l^2c^{*2} + 2lhc^*a^* \cos \beta^*]^{-\frac{1}{2}}$$

In the sanidine and albite types the parallelepiped is face centred on c (001), and is itself the unit cell. But in the anorthite and plagioclase types the true unit cell requires two or more such units (= large-cell feldspars with 14 Å c repeat). This large cell, and other large-cell structures give 'extra' x-ray reflections which are due to differences in the positions of the atoms in the sub-cells. Since the differences of position are small, these 'difference reflections' (more commonly known as 'superlattice reflections') are weak, and have been classified and named b, c and d type, the reflections at positions common to all feldspars being a (see section 4.2).

In anorthite the lattice is primitive, and in high anorthite it is body centred, see figure 3.2.

3.13 The atomic positions within the unit cell of sanidine

Sanidine may serve as an example of the detailed structure of feldspars: The four K atoms and four of the 32 oxygen atoms (which are called O_{A2}) occupy a set of four equivalent sites, the atomic coordinates of which are:

$$u, 0, v; \quad \bar{u}, 0, \bar{v}; \quad \tfrac{1}{2} + u, \tfrac{1}{2}, v; \quad \tfrac{1}{2} - u, \tfrac{1}{2}, \bar{v}$$

There are in the unit cell sixteen (Si + Al) atoms that are divided into two sets, called T_1 and T_2, of eight equivalent sites:

$$x, y, z; \quad \bar{x}, \bar{y}, \bar{z}; \quad \tfrac{1}{2} + x, \tfrac{1}{2} + y, z; \quad \tfrac{1}{2} - x, \tfrac{1}{2} - y, \bar{z}$$

$$x, \bar{y}, z; \quad \bar{x}, y, \bar{z}; \quad \tfrac{1}{2} + x, \tfrac{1}{2} - y, z; \quad \tfrac{1}{2} - x, \tfrac{1}{2} + y, \bar{z}$$

The same general sites are occupied by 24 oxygen atoms, which are divided into three sets of eight equivalent sites, called O_B, O_C and O_D. There still remain four oxygens, O_{A1}, whose atomic coordinates are:

$$0, u, 0; \quad 0, \bar{u}, 0; \quad \tfrac{1}{2}, u + \tfrac{1}{2}, 0; \quad \tfrac{1}{2}, \tfrac{1}{2} - u, 0, \text{ with } u = 0.15$$

The numerical values of these parameters are listed in table 3.3. In these positions, the oxygen atoms surround each Si and Al tetrahedrally. The distance from these cations to any of the four surrounding oxygen ions is in sanidine 1·645 Å. Ideally in this structure the Si—O and Al—O distances are 1·61 Å and 1·75 Å respectively. Note that the figure for sanidine (1·645) corresponds to Si: Al = 3:1 (which is in harmony with the chemical formula) by linear interpolation, see p. 102.

The interstitial cavities formed between the interlocking Si–Al–oxygen chains are, in the feldspar lattices, occupied by large cations: K, Na, Ca, the ionic radii of which are 1·33, 0·98, 1·06 Å respectively. The large size of the K ion inflates the framework which expands especially in the a

Table 3.3

Numerical values of the atomic coordinates in sanidine. (Cole and others, 1949)

Symbol	0000[a]	000c	00i0	00ic	m000	m00c	m0i0	m0ic
K	0·29 0 0·14	0·71 0 0·86	0·79 0·50 0·14	0·21 0·50 0·86	—	—	—	—
T_1^c	0·01 0·19 0·22	0·99 0·81 0·78	0·51 0·69 0·22	0·49 0·31 0·78	0·01 0·81 0·22	0·99 0·19 0·78	0·51 0·31 0·22	0·49 0·69 0·78
T_2^c	0·71 0·12 0·35	0·29 0·88 0·65	0·21 0·62 0·35	0·79 0·38 0·65	0·71 0·88 0·35	0·29 0·12 0·65	0·21 0·38 0·35	0·79 0·62 0·65
O_{A1}^b	0 0·15 0	0 0·85 0	0·50 0·65 0	0·50 0·35 0	—	—	—	—
O_{A2}^b	0·64 0 0·29	0·36 0 0·71	0·14 0·50 0·29	0·86 0·50 0·71	—	—	—	—
O_B	0·83 0·15 0·22	0·17 0·85 0·78	0·33 0·65 0·22	0·67 0·35 0·78	0·83 0·85 0·22	0·17 0·15 0·78	0·33 0·35 0·22	0·67 0·65 0·78
O_C	0·03 0·31 0·26	0·97 0·69 0·74	0·53 0·81 0·26	0·47 0·19 0·74	0·03 0·69 0·26	0·97 0·31 0·74	0·53 0·19 0·26	0·47 0·81 0·74
O_D	0·18 0·13 0·40	0·82 0·87 0·60	0·68 0·63 0·40	0·32 0·37 0·60	0·18 0·87 0·40	0·82 0·13 0·60	0·68 0·37 0·40	0·32 0·63 0·60

[a] Prototype.
[b] The symbols of these two atoms have 1 or 2 respectively replacing the first zero.
[c] These sites are shared between Al and Si, and are in the centres of the tetrahedra whose corners are occupied by oxygen atoms.

direction, see figure 3.2 (*b*). (Barium, which is another large ion, radius = 1·43 Å, has the same effect.) These large-cation frameworks show a tendency to assume monoclinic symmetry.

The structural pattern of (triclinic) albite is similar to that of K-feldspar, but the framework is somewhat distorted due to a slight collapse of the chains around the smaller Na ions. Similarly, in anorthite, but here the triclinicity is still more pronounced, and in addition the *c* axis is doubled, see figure 3.2 (*a*). Further complexities are found in the plagioclases that are solid solutions or submicroscopic intergrowths of albite and anorthite.

Figures 3.3 and 3.4 illustrate some of the geometric properties of the feldspar lattice. The two perfect cleavages, inclined exactly or nearly at

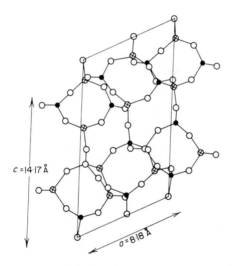

FIGURE 3.3 The tetrahedral framework of the anorthite lattice projected down the *b* axis on the plane (010). A Si–Al–oxygen chain runs parallel to the *a* axis. The anorthite unit cell is outlined; it has the long 14 Å *c* axis. The prominent cleavages parallel to (001) and (010) cut only the cross-linkages between the zigzag chains parallel to the *a* axis. Any other cleavage will rupture a greater number of powerful Al—O bonds and Si—O bonds

90°, are direct consequences of the configuration of the three-dimensional framework.

Likewise the various twin laws may be deduced from the topology of the lattice. The prerequisite condition for the formation of twins is that the crystal lattice is almost continuous across a twin boundary. This is not the place to go into all details or to discuss the various cases, suffice it to refer to chapter 2 and to figure 3.5 as an example of the nearly perfect continuation of the feldspar lattice across the composition face of a Manebach twin.

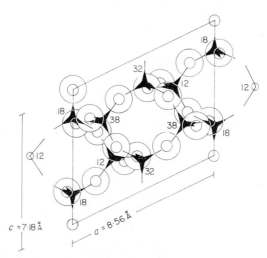

FIGURE 3.4 Portion of the tetrahedral framework projected on the plane (010)—the same as in figure 3.3. The sanidine unit cell is outlined; only atoms in the lower half of the cell are shown; due to a reflection plane those in the upper half present the mirror image of the lower half. The Al and Si ions are shown as black stars with their bonds pointing towards the four surrounding oxygen atoms. The oxygen atoms are shown as large white circles. Actually they are still larger—in the figure they are drawn with a radius of 0·7 Å; the true radius is about 1·4 Å, or twice the distance shown in the figure. If they had been shown in full size, they would have obscured the view of the unit cell with the characteristic interstices of the negatively charged framework in which are located the large K^+ ions (not shown). Similarly, in albite and anorthite the interstices are occupied by Na^+ and Ca^{2+} ions respectively, which are smaller than K^+ and cause a slight collapse of the framework, and a consequent shrinkage of the chain
(= contraction of the a axis)

3.14 Megaw's notations for feldspar structures

The lower symmetry of the triclinic feldspar species and the doubling of the c axis in the anorthite-type structures make it necessary to explain how the positions of the atoms in the sanidine structure can remain as standard for the other feldspars. This is done with the help of symbols invented for this purpose by Megaw (1956).

The symmetry operations producing the atomic sites in sanidine can be seen from the lists of atomic coordinates as given in table 3.4. The operations are those belonging to the space group $C2/m$ and are (1) a mirror plane at $y = 0$, (2) face centring on (001), (3) a centre of symmetry at (000). Neither this particular choice of operations nor the order of performing them is unique; however, Megaw proposes that the sets in this order should be taken as standard.

The eight sites derived from the prototype x, y, z, by these three operations are distinguished by the letters m, i and c respectively (m serving as a reminder of the mirror plane, c of the centre of symmetry and i of the body centring which in the 14 Å structures replace face centring in the 7 Å structures). Another operation is needed in the 14 Å structures (see below) and it is convenient that it should stand in second place. Thus a four-figure symbol is needed, the second figure in sanidine (and in the other 7 Å structures) always being zero.

This four-figure symbol is added to the symbol specifying the particular set of symmetry-related sites in sanidine, and specifies the individual site within the set. For example, the four K atoms receive the symbols

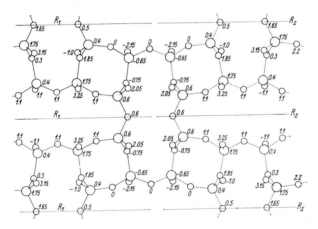

FIGURE 3.5 Manebach twin. Twin boundary (001) (from Taylor and others, 1934). Portions of the tetrahedral framework of two individuals in twin position are projected onto a plane normal to the twin boundary and normal to the a axis; the reciprocal axes c^* and b^* lie in the plane. c^* is twin axis and common to both individuals. In the monoclinic feldspars it coincides with the lines R_1 and R_2; $b^* = b$ is normal to these lines. R_1 and R_2 of the two individuals are the traces of the (010) cleavages, which are continuous (in the triclinic feldspars nearly continuous) through the twinned crystal. They are structural reflection planes. In the first individual the direct c axis slopes down from right to left, in the second it slopes up from right to left
Tetrahedron bonds in the first individual are drawn as a full line, in the second individual as a dotted line. Heights are given in angstrom units above the plane of the diagram

K(0000), K(000c), K(00i0), K(00ic). The use of these symbols is demonstrated by table 3.4 and figure 3.3.

In the triclinic feldspar structures, certain of the operations of symmetry or translation found in sanidine have disappeared. Nevertheless the actual sites are recognizable near those which would be given by such operations; hence the same nomenclature may be used.

TABLE 3.4

Atomic coordinates in the feldspar structures. (From Megaw, 1956)

Sanidine	Albite	Body-centred anorthite	Primitive anorthite	Symbol
x,y,z	x_1,y_1,z_1	x_{11},y_{11},z'_{11}	x_{111},y_{111},z'_{111}	0000
$\bar{x},\bar{y},\bar{z}$	$\bar{x}_1,\bar{y}_1,\bar{z}_1$	$\bar{x}_{11},\bar{y}_{11},\bar{z}'_{11}$	$\bar{x}_{111},\bar{y}_{111},\bar{z}'_{111}$	000c
$\frac{1}{2}+x,\frac{1}{2}+y,\bar{z}$	$\frac{1}{2}+x_1,\frac{1}{2}+y_1,z_1$	$\frac{1}{2}+x_{11},\frac{1}{2}+y_{11},\frac{1}{2}+z'_{11}$	$\frac{1}{2}+x_{112},\frac{1}{2}+y_{112},\frac{1}{2}+z'_{112}$	00i0
$\frac{1}{2}+x,\frac{1}{2}-y,\bar{z}$	$\frac{1}{2}-x_1,\frac{1}{2}-y_1,z_1$	$\frac{1}{2}-x_{11},\frac{1}{2}-y_{11},\frac{1}{2}-z'_{11}$	$\frac{1}{2}-x_{112},\frac{1}{2}-y_{112},\frac{1}{2}-z'_{112}$	00ic
—	—	$x_{12},y_{12},\frac{1}{2}+z'_{12}$	$x_{121},y_{121},\frac{1}{2}+z'_{121}$	0z00
—	—	$\bar{x}_{12},\bar{y}_{12},\frac{1}{2}-z'_{12}$	$\bar{x}_{121},\bar{y}_{121},\frac{1}{2}-z'_{121}$	0z0c
—	—	$\frac{1}{2}+x_{12},\frac{1}{2}+y_{12},z'_{12}$	$\frac{1}{2}+x_{122},\frac{1}{2}+y_{122},z'_{122}$	0zi0
—	—	$\frac{1}{2}-x_{12},\frac{1}{2}-y_{12},\bar{z}'_{12}$	$\frac{1}{2}-x_{122},\frac{1}{2}-y_{122},\bar{z}'_{122}$	0zic
$x,\bar{y},z$	$x_2,\bar{y}_2,z_2$	$x_{21},\bar{y}_{21},z'_{21}$	$x_{211},\bar{y}_{211},z'_{211}$	m000
$\bar{x},y,\bar{z}$	$\bar{x}_2,y_2,\bar{z}_2$	$\bar{x}_{21},y_{21},\bar{z}'_{21}$	$\bar{x}_{211},y_{211},\bar{z}'_{211}$	m00c
$\frac{1}{2}+x,\frac{1}{2}-y,z$	$\frac{1}{2}+x,\frac{1}{2}-y_2,z_2$	$\frac{1}{2}+x_{21},\frac{1}{2}-y_{21},\frac{1}{2}+z'_{21}$	$\frac{1}{2}+x_{212},\frac{1}{2}-y_{212},\frac{1}{2}+z'_{212}$	m0i0
$\frac{1}{2}-x,\frac{1}{2}+y,\bar{z}$	$\frac{1}{2}-x_2,\frac{1}{2}+y_2,\bar{z}_2$	$\frac{1}{2}-x_{21},\frac{1}{2}+y_{21},\frac{1}{2}-z'_{21}$	$\frac{1}{2}-x_{212},\frac{1}{2}+y_{212},\frac{1}{2}-z'_{212}$	m0ic
—	—	$x_{22},\bar{y}_{22},\frac{1}{2}+z'_{22}$	$x_{221},\bar{y}_{221},\frac{1}{2}+z'_{221}$	mz00
—	—	$\bar{x}_{22},y_{22},\frac{1}{2}-z'_{22}$	$\bar{x}_{221},y_{221},\frac{1}{2}-z'_{221}$	mz0c
—	—	$\frac{1}{2}+x_{22},\frac{1}{2}-y_{22},z'_{22}$	$\frac{1}{2}+x_{222},\frac{1}{2}-y_{222},z'_{222}$	mzi0
—	—	$\frac{1}{2}-x_{22},\frac{1}{2}+y_{22},\bar{z}'_{22}$	$\frac{1}{2}-x_{222},\frac{1}{2}+y_{222},\bar{z}'_{222}$	mzic

3.15 Albite and microcline

The plane of symmetry occurring in sanidine is no longer present in albite and microcline. Atomic sites which were related by it, i.e. sites whose symbols differ by m, are now independent; thus it is necessary to quote separately the coordinates of atoms such as 0000 and m000. The fourfold sets of which these are representative may be specified by dropping the last three figures of the complete symbol; thus, for example, instead of T_1 we have $T_1(0)$ and $T_1(m)$.

It should be noted that the prototype sites at 0000 and m000 are not in accordance with older usage; for albite Taylor and others (1934) recorded the values of the coordinates of atoms 0000 and m0i0, and other authors have followed them, see table 3.5.

TABLE 3.5

Various notations for the atomic sets of (Al + Si)

Feldspar	Reference	Notation			
Albite	Taylor (1933)	Si_1	Si_1'	Si_2	Si_2'
	Megaw (1956)	$Si_1(0)$	$Si_1(m)$	$Si_2(0)$	$Si_2(m)$
	Megaw (1959)	$B_1(0)$	$B_1(m)$	$B_2(0)$	$B_2(m)$
	Laves (1960)	B_2	B_1	A_1	A_2
Microcline	Megaw (1956)	$Si_1(m)$	$Si_1(0)$	$Si_2(m)$	$Si_2(0)$
Notation for all feldspars used in this book	Taylor (1962)	$T_1(0)$	$T_1(m)$	$T_2(0)$	$T_2(m)$

Graphically this is shown in figure 3.6.

It should also be noted that the old crystallographic orientation of microcline did not bring out the analogy with the structure of albite. Laves (1951, 1965) therefore revised the orientation of microcline by a 180° rotation around the b axis. In older notations, the $T_2(0)$ set of microcline is therefore identical to the $T_2(m)$ set of albite.

Microcline and low-temperature albite have analogous atomic arrangements. The principal difference from sanidine is that the Al and Si ions are ordered; in low albite and maximum microcline all Al ions are in the

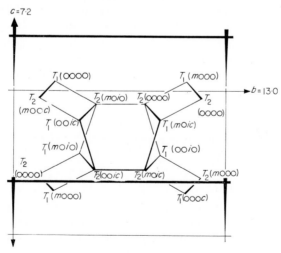

FIGURE 3.6 Schematic illustration of the relations of the point symbols used in this book

set $T_1(0)$, all Si ions are in the three remaining tetrahedral sets $T_1(m)$, $T_2(0)$ and $T_2(m)$. This distribution requires a triclinic symmetry.

The high-temperature albite exhibits some disorder in the Al/Si distribution. The degree of order is a function of the temperature; the distribution pattern is triclinic and probably similar to that of sodic plagioclase, see pp. 121 and 139.

The atomic coordinates of these structures are given by Ribbe and others (1962) and by Williams and Megaw (1964).

3.16 Anorthite

In the anorthite structures, the length of the c axis is doubled (~ 14 Å). If the sanidine structure were described with reference to this axis, sites at (x_1, y_1, z_1) and $(x_2, y_2, \frac{1}{2} + z_2)$ with x_1, y_1, z_1 equal to x_2, y_2, z_2 respectively would be crystallographically identical, see figure 3.2. In the 14 Å structures this identity disappears. The second site of such a pair is distinguished in the proposed notation by writing z in the second place of the symbol, for example, O_D (0z0c).

Coordinates of sites in the different structures, and the corresponding symbols, are given in table 3.4.

3.161 Body-centred anorthite

Referred to a 14 Å axis, albite had a repeat distance of $c/2$; this identity has disappeared in anorthite. It is now necessary to quote separately the coordinates of 0000 and 0z00 as well as m000 and mz00. The fourfold symmetry-related sets of which these are representative may be specified by dropping the last two figures of the complete symbol; for example, T_1 (00), T_1 (0z), T_1 (m0), T_1 (mz) are crystallographically distinct sets.

Values of coordinates for body-centred anorthite are given by Sörum (1951, 1953). There is no easily-recognized principle in his selection of prototype atoms. Fleet and others (1966) reinterpreted this structure: by assuming mistakes of an anti-phase-domain character it is possible to select a structure which is very closely similar to that of primitive anorthite, see p. 135.

3.162 Primitive anorthite

In primitive anorthite, body-centring translation has disappeared. The atoms whose coordinates must be separately quoted are 0000, 00i0, 0z00, 0zi0, m000, m0i0, mz00, mzi0. The pairs of symmetry-related atoms may be specified by dropping the last figure of the complete symbol, for example, T_1 (m0i).

Values of coordinates were published for this structure type by Kempster and others (1962); and a complete structural analysis by Megaw and others (1962) explained how the structure is completely ordered both in respect to the Ca positions and to the Al/Si distribution, see p. 134.

The *plagioclases* and the homogeneous mixed crystals of the *alkali feldspars* (anorthoclases, etc.) are important feldspar series which will be specially treated in section 3.4.

3.17 Disorder or anisotropic temperature vibration

In all structures the atoms show some thermal vibration; this will affect the intensities of the x-ray reflections, for the scattering power of an atom at rest is different from that of a vibrating atom. Temperature factors are therefore used to take account of the effective spreading out, or inflating of the atoms by thermal vibration. Vibration of uniform amplitude in all directions is represented by an isotropic temperature factor. But many atoms—and in the feldspar structure particularly the large cations—may require anisotropic temperature factors describing the effective 'shape' of an atom.

Another interpretation of atoms with elongation in one direction is assuming split-atom occupation of two slightly different lattice sites. This corresponds to a special case of partial disorder.

In all variants of potassium feldspar, the K atom is apparently disc shaped; this requires either some anisotropy of thermal vibration for the K atom or a partial disorder.

In the albite structures, the Na atom shows a marked elongation; this effect persists at $-180°$c, and can hardly be due to anisotropic thermal vibration. The split-atom model is therefore suggested. The separation between the two 'half atoms' in low albite at room temperature is 0·2–0·3 Å, at $-180°$c it is 0·27 Å, approximately parallel to the *b* axis. In high albite at room temperature the separation is 0·6 Å along the *b* axis, at $-180°$c it is 0·65 Å along a direction inclined at 35° to *b*, and nearly in the (100) plane.

In the primitive anorthite structure the Ca atom has an isotropic temperature factor; but the body-centred anorthite reveals elongated or doubled Ca peaks and 'half-atom splittings' for other atoms. The temperature factors for O, Al and Si are otherwise isotropic and small; this is interpreted as a perfection of the Al/Si ordering particularly since microcline, another highly ordered feldspar, exhibits the same properties. But the O ions in sanidine exhibit an appreciably higher temperature factor with stronger anisotropy (Hahn, 1962).

8

3.2 THE STRUCTURES OF THE ALKALI FELDSPARS

3.21 Potassium feldspars

A general picture of the feldspar structures is presented in section 3.1. A number of accurate structure analyses recently completed have given an unprecedented insight into the complexities and differences of the several kinds of feldspar. A key point of particular importance in the system of the alkali feldspars is the distribution of Al and Si atoms in the tetrahedral sets of the feldspar lattice. A thorough knowledge of the Al/Si distribution pattern is necessary to understand the existence of a range of transitional stages between the 'low-temperature' and the 'high-temperature' feldspars.

The difference in scattering power for the atoms Al and Si is very small, and the relative positions of Al and Si cannot, therefore, be determined by the relative intensities of the x-ray reflections, but have to be deduced from the size of the tetrahedron, the AlO_4 tetrahedron being slightly larger than SiO_4. Smith and Bailey (1963) found the distance Al—O to be 1·75 Å, the distance Si—O to be 1·61 Å. Similarly Finney and Bailey (1964) found the O—O distances to be 2·625 Å and 2·855 Å for Si and Al tetrahedra, respectively. The percentage Al occupation of a tetrahedron is found by linear interpolation between these end points. The latest figures are: Si—O = 1·603, Al—O = 1·761 (Jones, 1968; Ribbe and Gibbs, 1967).

3.211 The structures of the variants

In the potassium feldspar structure there are three extreme variants differing with respect to the degree of disorder of the Al/Si distribution (see figure 3.7).

1. Sanidine which is disordered monoclinic, $K(Al, Si)_4O_8$
2. Orthoclase which is partly ordered monoclinic, $K(Al, Si)_2Si_2O_8$
3. Microcline which is fully ordered triclinic, $KAlSi_3O_8$

A fourth mineralogical type is adularia (section 3.214) which is structurally variable.

There are four 'molecules' of the formula $KAlSi_3O_8$ in the unit cell, consequently there are sixteen, Z ions, i.e. 4Al + 12Si.

In the monoclinic system these ions must be distributed over two eight-fold sets T_1 and T_2.

The topology of the lattice is such that if all sites in T_1 (and in T_2) have the same probability a (and b respectively) of being occupied by an Al ion, monoclinic symmetry is possible. Monoclinic holohedral symmetry demands that at least one of the sets T_1 or T_2 have both Al and Si in a disordered arrangement. Therefore, two extreme monoclinic arrangements with all transitions between them are possible (see figure 3.7):

(1) $a = b = 0.25$. This structure may be symbolized by the formula $K(Al, Si)_4O_8$; it means that the Al/Si distribution is completely disordered; according to the $1:3$ ratio there are statistically 25% Al and 75% Si in each atomic site. To symbolize this it is expedient to consider the corresponding triclinic feldspar structure in which the two eightfold sets of tetrahedra break up into four fourfold tetrahedral sets: $T_1(0)$, $T_1(m)$, $T_2(0)$, $T_2(m)$. The aluminium occupancy referred to these sets is therefore 25, 25, 25, 25.

(2) $a = 0.5$, $b = 0$. This structure is symbolized by the formula $K(Al, Si)_2Si_2O_8$. One of the eightfold sets (= double fourfold sets, $T_2(0)$,

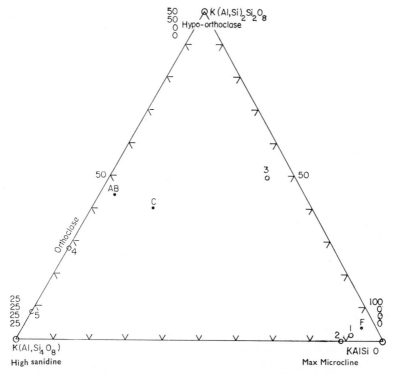

FIGURE 3.7 The ternary system of potassium feldspar. The names and the aluminium distribution pattern are given for each corner. The positions of five fully analysed K-feldspars are indicated (1–5) as in tables 3.6 and 3.7. Plots AB, C and F from J. M. Rhodes (personal communication)

$T_2(m)$) is occupied only by silicon ions. In the sites of the remaining set, $T_1(0)$ plus $T_1(m)$, there is a statistical distribution of 50 % Si and 50 % Al. The aluminium occupancy of the four sets (in the same sequence as above) is 50, 50, 0, 0.

(3) *In triclinic feldspars* the two eightfold sets of atomic sites are now actually split into four fourfold sets $T_1(0)$, $T_1(m)$, $T_2(0)$, $T_2(m)$. If this splitting takes place without changing the Al–Si distribution, i.e. $a_1 = a_2$ and $b_1 = b_2$, the result is a *displacive inversion* (this happens in Na-rich alkali feldspars). If the transition induces a concomitant change in the Al–Si distribution, i.e. a_1 becomes $\neq a_2$ and/or b_1 becomes $\neq b_2$, then a diffusive transformation takes place (Laves, 1952). The resulting structure in natural maximum triclinic microcline is:

$$a_1 = 1; \quad a_2 = b_1 = b_2 = 0$$

This structure may be symbolized by the formula $KAlSi_3O_8$. It means that the Al ions have concentrated in one fourfold set, $T_1(0)$, which exhibits large cation–O distances ($= 1·75$ Å), whereas the remaining three of the fourfold sets are occupied by Si and exhibit small cation–O distances ($= 1·61$ Å), (these distances directly indicate that the sites in the one set are occupied only by aluminium atoms). This structure is, therefore, fully ordered, and the aluminium distribution pattern is 100, 0, 0, 0.

These three 'end members' of the potassium feldspar structure are taken as corners in the diagram of figure 3.7.

The diagram does not, however, display all possible arrangements in triclinic feldspars. Any distribution satisfying the relation:

$$a_1 + a_2 + b_1 + b_2 = 1 \qquad (3.1)$$

is theoretically possible. This is graphically shown in figure 3.8, representing the three-dimensional variation in the order/disorder structure in feldspars. The corners of the shaded plane inside the tetrahedron represent the three structural variants so far discussed. It is hypothesized that all stable transitional structures lie in this plane (Barth, 1959). Thus, there exists a twofold infinity of K-feldspar structures, while there is a threefold infinity of possible structural variants in the whole feldspar system.

Five potassium feldspar variants have been subjected to complete structural analyses. Pertinent data are listed in tables 3.6 and 3.7.

(*a*) The maximum microclines (nos. 1 and 2 in tables and figure) come very near to full Al/Si order; almost all Al atoms have congregated in the $T_1(0)$ tetrahedron sites. (*b*) The intermediate microcline (no. 3) is less ordered; obviously the $T_1(0)$ set is favoured by Al, but it is interesting that also $T_1(m)$ is conspicuously more favoured than are any of the T_2

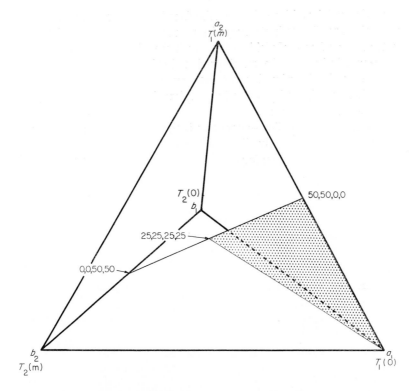

FIGURE 3.8 The tetrahedral space representing the possible structural disorder relations of Al and Si in the quaternary system of potassium feldspar, being a graphical representation of equation (3.1)

The four extreme Al/Si distribution possibilities, corresponding to 100% Al in $T_1(0)$, $T_1(m)$, $T_2(0)$ or $T_2(m)$ are plotted at the four corners, which, therefore, represent the probabilities $a_1 = 1$, $a_2 = 1$, $b_1 = 1$ and $b_2 = 1$ respectively. Any one point inside the tetrahedron thus satisfies equation

(3.1)

Monoclinic holohedral symmetry demands that $a_1 = a_2$ and $b_1 = b_2$. This happens only along the line connecting the points 50, 50, 0, 0 and 0, 0, 50, 50 as marked on the figure; the point at the middle of this line (= the centre of the tetrahedron) represents the arrangement 25, 25, 25, 25

The total remaining space inside the tetrahedron represents various triclinic possibilities, but the actual K-feldspar structures are probably confined to the plane shaded; it is just possible that some adularias may be located in the space outside the plane

It should be added that although monoclinic symmetry can develop with $a_1 = a_2$ and $b_1 = b_2$, this is not necessary. In soda-rich alkali feldspar (anorthoclase) this arrangement gives triclinic symmetry

Feldspars

sets, see figure 3.9 and legend. (3) Orthoclase is typically partly disordered (no. 4), the two T_1 sets have merged into one (eightfold) set and the two T_2 sets into another (eightfold) set in which the Al occupancy is 32% and 18%, respectively. (*d*) The sanidinized orthoclase (no. 5) was prepared from the partly disordered orthoclase by extended heat treatment at 1000°C. It thus achieved practically complete disorder with close to 25% Al in all available positions.

The transition microcline → sanidine is thus a disordering process; the Al atoms become completely 'dissolved' in the feldspar lattice. Laves (1952) called this a diffusive transition.

TABLE 3.6

Crystallography of potassium feldspars exhibiting various degrees of order

	1	2	3	4	5
a (Å)	8·560	8·573	8·578	8·562	8·564
b (Å)	12·964	12·962	12·960	12·996	13·030
c (Å)	7·215	7·219	7·211	7·193	7·175
α (°)	90° 39'	90° 34'	90° 18'	90	90
β (°)	115° 50'	115° 55'	115° 58'	116° 01'	116° 00'
γ (°)	87° 42'	87° 45'	87° 08'	90	90
a^* (Å)	0·1299	0·1298	0·1297	0·1300	0·1299
b^* (Å)	0·0772	0·0772	0·0772	0·0769	0·0767
c^* (Å)	0·1540	0·1541	0·1643	0·1547	0·1551
α^* (°)	90° 23'	90° 28'	90° 05'	90	90
β^* (°)	64° 10'	64° 04'	64° 02'	63° 59'	64
γ^* (°)	92° 14'	92° 13'	90° 50'	90	90
$2V$ (°)	82	71	76	43 ⊥ (010)	43 ∥ (010)
Order index (S)	92	86	61	19	5

1 Maximum microcline, Pellotsalo, Brown and Bailey (1964).
2 Authigenic maximum microcline, Pontiskalk, Finney and Bailey (1964).
3 Intermediate microcline, 'Spencer U', Bailey and Taylor (1955).
  The 'new setting' of microcline is used in the table; the values given by Bailey and Taylor for the direct and the reciprocal angles α and γ are the complements of those given here, see text.
4 Orthoclase, 'Spencer C', Jones and Taylor (1961).
5 Sanidinized orthoclase, 'Heated Spencer C', Ribbe (1963).

TABLE 3.7

Disorder patterns in potassium feldspars

	1	2	3	4	5
% Al occupancy in $T_1(0)$	94	92	69	32	27
% Al occupancy in $T_1(m)$	03	02	27	32	27
% Al occupancy in $T_2(0)$	01	06	03	18	23
% Al occupancy in $T_2(m)$	02	00	01	18	23
Order index (S)	0·92	0·86[a]	0·61	19	5
High sanidine (%)	8	12	8	72	92
Hypo-orthoclase (%)	2	0	50	28	8
Max. microcline (%)	90	88	42	0	0
$\Delta = 12 \cdot 5 \ (d_{(131)} - d_{(1\bar{3}1)})$	0·98	0·97	—	0	0
$a : \alpha$ on (001) (°)	17	16·5	9	0	0
$2V_\alpha$ (°)	82	71[b]	76	43 $\perp$ (010)	44 $\parallel$ (010)

[a] Considering O—O distances.
[b] Spencer (1937) gave $2V = 76°$. It was redetermined by Finney and Bailey (1964) to $2V = 70 \cdot 5°$.

The opposite process, the transition from sanidine to microcline, is an ordering process during which the randomly distributed Al ions diffuse into one of the four possible sets of tetrahedra. This is obviously a segregation process similar to exsolution, which takes place with decreasing temperature.

A quantitative measure of the degree of order is the long-range order function (S) of Smith and MacKenzie (1961).

$$S = \frac{\sum_{i=4}^{i=1} |0 \cdot 25 - T_i|}{1 \cdot 5} \times 100$$

The function is unity for full order, zero for complete disorder. It gives the percentage of Al/Si order for a sample, if the ratios Al/Al + Si in each of the four tetrahedra $T_1(0)$, $T_1(m)$, $T_2(0)$, $T_2(m)$ are known. The only way to determine this function was, thus far, a full-scale structural analysis. But recently rapid methods for a rough determination have been proposed, see figure 3.9.

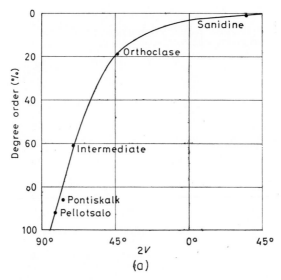

FIGURE 3.9 (*a*) Variation of optic angle with degree of Al/Si order in
K-feldspar. (Finney and Bailey, 1964)

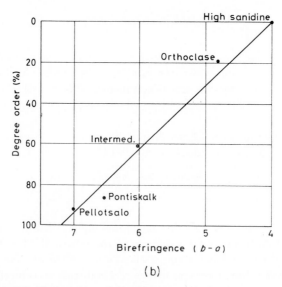

FIGURE 3.9 (*b*) Variation of birefringence ('*b*'-α) with degree of Al/Si
order. (Hewlett, 1959)

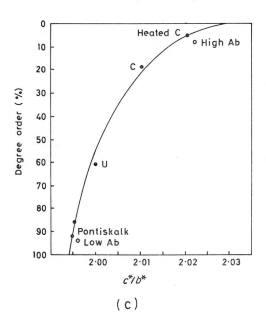

FIGURE 3.9 (*c*) Variation of the ratio of the reciprocal axes c^*/b^* with degree of Al/Si order. (Jones, 1966)

(*a*) Measurement of the obliquity using the separation of the (131) and (1$\bar{3}$1) reflections. The triclinicity is defined by $\Delta = 12\cdot5(d_{(131)}-d_{(1\bar{3}1)})$; this term is unity for maximum microcline, zero for a monoclinic crystal (Goldsmith and Laves, 1954b). This method is applicable only to triclinic crystals. (*b*) Measurement of $2V$ (Finney and Bailey, 1964). This method is rather inaccurate, for $2V$ is influenced by too many other factors, e.g. by submicroscopic twinning or by incomplete ordering along an atypical ordering path. See Ohta and Kizaki (1966a) who determined a great number of optic angles and found that $2V$ may vary in the range 40°– 70° within a single crystal. (*c*) Measurement of the partial birefringence ('*b*'–α) (Hewlett, 1959; Brown, 1962). This method looks promising, but has not yet been tested sufficiently to demonstrate its usefulness. (*d*) Most promising is the method of Jones (1966) using the ratio c^*/b^* as a direct measure of the degree of order as defined by the long-range order function, see figure 3.9.

These parameters are plotted into the composition triangle in figure 3.10. It is obvious that by using the triclinicity function Δ in combination with $2V$ and the long-range order function (S), the Al/Si disorder pattern of a crystal of potassium feldspar can be approximately determined without a full-scale structural analysis.

If the five potassium feldspar crystals which so far have been subjected to full structural analysis are representative, very interesting inferences concerning the actual disorder relations of the potassium feldspar variants are indicated, see figure 3.11 and its legend. Note that there are no orthoclases of greater ordering than ca. 33%. All theoretical variants with order indices above 33% and up to 'hypo-orthoclase' (50, 50, 0, 0) with 67% order would seem to be unstable and unknown. The stable path breaks into triclinic symmetry at $\backsim 500°$c, crosses the composition field of the triangle in figure 3.10 and reaches 67% order at a distribution (75, 25, 0, 0) and a triclinicity value of $\Delta = 0.50$; this probably corresponds to about 400°c. At still lower temperatures the order increases, the triclinicity increases, and maximum microcline (100, 0, 0, 0) becomes stable at around 300°c.

McConnell and McKie (1960) described the ordering of Al/Si in albite as a *smeared* transformation, implying the stable coexistence of two (or more) closely related structural modifications over a range of temperature (definition of Ubbelohde). The ordering of Al/Si in the potassium feldspar variants should be susceptible to description in the same kinetic terms. It is implied in a statistical structure, i.e. a structure with variate atom equipoints, that on an atomistic scale at least two modifications coexist. One way to visualize the structure of the completely disordered sanidine (25, 25, 25, 25) could be to imagine a 'mixed crystal' consisting of equal amounts of the four components (= modifications) represented by the four corners of the tetrahedron of figure 3·8: (100, 0, 0, 0), (0, 100, 0, 0), (0, 0, 100, 0), (0, 0, 0, 100). For it is obviously 'wrong' to imagine a crystal in which the crystallographic sites (= equipoints) are occupied by fractions of atoms. Notice, however, that in table 3.7 the 'compositions' of five natural feldspars are conveniently given in terms of three end members: high sanidine (25, 25, 25, 25), hypo-orthoclase (50, 50, 0, 0), maximum microcline (100, 0, 0, 0).

However, for kinetic studies it seems best to look upon these feldspars as representing a single stable crystal lattice in which there are domains of fluctuations of order; this is in direct accordance with the x-ray patterns which show only one phase. More akin to smeared transformations are possibly some processes occurring in unstable crystals: in the randomly disordered potassium feldspars of many augen gneisses, etc. (see p. 116

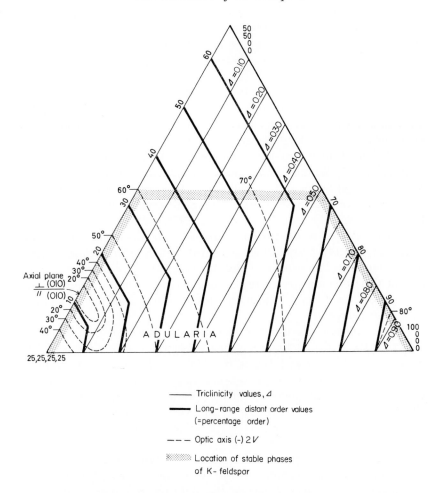

FIGURE 3.10 Properties of the various structural variants of K-feldspar
The shaded band from the lower left corner, up half the left edge, across
the triangle and down the right edge to the lower right corner locates the
stable phases of the K-feldspars. Along the left edge is the field of sanidine
and orthoclase; across the ternary field and down the right edge is the field
of intermediate to maximum microcline. The field of adularia represents
unstable (metastable) phases. Microclines may pass through the adularia
field if they develop disorder in response to quick heating

and figure 3.12), and in crystals prepared during the non-equilibrium transformation from low feldspar to high feldspar by heating above 1000°c. The x-ray patterns of such crystals show two (or more) sets of reflections corresponding to low-temperature and high-temperature forms.

The conclusion that orthoclases with order index $\gtrsim 33\%$ are unstable is in harmony with Hafner and Laves (1957) maintaining that it would be highly improbable to find an orthoclase with the theoretical maximum of monoclinic order. Taking Bailey and Taylor's intermediate microcline into account, Hafner and Laves deduced an Al distribution pattern of (38, 38, 12, 12) for the *actual* case of maximum monoclinic ordering. MacKenzie and Smith (1959), Smith and MacKenzie (1961) pointed out that if the local electric balance of charge determines the stability (see Ferguson, 1960; Ferguson and others, 1958, 1959), the most stable potassium feldspar would be monoclinic with an Al distribution pattern of (36, 36, 14, 14). They further suggested that most orthoclases might, in fact, represent this structure ('ideal orthoclase'). They added, however, that in their opinion free-energy considerations are more important in determining the form stable at low temperatures than the long-range balance of charge.

These conclusions are tentative; in particular, they depend on the structure analysis of the intermediate microcline, the so-called 'Spencer U' determined by Bailey and Taylor in 1955. This is the only structurally analysed feldspar intermediate between full triclinicity and full monoclinic symmetry. An important step forward would now be to study additional intermediate microclines with a view to accurately establishing the consecutive disorder patterns of the stable members of the potassium feldspar series.

The details of these patterns are graphically shown by figure 3.11 displaying the successive variation of the Al occupancy of each of the four individual tetrahedral sets during the diffusive transition sanidine → orthoclase → microcline.

3.212 The names of the variants of potassium feldspar

It is consistent with mineralogical nomenclature to use the names sanidine and orthoclase for the monoclinic members of the potassium feldspar system. Typical sanidine is glassy K-feldspar, and is highly disordered. Orthoclase is not glassy, is usually partly ordered but can be rather highly disordered. If the high disorder is taken as the fundamental criterion, it should be called sanidine without being glassy. Jones (1966) puts the boundary at an order index of ~ 0.1, but this may be rather low.

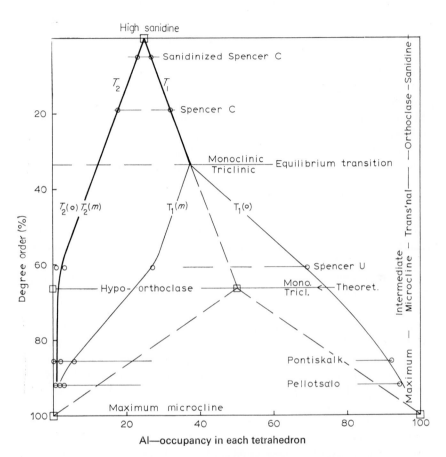

FIGURE 3.11 A graphical presentation of the change of the Al occupancy in each of the four tetrahedral groups during the diffusive transformation sanidine → orthoclase → microcline

At zero order (high sanidine at top of diagram) all four groups, $T_1(0)$, $T_1(m)$, $T_2(0)$, $T_2(m)$ have statistically the same content of Al. By cooling, a process of ordering is initiated: (1) Both T_2 groups lose Al, and both T_1 groups gain Al until about one-third order is achieved; this represents maximum order in natural orthoclase; (2) The T_1 groups now split into $T_1(0)$ and $T_1(m)$; $T_1(0)$ collects Al from the other three groups ($T_1(m)$, $T_2(0)$, $T_2(m)$) all of which lose Al at the *same* rate, until $T_2(0)$ and $T_2(m)$ have lost all Al (at about 60% order); (3) Now $T_1(m)$ quickly transfers to $T_1(0)$ what is left of the Al content, until practical order is reached with 90–100% of the total Al in $T_1(0)$; this is natural maximum microcline

Laves (1960) proposed to use the name 'sanidine' for *all* stable monoclinic feldspars and to distinguish the variants by adjective phrases. As names for the intermediate microclines having their projection points inside the triangle of figure 3.7, i.e. for triclinic species, he recommends 'microclinic pseudo-sanidine' and 'sanidine microcline', the name 'common orthoclase' being restricted to potassium feldspars that are built up of submicroscopically small twin units of triclinic symmetry according to the M-law (Mallard's hypothesis, 1876). The optics of common orthoclase are influenced by twinning of submicroscopically small microcline individuals. If the twin lamellae are 'balanced' monoclinic optics result, if not, the crystals exhibit triclinic optics and should, according to Laves, be called 'common orthoclases, unbalanced'. Nissen (1967) found in orthoclases from plutonic granitic rocks in Japan a submicroscopic domain texture consisting of small lamellae showing cross-hatched albite–pericline twins, resembling the domain texture of optically monoclinic adularia. He concluded that these feldspars grew as sanidine crystals.

Marfunin (1961, 1966) uses terms like triclinic sanidines and triclinic orthoclases, and Taylor (1965) includes 'nearly monoclinic' feldspars in the orthoclase group.

In the opinion of the author, sanidines and orthoclases are truly monoclinic phases of K-feldspar and should so remain; microclines are the triclinic phases which may be further defined by giving the triclinicity index Δ or the extinction on (001). For details of adularia and the alkali feldspars, see p. 118 and legend to figure 3.20 respectively.

3.213 Stability and frequency of the structural variants

A temperature of 500°c for the transition triclinic–monoclinic has been more or less accepted since Goldsmith and Laves (1954a) found that microcline could be hydrothermally altered to orthoclase at 525 but not at 500°c. Barth (1959) concluded from observations on natural K-feldspar that the transition occurs over a range from about 300 to 500°c. Accordingly, MacKenzie and Smith (1961) proposed a range of approximately 300°c, starting at about 250°c. Tomisaka (1962) found by hydrothermal experimentation that, according to the water pressure, the symmetry transition took place at temperatures between 360 and 470°c. Hart (1964), Steiger and Hart (1967), studied a Tertiary contact zone in the Precambrian rocks (gneisses, schists and amphibolites) at Eldorado in the Front Range, Colorado, and found, on approaching the contact, an abrupt change from the unaltered highly triclinic microcline to orthoclase. This change probably took place at a temperature of less than 400°c, and did not involve solution–redeposition, because the orthoclases near the contact had retained appreciable amounts of their radiogenic argon. Wright (1967) studied Precambrian pegmatites within the same contact zone and observed the transformation from maximum microcline to orthoclase by contact metamorphism. He concluded that the upper stability limit of maximum microcline is at $375° \pm 50°c$. A first-order transformation is suggested by the absence of microcline of intermediate obliquity but a higher-order transformation occurring over a small range of temperature is also possible.

Faced with such conflicting evidence it is impossible to propose an accurate temperature value of either the initiation of the disorder (which may well be as low as 250°c) or of the point of the transition triclinic $\rightleftharpoons$ monoclinic (which would seem to be around 400°c). It is worth mentioning that the transition triclinic $\rightleftharpoons$ monoclinic will vary according to the degree of disorder of the actual monoclinic phase, see figure 3.11 and legend.

A number of geologists have reported that K-feldspars from migmatites, crystalline schists, gneisses and particularly from augen gneisses show no sharp transition but exhibit extreme ranges of triclinicity. Many of these feldspars may have formed metastably within the stability field of maximum microcline (analogous to the low-temperature formation of authigenic orthoclases and monoclinic adularias).

Hafner and Laves (1957) found evidence of the existence of various microclines exhibiting many different intermediate structures. Many of these structures would seem to have no real stability field.

Data for the free-energy relations, which determine the stability of the various members, are hard to obtain from natural feldspars because of the impurity of the available material, perthite formation, uncertainty of the physical conditions during crystallization and cooling, etc. Experimental data are of even less value: the reactions are slow except at relatively very high temperatures, equilibrium is therefore difficult to establish in the laboratory (see Goldsmith, 1967).

Hafner and Laves (1957) concluded on the basis of infrared absorption spectra that if microcline is slowly heated it will assume monoclinic symmetry at partial disorder (= orthoclase close to point Ab of figure 3.7). By prolonged heat treatment this orthoclase eventually becomes fully disordered sanidine. These authors emphasize, however, that rapidly heated microcline, which at elevated temperatures strives to attain the stable state of disorder, passes through various intermediate stages that are unstable at all temperatures. Pertinent experiments were performed by P. Maillard (*Thesis*, Zurich, 1957—see Bambauer and Laves, 1960). He

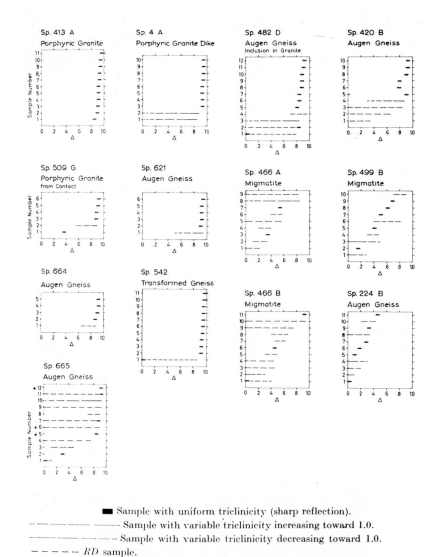

■ Sample with uniform triclinicity (sharp reflection).

—— —— —— ——— Sample with variable triclinicity increasing toward 1.0.

——— —— ——— — Sample with variable triclinicity decreasing toward 1.0.

— — — — — *RD* sample.

■■— — — — Sample with dominantly uniform triclinicity and some *RD* domains.

FIGURE 3.12 The obliquity of K-feldspars within single hand specimens.
Each square represents one sample

heated microcline from Crystal Park at 1050°c for 650 hours. During this heating the indicatrix migrated from the microcline position (with $2V_\alpha = 80°$) continuously into the sanidine position (with $2V_\alpha = 44°$ and the optic plane parallel to (010)); in the course of this migration the optic angle passed through a minimum of $2V_\alpha = 39°$. Interesting heating experiments were also performed on adularia.

The conclusion seems to be that the path of transformation is different according to whether the crystal is heated or cooled, rapidly or slowly within various temperature ranges. If this is true, the existence of an infinite number of intermediate microclines can be explained; indeed, potassium feldspar structures corresponding to any point within the area of the triangle of figure 3.7 can easily be understood.

The most common natural monoclinic feldspars are sanidines with $(-)2V$ in the range 20–40° $\perp$ (010) and orthoclases with $2V = 40$–60° corresponding to 15–33% order; sanidines of lower degrees of order are also found, so that the lower half of the edge high sanidine–hypo-orthoclase of figure 3.7 is covered.

Microcline with $(-)2V$ around 80° is most common. High triclinicity values, $\Delta = 0.80$–1.00, are more common than lower values (Barth, 1959; Dietrich, 1962; Hart, 1964; Ohta and Kizaki, 1966b; Wright, 1967). Consequently, most microclines plot close to the $KAlSi_3O_8$ corner (= corner of ideal maximum microcline).

However, in a great many Precambrian gneisses and granites, randomly disordered microclines are found. In addition to Δ with a definite value, diffuse reflections which represent variable Δ values within a crystal are encountered (Goldsmith and Laves, 1954b). These may vary from reflections which are diffuse about a definite Δ value to reflections that are evenly diffuse up to a certain Δ value. The latter has been called randomly disordered (RD) by Christie (1962). The RD potassium feldspar crystals are composed of small domains that have every possible Δ value between 0 and a fixed maximum value.

Smithson (1962) investigated the distribution of obliquity within single hand specimens of Precambrian granitoid rocks from Flå, Norway. The rather surprising results are displayed in figure 3.12.

Smithson concluded that amphibolite facies gneisses and particularly augen gneisses are characterized by microcline with a wide range of obliquities (cf. Guitard and others, 1960; Heier, 1961; Marmo and others, 1963), and that RD microclines form by a delicate interplay of growth rate, shear, temperature and volatiles present. They probably represent phases arrested at certain temperatures (or oscillating temperature intervals) during the vane of the metamorphism.

9

3.214 The problem of adularia

Many feldspars growing at low temperatures develop metastably a highly disordered (monoclinic or near-monoclinic) lattice, because the thermal energy is insufficient to organize the growth of a more ordered structure. Not only does this apply to the truly authigenic low-temperature K-feldspars, but also to late replacement feldspars that are frequently

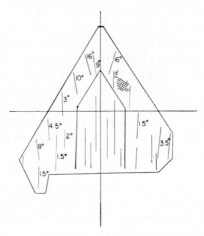

FIGURE 3.13 Adularia crystal from St. Gotthard normal to the *c* axis displaying the characteristics described by Mallard (1876): core shows optical extinction parallel to (010), edges show oblique extinctions provoking false zoning. Core and mantle show no compositional differences. (From Chaisson, 1950)

observed in the groundmass of many gneisses, and, last but not least, to the feldspars represented by adularias of the Alpine veins.

There is a copious literature on adularia. It was regarded as a monoclinic mineral, but recent investigations (optical and roentgenographic) indicate that triclinic structures are more characteristic (for references see Bambauer and Laves, 1960).

Adularia may consist of a great variety of lamellar domains exhibiting different structural states (see figure 3.13). In one and the same crystal the optical properties of the lamellae have been known to range from those characteristic of sanidine (axial plane $\parallel$ (010), $2V_\alpha \simeq 45°$) to those of microcline (axial plane $\perp$ (010), $2V \simeq 50°$).

The transition sanidine optics → microcline optics is particularly interesting. In adularia from Val Casatscha, Bambauer and Laves (1960) found that the sharp lamellae usually $\parallel$ (201) or $\parallel$ (110) display approximately

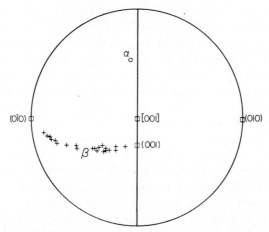

FIGURE 3.14 Stereogram showing the variation of the position of the indicatrix in a series of lamellae parallel to (hkl) and to ($h\bar{k}l$) in adularia from Val Casatscha. (Bambauer and Laves, 1960)

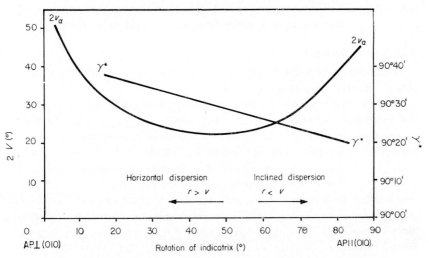

FIGURE 3.15 Range of variations in adularia optics. The optic axis, $2V$ and the reciprocal lattice angle γ^* as functions of the rotation of the indicatrix around the smaller axis α. The position of the axial plane (AP) changes from normal to parallel (010). (Bambauer and Laves, 1960)

either sanidine or microcline optics. But transitional optics are characteristic of the so-called 'diffuse' lamellae parallel to (hkl) and ($h\bar{k}l$).

The directions α and β of the optic indicatrix are plotted into the stereogram of figure 3.14. It should be noted that the position of α is practically constant, and that β (as well as the poles of the optic axes, which are not shown in the diagram) migrate along regular curves. This means that the optical changes are explained by a rotation of the indicatrix around the α axis. Figure 3.15 gives the correlation of the rotation of the indicatrix, the optic axial angle, and the optical dispersion. This kind of optical orientation is not known in any other variety of potassium feldspar.

Not all adularias show the same pattern of optical correlation or optical orientation. Measurements by, for instance, Chaisson (1950), Ansilewski (1958), Nowakowski (1959), deviate considerably from those of Bambauer and Laves (1960). But in view of the threefold infinity of possibilities of the Al/Si distribution—as demonstrated by equation (3.1)— it should not be surprising that different adularias exhibit vastly different optical orientations in spite of being chemically identical.

Laves thinks that the material of adularia originally grew (metastably) at rather low temperatures as a completely disordered feldspar (sanidine), and later underwent changes tending *directly* towards the maximum microcline state, see figure 3.10. During this process structural states were realized that hardly correspond to a stable equilibrium at any temperature. Thus, the 'field of adularia' is different from the 'field of microcline'.

3.22 Sodium feldspar

Two variants of sodium feldspar are known, viz. low albite and high albite. The transition point is at about 450°C.

Merwin (1911), during heating of albite, observed abrupt changes in the birefringence, and suggested that albite had two forms. Further experiments showed that permanent changes of the optical properties took place in natural albite exposed to heat (Barth, 1931; Spencer, 1937).

In 1950 Tuttle and Bowen showed that there were two modifications of $NaAlSi_3O_8$, which they described as high-temperature albite and low-temperature albite (the abbreviated names high albite and low albite are now in use). MacKenzie (1957) systematically investigated the polymorphism of $NaAlSi_3O_8$. Subsequent authors have determined the detailed crystal structures. MacKenzie and Smith (1961) and Gay (1962) have excellent summaries; Gay also includes plagioclases. Final conclusions were reached by Stewart and von Limbach (1967).

Low albite is structurally analogous to microcline: it has a completely ordered lattice, see table 3.8. Ideally, all Al ions are gathered in the $T_1(0)$ set of atomic sites (which has been known since 1951 from Laves' experiments on alkali interdiffusion). This structure is stable up to about 450°C.

Martin (1967) succeeded in synthesizing low albite from glasses of composition $NaAlSi_3O_8 + 5\% Na_2Si_2O_5$ at 200°C and 10 kbar P_{H_2O}. The

TABLE 3.8

Crystallographic data for albite

	Low albite[a]	High albite[b]	Synthetic materials[c]
a (Å)	8·138	8·149	8·160
b (°)	12·789	12·880	12·870
c (Å)	7·156	7·106	7·106
α (°)	94° 20′	93° 22′	93° 33′
β (°)	116° 34′	116° 18′	116° 22′
γ (°)	87° 39′	90° 17′	90° 11′
$T_1(0)$	94	30	39
$T_1(m)$	0	21	14
$T_2(0)$	4	22	18
$T_2(m)$	2	27	29
Order index	92	9	24

[a] From pegmatite at Ramona, California. Composition $Ab_{98.5}$, Or_1, $An_{0.5}$. Lattice parameters according to Ferguson and others. Al contents of the tetrahedral sets from a three-dimensional refinement of the structure by Ribbe and others (1962).

[b] Amelia albite heated at 1065°C (Ferguson and others, 1958).

[c] Cell dimensions from glass crystallized at 925°C and 250 bar H_2O pressure (Stewart and von Limbach, 1967). Disorder pattern from glass crystallized at 700°C and 1000 bar H_2O pressure (Williams and Megaw, 1964).

initial, metastable phase was high (or intermediate) albite that gradually recrystallized with time to low albite. The marked kinetic effect of excess soda on the transition may explain the presence of low albite in most plutonic, pegmatitic, metamorphic and hydrothermal rocks, whereas authigenic albites in dolomite often exhibit intermediate optics and lattice parameters. The inversion of these albites was impeded due to lack of excess soda in the environment of crystallization.

High albite is stable above 450°C. At about this temperature some disorder in the Al/Si distribution is introduced. The degree of disorder is a function of the temperature; this is graphically demonstrated by Stewart and von Limbach's measurements given in figure 3.16. With increasing temperature the disorder increases. But as seen from figure 3.17 high albite has no counterpart in the potassium feldspars. Obviously the *kind* of disorder in high albite is different from that in any other alkali feldspar; it rather approaches that in plagioclase. Referring to the general discussion

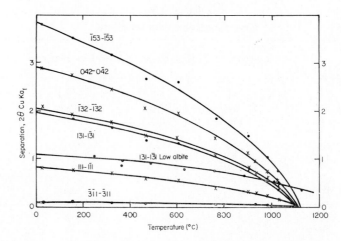

FIGURE 3.16 Angular separation of symmetrically related pairs of diffraction lines of high albite measured at high temperature. (Stewart and von Limbach, 1967)

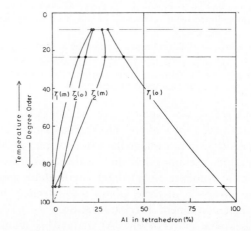

FIGURE 3.17 The change of the Al occupancy in each of the four tetrahedral groups during the diffuse transformation high albite → low albite. The presentation is analogous to that given in figure 3.11 for K-feldspar. A direct comparison shows that the disorder relations in Na-feldspar are of a different kind

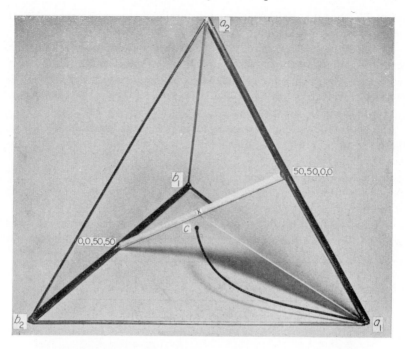

FIGURE 3.18 The tetrahedral space, as in figure 3.8, giving the types of
Al/Si disorder in the feldspar structures. The K-feldspar structures are
confined to the solid plane inside the tetrahedron, the Na-feldspar structures
lie along the line a_1–c

of the Al/Si distribution in feldspar structures on p. 104, particularly to
equation (3.1) and to figure 3.8, it is seen that the disorder pattern of high
albite can be represented graphically by the path a_1–c of figure 3.18.
McConnell and McKie (1960) studied the kinetics of this transformation
and described it as smeared, see discussion on p. 110.

It is questionable whether pure sodium feldspar has a monoclinic
modification (see Grundy and others, 1967; Stewart and von Limbach,
1967). But slightly potassian albite does become monoclinic close to its
melting point (see below).

3.221 On the monoclinic sodium feldspar

A monoclinic feldspar with the chemical composition of albite has
repeatedly cropped up in the mineralogical literature. It would seem
appropriate, therefore, to give a survey of the circumstances.

Barbier and Prost in 1908 were the first to claim the discovery of a
monoclinic albite—it was later called barbierite and eventually monalbite,

see p. 127, but this claim was not substantiated; the data reported were found to be inconsistent and faulty.

About 20 years later, large crystals of an apparently monoclinic anti-perthite—lamellae of orthoclase in a host of monoclinic albite—were reported from a pegmatite at Seiland (N. Norway) by Barth (1929). The bulk chemical composition of the antiperthite is $Or_{26.5}$, $Ab_{69.3}$, $An_{3.0}$, 1·0 Ba-feldspar, 0·2 Sr-feldspar.

The photomicrograph in figure 1.19 shows that the groundmass between the orthoclase lamellae is homogeneous, no twins can be seen, and the extinction on (001) is zero.

In the following table some optical data for this groundmass are compared with those of ordinary low albite; figure 3.19 gives a comparison of the positions of the corresponding indicatrices.

A Laue diagram taken of the large 'monoclinic' area in the centre of figure 1.19 proved that this area was made up of submicroscopic triclinic

	Seiland albite	Low albite
Extinction on (001) (°)	0	3·5
Extinction on (010) (°)	18	18
$2V_\gamma(°)$	88	78

twin lamellae. It can be calculated, mathematically, that the monoclinic optical properties are simple results of the twin structure (theory of Mallard, see p. 4).

There can be no doubt that very small amounts of potassium will make the albite lattice truly monoclinic at high temperatures, but by cooling, a displacive spontaneous inversion takes place. Ito (1939) showed by oscillation and Weissenberg diagrams that pericline twins in albite have the direct axis b parallel to the reciprocal axis b^*, and concluded an inheritance of monoclinic symmetry. Heating experiments have been performed by various workers. In some of these experiments uncontrolled amounts of potassium had contaminated the albite lattice, and it was erroneously believed that a monoclinic, pure albite could persist at room temperature, the so-called monalbite (Schneider and Laves, 1957). In effect, some 5% K_2O, corresponding to Or_{33}, is necessary to stabilize a monoclinic phase at room temperature.

Truly monoclinic cryptoperthitic lamellae were observed in a host of orthoclase by Jung and by Soldatos, see p. 24. The lamellae were probably exsolved at high temperatures ($\sim 650°c$) as monoclinic potassian albite.

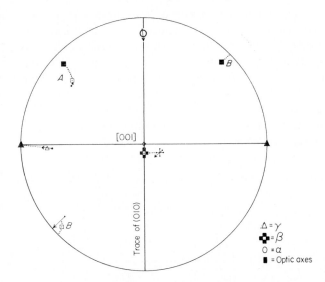

FIGURE 3.19 Stereographic projection of the optical orientation of the monoclinic albite from Seiland. The deviation from the normal attitude of the indicatrix is indicated by dotted lines. The arrows show the corresponding optical orientation of a triclinic albite with $0 \to 10$ An

In order for potassian albite to stay monoclinic at room temperature, an admixture of Or_{33} is necessary. But even with a smaller Or content an inversion to triclinic symmetry could fail to appear, for the monoclinic host forming coherent interfaces with the exsolved lamellae so strongly influences the symmetry and lattice parameters of the lamellae that an inversion is prevented.

It is interesting to note that, in like manner, small crystals of high cristobalite crystallizing in silica glass at elevated temperatures remain as high cristobalite at room temperature so long they are imbedded in the glass (Greig, 1932).

3.23 Alkali feldspar mixed crystals

Stable mixed crystals of $NaAlSi_3O_8$–$KAlSi_3O_8$, exist only at elevated temperatures. Under equilibrium conditions exsolution takes place below $\simeq 700°$c. However, diffusion rates are low, and the undercooled mixed crystals persist indefinitely in a metastable state at room temperature.

The subsolidus relations are shown in figure 3.20. The Ab end member is triclinic, the Or end member is monoclinic. The transition point changes rapidly with temperature. The transition is spontaneous and it was

discovered by Förstner (1884) who experimented with natural anorthoclases. More recently, it was investigated independently by Laves (1952),
MacKenzie (1952) and by Donnay and Donnay (1952). Laves showed
unequivocally that the transition is of the displacive type (such as high $\rightleftharpoons$
low quartz, or high $\rightleftharpoons$ low cristobalite) which leaves the Al distribution
pattern unaffected, i.e. it is identical on either side of the transition line.
MacKenzie accurately located this line of transition and also investigated
Ca-bearing (ternary) mixed crystals. Recently, Orville (1967) investigated
the same series (see below).

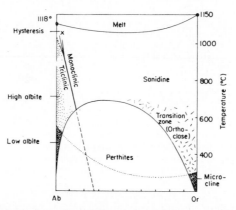

FIGURE 3.20 Subsolidus relations in the system Ab (NaAlSi$_3$O$_8$)–Or (KAlSi$_3$O$_8$)
An interesting modification of the solvus involving a minimum at high Or
contents was suggested by Wright (1964), but it is not shown in this diagram.
The displacive transformation monoclinic–triclinic is marked by a sharp line that
crosses the solvus and continues as a dashed line into the metastable region of
the mixed crystals. In this region below the solvus, the mixed crystals persist
            indefinitely at room temperature in a metastable state
Densely shaded areas: Microcline and low albite having the same crystal structure,
viz. an ordered distribution of Al and Si with Al occupying the points of one
            of the four structurally equivalent fourfold positions, $T_1(0)$
Dashed area: Orthoclase of partly disordered structure. Al migrates into two of
the fourfold positions. By increasing diffusional disorder it passes into the white
            area above the solvus representing sanidine with full disorder
Faintly shaded area: High albite which is partly disordered, but the kind of
            disorder is different from that in orthoclase
No change in disorder takes place at the monoclinic/triclinic line of displacive
transition, but if the line is crossed from right to left a further increase in Na
        will gradually change the sanidine disorder pattern into that of high albite
If a monoclinic mixed crystal, x, at 1050°c containing Or$_5$ is quenched, it will at
about 1000°c invert into triclinic symmetry, although the Al/Si distribution
pattern remains as before. By further cooling this structure becomes increasingly
unstable (even above the solvus) and by diffusive transitions it passes into a
structure of the high-albite type. If this is true, one should expect to find in lavas
            Na-rich anorthoclases of different structural states

Donnay and Donnay (1952) measured the six chief crystallographic constants at room temperature of a series of mixed crystals prepared at about 700°c across the field from the pure sodium feldspar to the pure potassium feldspar. The values of the constants plotted against composition give smooth curves. At the transition point, the curve of the interaxial angle α shows a discontinuity in its first derivative. The other curves were believed to show no break. But actually the curve of the cell volume does exhibit a break (see below). No two-phase region was found (in which triclinic and monoclinic forms exist); to escape detection it would have had to be less than one atomic per cent wide. The phase transitions are, therefore, of second or higher order; the mixed-crystal series may be considered complete.

The great difference in size of K^+ and Na^+ makes a complete series of mixed crystals remarkable. The radii at room temperature are 1·33 Å and 0·98 Å respectively, and the difference $1·33 - 0·98 = 0·35 = 36\%$ of the smaller ion. The usual limit for a complete series of mixed crystals is 15%. A possible explanation is that the *effective* radii change with temperature. If the thermal expansion of sodium was greater than that of potassium, the difference would then be reduced to 15% at about 700°c. Therefore the mixed-crystal series is stable only above 700°c. Barth had previously tried to explain the general laws of polymorphism in ionic lattices by assuming a differential thermal expansion of the individual ions (see Goldschmidt and others, 1926).

If K is replaced by the smaller Na, strain develops that is strong enough to transform the monoclinic lattice into triclinic symmetry if Na enters beyond a certain limit. The large K ions block up the cavities of the lattice much better than do the much smaller Na ions. If too much Na is introduced, the structure will collapse and become triclinic to suit the modest space requirements of Na; the Al/Si distribution is not affected by this collapse.

Figure 3.20 shows how the line of inversion rises obliquely toward the albite side. This means that the higher the temperature the more Na is tolerated by the monoclinic lattice, which accords with the theory that the relative size of the Na ion is greater at high temperatures.

The intersection of the line of inversion with the albite axis gives the temperature of inversion of pure albite. It is seen from figure 3.20 that this point is very close to the melting point of albite, but whether it is just above or just below the melting point (1118°c) is not yet definitely settled. The question is decisive for the existence of a monoclinic form of pure albite, see Brown (1967), Grundy and others (1967), Hall and Quareni (1967), Stewart and von Limbach (1967).

The unit volumes and density of the mixed crystals (table 3.9), if plotted against composition (figure 3.21), give lines of peculiar curvature indicating internal strains of great magnitude. This is not surprising when it is remembered that the measurements were made at room temperature, and the mixed-crystal series is actually unstable below 700°c.

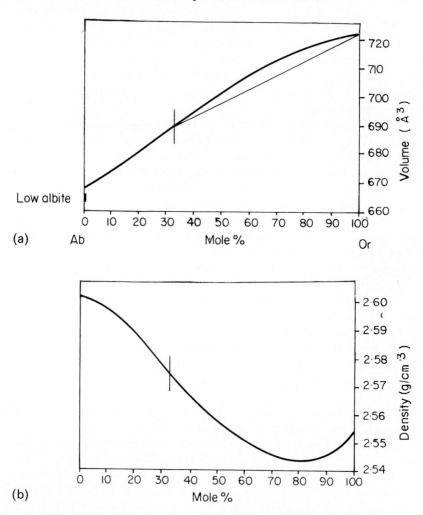

(a)

(b)

FIGURE 3.21 (*a*) Volume of the unit cell in the high-temperature mixed-crystal series Ab–Or at room temperature; (*b*) Specific gravity of the high-temperature mixed-crystal series Ab–Or at room temperature Vertical line marks the transition triclinic–monoclinic. (Data after Donnay and Donnay, 1952)

TABLE 3.9

Cell volume and density of the synthetic alkali feldspar series

Ab Or (wt. %)		Cell volume (Å)		Density (g/cm³) Stable
		Unstable[a]	Stable[b]	
0	100	722·52	722·6	2·558
20	80	714·98	715·1	2·555
40	60	704·93	704·9	2·562
50	50	700·30	699·7	2·566
60	40	694·80	693·6	2·573
70	30	686·38	687·2	2·581
80	20	678·60	679·6	2·594
90	10	669·23	672·7	2·610
100	0	663·67	666·1	2·615

[a] The unstable cell volumes refer to the unstable microcline–low albite solid solutions.
[b] The stable cell volumes refer to the sanidine–high albite solid solutions, see text (from Orville, 1967).

The shape of the solvus has been difficult to determine (see p. 218). Figure 3.22 shows three solvi as explained in the legend.

Experiments conducted by Yoder and others (1957) show that the solvus is affected by pressure: the maximum on the solvus rises about 14°/1000 bar. Barth (1967) calculated the magnitude of this effect from values for H_f and ΔV; H_f being the molar heat of the formation of solid solutions between high albite and orthoclase, ΔV the difference between the actual volumes and the volumes corresponding to a linear relation between the components. The results of these calculations are presented in figure 3.22. Several interesting facts emerge.

(1) The effect of high pressure—which as usual is similar to that of low temperature—is a general expansion of the field of exsolution. The maximum rise in the solvus with increasing pressure takes place rather close to the Or side, whereas the solvus in the region Ab_{90-100} is depressed. Luth and Tuttle (1966) found exactly the same value of increase on the Or side but a slightly higher value on the Ab side. Thus the shape of the whole solvus is changed; the characteristic skewness of the low-pressure solvus is reduced and the high-pressure solvus becomes more symmetric.

(2) The curve for ΔV is shown in the middle part of figure 3.22. In various ways this curve reflects the fine structure of the feldspars.

(a) The high positive values (with a maximum at Ab_{37}, Or_{63}) are due to a small coefficient of thermal expansion of the monoclinic alkali feldspar

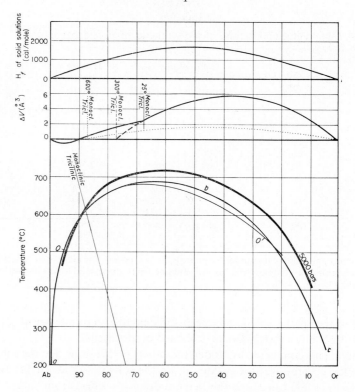

FIGURE 3.22 Upper diagram: Heat of solid solution between K- and Na-feldspar. (Data from Kracek and Neuvonen, 1952)

Middle diagram: The change of unit cell volumes due to the formation of solid solutions between high albite and orthoclase

ΔV = change of volume in terms of the difference between observed volume and volume calculated by linear interpolation of the component volumes. The curve for ΔV has a break at the monoclinic/triclinic inversion which divides the curve into two parts: a monoclinic part with a regular shape and a triclinic part with an irregular shape. This suggests that the monoclinic solid solutions are crystallographically homogeneous, whereas the crystal structure of the triclinic solid solutions changes with the composition

Lower diagram: Subsolidus equilibrium diagram for the alkali feldspars
Heavy line: Solvus calculated for a pressure of 5000 bar
a–b–c: Solvus as determined by analyses of natural feldspars. (Barth, 1962)
O–O: Solvus of synthetic feldspars at 1 atmosphere. (After Orville, 1963)
The thin and straight oblique line marks the displacive transition monoclinic ⇌ triclinic

structures; recent experiments by Stewart and von Limbach (1964) show the triclinic (anorthoclase) structures to have a greater coefficient of expansion. It must be assumed, therefore, that at high temperatures the monoclinic mixed crystals show more normal volumes, and only by cooling do they develop the high positive values. If the volume measurements had been done at, say 300°C, the ΔV curve of the monoclinic part should have shown a smaller convex bulge. At 600°C the bulge would have been still smaller, as indicated by the dotted curve. At 600°C the transition mono-clinic/triclinic is at approximately Ab_{87}, Or_{13}, which is close to the com-position at which the pressure has no effect on the position of the solvus, see figure 3.22, lower diagram.

(b) At the transition point monoclinic/triclinic, the ΔV curve shows a discontinuity in its first derivative. Obviously, the volume relations of the

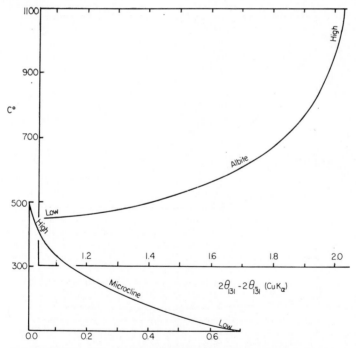

FIGURE 3.23 Variation in the triclinicity of albite and microcline with temperature

The parameter $2\theta_{(131)} - 2\theta_{(1\bar{3}1)}$ in low albite changes from 1·06 to 2·03 degrees of arc in the temperature range 450–1100°C. The albite curve is after MacKenzie (1957). The microcline curve has not been accurately determined but is sketched here after qualitative data; it is displaced one degree of arc in relation to the albite curve; see scale on the abscissa

monoclinic part of the solid solution series contrast with those of the triclinic part. In the monoclinic part, the ΔV curve has a regular shape indicating that all mixed crystals of this part are similar in structure. In the triclinic part, however, the irregular ΔV curve would seem to reflect a gradual change of the crystal structure from the completely disordered Al/Si pattern of the mixed crystals close to the transition point into a plagioclase-like pattern close to the Ab side. At room temperature, the transition point is according to Donnay at Or_{33}; according to Orville (1967) it is at Or_{42}.

Low albite with an ordered Al/Si distribution as in microcline will on prolonged heating develop diffusional disorder with respect to Al–Si and gradually transform into high albite. The higher the temperature, the higher the disorder, and the greater is the deviation from the structure of

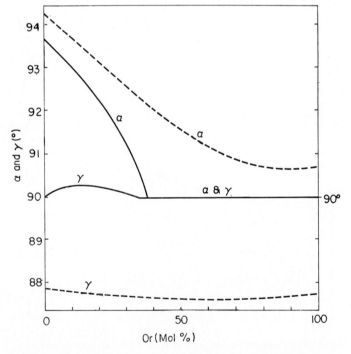

FIGURE 3.24. The interaxial angles α and γ of the alkali feldspar mixed-crystals series. Solid curves represent sanidine–high albite solid solution stable at elevated temperature. Dashed curves represent microcline–low albite solid solution unstable at all temperatures. (Data from Orville, 1967)

low albite. The diffusional synthesis of high albite takes time, because diffusion of Al and Si ions in the lattice is a slow process. Baskin's (1956) experiments suggest that in the range 1000–1100°c equilibrium will be attained within about 10 days, see figure 2.11. In MacKenzie's experiments, the parameter $2\theta_{131}-2\theta_{1\bar{3}1}$—which should become zero at monoclinic symmetry—actually increases from about one to two by heating up to 1000°c. These observations demonstrate that the crystal structure of albite does not approach monoclinic symmetry upon heating. Consequently, the transition is not analogous to that from microcline to sanidine.

How does this harmonize with the fact that albites with very small amounts of K in the lattice do become monoclinic with a truly ideally disordered structure in the range 1000–1100°c? Stewart and von Limbach (1964) showed that synthetic albite (containing traces of K) became monoclinic at 1044°c on heating; it remained monoclinic on cooling to 970°c, when it again became triclinic. Thus a hysteresis loop at about 80°c was established, a fact which excludes a displacive transformation. The explanation favoured by the author is indicated in figure 3.20.

Unstable triclinic mixed crystals from low albite to microcline can be prepared by alkali interdiffusion in the solid state (Goldsmith and Laves, 1957, 1961; Hafner and Laves, 1957; Laves, 1951). Orville (1963, 1967) used the reaction maximum microcline $\rightleftharpoons$NaCl at 900°c. These mixed crystals are very unstable under all physical conditions and will at room temperature within a few days break up and exsolve into the component phases. The lattice angles and spacings show a non-linear change with composition, see table 3.9 and figure 3.24. Orville reports positive volumes of mixing with a maximum of 19 cm^3/mole near 50% albite. This would correspond to a coefficient of repulsion even higher than that calculated for the high-temperature feldspar mixed-crystal series.

3.231 Summary

The high-temperature solid solution series from albite to orthoclase (from NaAlSi$_3$O$_8$ to KAlSi$_3$O$_8$) exists at room temperature in a metastable state. The first third of the series shows triclinic symmetry, at Or$_{33}$, Ab$_{67}$ there is a displacive transition into monoclinic symmetry.

The volumes of mixing show a non-linear and irregular change with composition. In the monoclinic part of the series, the change is regular and high positive values are attained with a maximum of 6 Å^3 per unit cell at Or$_{63}$, Ab$_{37}$. In contrast, the triclinic part displays irregular changes and, in part, negative volume relations. At the transition point the volume itself is continuous, but shows a discontinuity in its first derivative (see curve for V in figure 3.22).

These volume relations can be explained by assuming that all mono-clinic mixed crystals are of similar structure, viz. sanidine structure with a tendency to complete Al/Si disorder, whereas the triclinic mixed crystals exhibit structures that change with the composition: at the transition point they show sanidine structure, but, as Na increases, some sort of order will develop that is different from that of other alkali feldspars and probably similar to that in plagioclase (= high-albite structure, see figure 3.19).

On the basis of known values for the heat of mixing and for the change in volume, the effect of pressure on the solvus has been calculated, see figure 3.22.

3.3 THE STRUCTURE OF ANORTHITE, $CaAl_2Si_2O_8$

The compound $CaAl_2Si_2O_8$ is polymorphous (Davis and Tuttle, 1952; Donnay, 1952; Goldsmith and Ehlers, 1952; Takéuchi and Donnay, 1959) and demonstrates that a feldspar composition can crystallize as a non-tectosilicate: (1) A metastable hexagonal modification, space group 6_3 mcm, isostructural with the hexagonal Ba-feldspar—at least the lattice geometry and space group are similar—is a sheet silicate with a two-dimensional double layer, $\sim[Al_2Si_2O_8]$ as the main structural element. Ca^{2+} ions enter between the layers to balance the charges. (2) A metastable orthorhombic modification, space group $P_{2,2,2}$, not related to the ortho-rhombic form of Ba-feldspar. (3) A stable triclinic modification called anorthite, which again exhibits a high- and a low-temperature variant, mutually related through a gradual order–disorder transformation. The refractive indices, optic axial angle and density are:

	α	β	γ	$2V$	g/cm^3
Natural anorthite	1·577	1·585	1·590	−77	2·76
Rhombic $CaAl_2Si_2O_8$	1·553	1·580	1·584	−39	2·70
Hexagonal $CaAl_2Si_2O_8$	1·585	1·585	1·590	0	2·77

Gay and Taylor (1953) suggested that in anorthite the disorder develops in the distribution of the Ca ions. By partially substituting Ga for Al and Ge for Si in an anorthite lattice Goldsmith and Laves (1955) were able to verify this kind of disorder: As distinct from all other feldspars, the Al and Si atoms are ordered in anorthite, even at high temperatures. But the Ca ions are not as symmetrically arranged in the lattice 'holes' as are the Na or K atoms of the alkali feldspars. Furthermore, with increasing temperature, the Ca ions gradually become disordered, the degree of disorder being a continuous and reversible function of temperature; at the melting point (1554°), the disorder is practically complete (Laves and Goldsmith, 1954).

There are two equivalent sets of lattice complexes that can be occupied by Ca ions; either arrangement produces an identical anorthite structure. If all Ca ions were contained in the one set, the crystal would be fully ordered. If the Ca ions are distributed at random over both sets, the crystal is disordered with respect to Ca (Laves and Goldsmith, 1954a).

With decreasing temperature, anorthite suffers a *districtive transformation* (see Laves's discussion to Megaw, 1962). The structure of the high-temperature, disordered variant used to be regarded as body centred and was designated anorthite (B). It reveals sharp reflections of two types only, *a* and *b* (in contrast to the low-temperature primite anorthite P where *c* and *d* also occur). Fleet and others (1966) have produced evidence that the apparent body centring in bytownite, An_{80}, is an effect of disorder. Half-Ca atom peaks resolve into 'half'-sites about 0.85 Å apart on the electron-density maps parallel to (100). The absence of *c* and *d* reflections can be explained by assuming the existence of out-of-phase domains. This is physically reasonable because of the close resemblance which must exist between two halves of the unit cell along the [111] direction, as shown by the small magnitudes of the 'half-atom splittings'; consequently a mistake in the sequence is not unlikely. Further support for this explanation comes from the existence of the transitional anorthites. At about $350°c$, domains develop with a modified Ca distribution; with further decrease in temperature the domain sizes grow until the crystal becomes one single domain; this crystal, called low anorthite or anorthite (P), has a primitive lattice (presence of reflections *a*, *b*, *c* and *d*), see p. 100. The districtive transformation is a continuous and reversible function of temperature (Brown and others, 1963; Bloss, 1964).

At the feldspar symposium organized by the International Mineralogical Association in Copenhagen, 1960, some interesting ideas on the structure of anorthite were offered for consideration (see Kempster and others, 1961; Chandrasekhar and others, 1961; Laves and Goldsmith, 1961).

3.4 THE STRUCTURE OF THE PLAGIOCLASES

Plagioclases are mixed crystals between albite and anorthite and used to be considered as an ideal example of continuous solid solutions. Bowen (1913) published the results of his studies of the melting phenomena on plagioclase feldspars—he calculated thermodynamically the latent heat of melting of albite and anorthite and the shape of the liquidus of the plagioclases—and proved in this way that the plagioclases represent near-ideal solid solutions at high temperatures. From this it does not follow, however, that ideality persists at lower temperatures, although many mineralogists erroneously supposed it to be valid for all plagioclase mixed crystals at all temperatures.

The development after 1934 has shown that the plagioclases at room temperatures are extremely complicated mixed crystals in which the crystallographic and optical properties (unit cell dimensions, interaxial angles, indices of refraction, etc.) and other physical properties (volume relations, density, etc.) change in a very irregular manner with the composition, see sections 2.4, 3.13, 4.2. Incipient exsolution also takes place (peristerites, p. 37, labradorization, p. 42).

The structural differences in the various types of plagioclases may be classified by peculiarities in the reciprocal lattice. The following types of reflections in single-crystal photographs can be distinguished (Gay, 1953).

(*a*) Chief reflections present in all feldspars (*hkl*) with $h + k$ even and l even. The next types, *b*, *c* and *d* are called subsidiary reflections.

(*b*) Superlattice reflections (*hkl*) with $h + k$ odd and l odd. They imply a body-centred cell and a doubling of the *c* axis as compared to that determined by *a*.

(*c*) $h + k$ even, l odd, and

(*d*) $h + k$ odd, l even. Both *c* and *d* reveal a primitive cell with doubled *c* axis.*

(*e*) Pairs of reflections, the so-called '*b*-split', which may appear instead of simple *b* reflections.*

(*f*) Pairs of reflections as satellites to *a*.

Additional reflections, called super satellites, corresponding to a periodicity of 1800 Å were observed by Korekawa and Jagodzinski (1967) in labradorites with schiller, see p. 43. The *e* and *f* reflections do not correspond to rational indices, but they correlate, in position and intensity, with the composition of the plagioclase (Gay, 1962).

Figure 3.25 gives a survey of the subsolidus relations of the plagioclases.

Additional complications in the plagioclases are disorder phenomena. There are three types:

(1) Substitutional disorder
(2) Position disorder
(3) Stacking disorder

(1) Substitutional disorder: In low albite and microcline, $T_1(0)$ is occupied by Al, the other sites by Si. In anorthite half the four sets derived from *each* of the original four $T_1(0)$, $T_1(m)$, $T_2(0)$, $T_2(m)$ are occupied

---

* The reflections that are here called *c*, *d*, *e* and *f* (following Bown and Gay, 1958) are by Laves and Goldsmith (1954) called c_1, c_2, *d* and *e*, respectively.

by Al and half by Si—and exactly the same distribution is found in celsian in spite of its different symmetry. This distribution is characterized by a perfect alternation of Si and Al along any line of T—O bonds. It incorporates the 'aluminium avoidance' rule suggested by Loewenstein (1954). It can be predicted on electrostatic grounds, as it tends to equalize the electrostatic valence bonds to all oxygens. Both the 14 Å repeat period and the 1:1 ratio of Si:Al are necessary to allow this arrangement.

It should be emphasized that the arrangement of albite cannot be derived from that of anorthite by continuous replacement of Al by Si, but requires also the replacement of Si on half the $T_1(0)$ sites by Al. This is likely to be a more difficult reorganization, and its onset should therefore be recognizable as corresponding to some break in the continuity of the series.

Changes in the *degree* of order occur continuously with temperature and composition. Changes in *kind* of order may be discontinuous. A particular kind of atom contained in one site will generally affect the probability of occupation of the next equivalent site by the same kind of atom. However, if this effect is weak, the difference of probability may be negligible. The crystal is *homogeneously disordered.* By contrast, the arrangement in one unit cell may be strongly correlated with the arrangements of its neighbours. If atoms of the one kind prefer the other kind as neighbours, a structure in which they alternate is that of lowest energy; then an ordered homogeneous crystal with *domain* texture may form; the original unit cell is doubled. Alternatively, in different growth conditions, a texture of *antiphase* domains will form. The domain sizes are in the range 3–30 unit cells. The size and shape of the diffuseness of the x-ray reflections give information about the size and shape of the domains.

(2) Position disorder: Experimentally, this effect has been observed for Na in high albite. The interpretation is that Na is 'split', i.e. it occupies two slightly different lattice sites (section 3.17). Similarly the Ca atom in high anorthite is split over the two lattice sites, p. 135.

(3) Stacking disorder: can be described as pseudo-translation repeats forming faulted subunits.

Megaw (1960) has explained the non-Bragg reflections as due to stacking faults that nucleate within an ideal intermediate plagioclase structure (near An_{77}) as a result of misfit inherent in the substitution NaSi–CaAl. Her ideal structure consists of 18 subcells (9 subcells long and 2 subcells wide) differing from one another in Al/Si pattern, and in distortion of the framework structures. These stacking faults would be spaced at intervals of several unit cells.

The distribution pattern of Si/Al in plagioclases is complicated because the ratio Si:Al changes from 3 at the composition of albite to only 1 at anorthite. In anorthite and contiguous feldspars with Si:Al = 1:1, order is so easily achieved that it persists even at very high temperatures. Andesine, An_{33}, with Si:Al = 2:1, marks one of the chief discontinuities in the plagioclase series (Doman and others, 1965; Bambauer and others, 1967). Also labradorite, An_{50}, marks a chief discontinuity; Si:Al is 1·67, the ratio Na:Ca is 1:1.

Niggli (1967) calculated the theoretically possible ordered distributions of Si and Al in plagioclases by applying a topological transformation; his general results—see table 3.10—reflect sudden changes, discontinuities and gaps (such as the peristerite gap) in the lattice constants vs. composition.

In spite of these complications a common tendency can be spotted in the Si/Al distribution of all plagioclases. As seen from table 3.11, $T_1(0)$ and

TABLE 3.10

Stoichiometric composition of the possible states of Si/Al order in the plagioclases

	c ~ 7 Å				c ~ 14 Å				
Si per cell	12	11	10		20	19	18	17	16
Al per cell	4	5	6		12	13	14	15	16
Si:Al	3·0	2·2		1·67		1·46	1·3	1·13	1·0
Composition (An)	0	25		50		62·5	75	87·5	100

TABLE 3.11

Average Al contents of the tetrahedra sites of various plagioclases

	$T_1(0)$	$T_1(m)$	$T_2(0)$	$T_2(m)$
Anorthite (Monte Somma)	0·50	0·51	0·49	0·52
Bytownite, An_{80}	0·51	0·44	0·40	0·45
Andesine, An_{48}	0·56	0·28	0·27	0·34
Oligoclase, An_{22}	0·42	0·18	0·16	0·31
Albite (Amelia, heated)	0·30	0·16	0·22	0·27

Values for bytownite are from Fleet and others (1966); for albite see table 3.8; all others are from Taylor (1962).

$T_2(m)$ contain most of the Al ions. This is true even for high albite, as discussed on p. 122, and explains that high plagioclase passes continuously into high albite.

However, we have no detailed knowledge of the Si/Al distribution and its variation with temperature and composition of the plagioclase. Example: a plagioclase with Si/Al ratio of $9:7 (= An_{75})$: Do the excess Si atoms go into only one of the 8 original Al sites, or into all 8 at random?

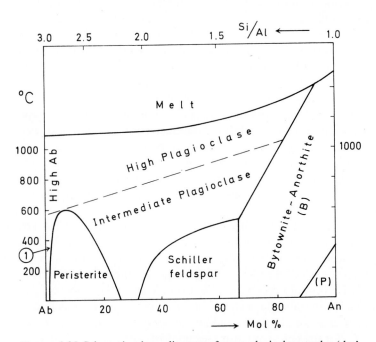

FIGURE 3.25 Schematic phase diagram of pure plagioclase under 'dry' conditions. Except for the melting curve the phase boundaries are uncertain and tentative. (1) = field of low albite; (P) = field of primitive anorthite; (B) = field of body-centred anorthite. Anorthite with 'Ca domains' (has been called transitional anorthite and is revealed by the diffuseness of the c reflections) is located in the border field between (B) and (P); at low temperature it tolerates additional amounts of Na and extends to An_{70}, see text

High plagioclase is more or less disordered with respect to the Si/Al distribution. With decreasing temperature it passes by gradation into the partly ordered intermediate plagioclase. At the Na-rich end complete exsolution takes place: the peristerite immiscibility gap is formed bounded by low albite and intermediate plagioclase. Another exsolution area, or near-exsolution area—disclosed in optical schiller and in the appearance of super-satellite x-ray reflections—exists at low temperature in the approximate range An_{30-70}, see text

Do quasi-ordered structures exist in which certain sites admit only Si, others only Al, and others are occupied at random? Generally, such questions cannot be answered.

At the symposium on feldspars in Copenhagen, 1960, some interesting ideas on the constitution of the plagioclases were discussed (see Megaw, 1961; Gay, 1961).

With reference to figure 3.25 the following details are relevant:

Transitional anorthite develops in the boundary region between anorthite (P) and anorthite (B): Domains of anorthite (P) occur in an anti-phase relationship such that the perfect Al/Si alteration is not interrupted at the domain walls; there is no evidence of other disorder (Ribbe and Megaw, 1962; Fleet and others, 1966).

The difference between high plagioclase and the variants stable at lower temperature lies—as in the alkali feldspars—in the order–disorder relations; both the Al/Si and the Na/Ca distributions depend on temperature and can only be changed through a diffusive transformation (Gay, 1954).

With decreasing temperature a more perfect lattice order is pursued, but diffusion is a slow process and, once cooled, the disordered high plagioclase structure remains metastably for geological eras. But in this way stresses develop that are reflected in quite abnormal physical properties of the crystals, see p. 161.

By passage into the intermediate plagioclases the detailed structure becomes extremely complicated. Stacking disorder may play an important part. Calcic intermediate plagioclases exhibit both e and f reflections; in the more sodic members (range An_{60-25}), the reflections fade away, and the e reflections become diffuse (as they also do by increasing temperature), until in sodic plagioclases they, too, vanish completely (Gay, 1956).

In the areas of peristerite and labradorization, incipient exsolution has started. For further description, see pp. 37ff. and 43.

REFERENCES

Ansilewski, J. (1958). On microcline and triclinic adularia from Bialskie Gory gneisses. *Bull. Acad. Polon. Sci., Ser. Sci. Geol. Geograph.*, *VII*, **10**, 275.

Bailey, S. W. and Taylor, W. H. (1955). The structure of triclinic potassium feldspar. *Acta Cryst.*, **8**, 621.

Bambauer, H. U., Eberhard, E. and Viswanathan, K. (1967). The lattice constants and related parameters of plagioclases (low). *Schweiz. Mineral. Petrog. Mitt.*, **47**, 351.

Bambauer, H. U. and Laves, F. (1960). Zum Adular-Problem. *Schweiz. Mineral. Petrog. Mitt.*, **40**, 177.

Barbier, D. and Prost, A. (1908). Sur l'existence d'un feldspath sodique monoclinic isomorphe de l'orthose. *Bull. Soc. Chim.*, **3**, 894.

Barth, T. F. W. (1929). Über den monoklinen Natronfeldspat. *Z. Krist.*, **69**, 476.

Barth, T. F. W. (1931). Permanent changes in the optical orientation of feldspars exposed to heat. *Norsk Geol. Tidsskr.*, **12**, 57.

Barth, T. F. W. (1934). Polymorphic phenomena and crystal structure. *Am. J. Sci.*, **27**, 273.

Barth, T. F. W. (1959). The interrelations of the structural variants of the potash feldspars. *Z. Krist.*, **112** (Laue Vol.), 263.

Barth, T. F. W. (1962). Feldspar solid solutions. *Chem. Erde*, **22**, 31.

Barth, T. F. W. (1963). The composition of nepheline. *Schweiz. Mineral. Petrog. Mitt.*, **43**, 153.

Barth, T. F. W. (1965). On the constitution of the alkali feldspars. *Tschermaks Mineral. Petrog. Mitt.* [3], **10** (Machatsohki Vol.), 14.

Barth, T. F. W. (1967). Structure and volume relations of the alkali feldspar mixed crystals. *Schweiz. Mineral. Petrog. Mitt.*, **47**, 121.

Barth, T. F. W. and Posnjak, E. (1931). The spinel structure. A case of variate atom equipoints. *J. Wash. Acad. Sci.*, **21**, 255.

Baskin, Y. (1956). Observations on heat-treated authigenic microcline and albite crystals. *J. Geol.*, **64**, 219.

Bloss, F. D. (1964). Optical extinction of anorthite at high temperature. *Am. Mineralogist*, **49**, 1125.

Bowen, N. L. (1913). The melting phenomena of the plagioclase feldspars. *Am. J. Sci.*, **35**, 577.

Bown, M. G. and Gay, P. (1958). The reciprocal lattice geometry of the plagioclase feldspar structures. *Z. Krist.*, **111**, 1.

Brown, B. E. (1962). Aluminium distribution in the igneous maximum microcline and the sanidine microcline series. *Norsk Geol. Tidsskr.* **42**, II (Feldspar Vol.), 25.

Brown, B. E. and Bailey, S. W. (1964). The structure of maximum microcline. *Acta Cryst.*, **17**, 1319.

Brown, W. L. (1967). A reinterpretation of monalbite. *Mineral. Mag.*, **36**, 80.

Brown, W. L., Hoffman, W. and Laves, F. (1963). Überkontinuierliche und reversible Transformationen des Anorthites ($CaAl_2Si_2O_8$) zwischen 25 und 350°C. *Naturwissenschaften*, **50**, 221.

Chaisson, U. (1950). The optics of triclinic adularia. *J. Geol.*, **58**, 537.

Chandrasekhar, S., Fleet, S. G. and Megaw, H. D. (1961). Structure of body-centred anorthite. *Inst. "Lucas Mallada" Curs. Conf.* **VIII**, 141.

Chao, S. H., Hargreaves, A. and Taylor, W. H. (1940). The structure of orthoclase. *Mineral. Mag.*, **25**, 498.

Christie, O. H. J. (1962). Observations on natural feldspars: Randomly disordered structures and a preliminary suggestion to a plagioclase thermometer. *Norsk Geol. Tidsskr.*, **42**, II (Feldspar Vol.), 383.

Cole, W. F., Sörum, H. and Kennard, O. (1949). The crystal structure of orthoclase and sanidinized orthoclase. *Acta Cryst.*, **2**, 280.

Cole, W. F., Sörum, H. and Taylor, W. H. (1951). The structure of the plagioclase feldspars. *Acta Cryst.*, **4**, 20.

Davis, G. L. and Tuttle, O. F. (1952). Two new crystalline phases of the anorthite composition—$CaO \cdot Al_2O_3 \cdot 2SiO_2$. *Am. J. Sci.* (Bowen Vol.), 107.

Dietrich, R. V. (1962). K-feldspar structural states as petrogenetic indicators. *Norsk Geol. Tidsskr.*, **42**, II (Feldspar Vol.), 394.

Doman, R. C., Cinnamon, C. G. and Bailey, S. W. (1965). Structural discontinuities in the plagioclase feldspar series. *Am. Mineralogist*, **50**, 724.

Donnay, G. (1952). Hexagonal $CaAl_2Si_2O_8$. *Acta Cryst.*, **5**, 153.

Donnay, G. and Donnay, J. D. H. (1952). The symmetry changes in the high-temperature alkali-feldspar series. *Am. J. Sci.* (Bowen Vol.), 115.

Ferguson, R. B. (1960). The low-temperature phases of the alkali feldspars and their origin. *Can. Mineralogist*, **6**, 415.

Ferguson, R. B., Traill, R. J. and Taylor, W. H. (1958). The crystal structures of low-temperature and high-temperature albites. *Acta Cryst.*, **11**, 331.

Ferguson, R. B., Traill, R. J. and Taylor, W. H. (1959). Charge balance and the stability of alkali feldspars: a discussion. *Acta Cryst.*, **12**, 716.

Finney, J. J. and Bailey, S. W. (1964). Crystal structure of an authigenic maximum microcline. *Z. Krist.*, **119**, 413.

Fleet, S. G., Chandrasekhar, S. and Megaw, H. D. (1966). The structure of bytownite (body-centred anorthite). *Acta Cryst.*, **21**, 782.

Förstner, H. (1884). Über künstliche physikalische Veränderungen der Feldspäthe von Pantelleria. *Z. Krist.*, **9**, 333.

Gay, P. (1953). The structures of the plagioclase feldspars: III. An x-ray study of anorthites and bytownites. *Mineral. Mag.*, **30**, 169.

Gay, P. (1954). The structures of the plagioclase feldspars: V. The heat treatment of lime-rich plagioclases. *Mineral. Mag.*, **30**, 428.

Gay, P. (1956). The structures of the plagioclase feldspars: VI. Natural intermediate plagioclases. *Mineral. Mag.*, **31**, 21.

Gay, P. (1961). Some recent work on the plagioclase feldspars. *Inst. "Lucas Mallada" Curs. Conf.*, **VIII**, 159.

Gay, P. (1962). Sub-solidus relations in the plagioclase feldspars. *Norsk. Geol. Tidsskr.*, **42**, II (Feldspar Vol.), 37.

Gay, P. and Bown, M. (1956). The structures of the plagioclase feldspars: VII. The heat treatment of intermediate plagioclases. *Mineral. Mag.*, **31**, 306.

Gay, P. and Taylor, W. H. (1953). The structure of the plagioclase feldspars: IV. Variations in the anorthite structure. *Acta Cryst.*, **6**, 647.

Goldschmidt, V. M., Barth, T. F. W., Lunde, G., Zachariasen, W. H. (1926). Geochemische Verteilungsgesetze der Elemente VII. *Skrifter Vid. Akad. Oslo*, No. **2**, 92.

Goldsmith, J. R. (1967). Metastability and hangovers in crystals. *Geochim. Cosmochim. Acta*, **31**, 913.

Goldsmith, J. R. and Ehlers, E. G. (1952). The stability relations of anorthite and its hexagonal polymorph in the system $CaAl_2Si_2O_8$–H_2O. *J. Geol.*, **60**, 386.

Goldsmith, J. R. and Laves, F. (1954a). The microcline stability relations. *Geochim. Cosmochim. Acta*, **5**, 1.

Goldsmith, J. R. and Laves, F. (1954b). Potassium feldspars structurally intermediate between microcline and sanidine. *Geochim. Cosmochim. Acta*, **6**, 100.

Goldsmith, J. R. and Laves, F. (1955). Cation order in anorthite ($CaAl_2Si_2O_8$) as revealed by gallium and germanium substitutes. *Z. Krist.*, **106**, 213.

Goldsmith, J. R. and Laves, F. (1957). Über die Mischkristallreihe Mikroklin–Albit. *Fortschr. Mineral.*, **35**, 18.

Greig, J. W. (1932). The existence of the high-temperature form of cristobalite at room temperature and the crystallinity of opal. *J. Am. Chem. Soc.*, **54**, 2846.

Grundy, H. D., Brown, W. L. and MacKenzie, W. S. (1967). On the existence of monoclinic NaAlSi$_3$O$_8$ at elevated temperatures. *Mineral. Soc. Notice*, No. **145**, London (1966); *Mineral. Mag.*, **36**, 83.

Guitard, G., Raguin, E. and Sabatier, P. (1960). La symétrie des feldspaths potassiques dans les gneisses et les granites des Pyrenées orientales. *Bull. Soc. Franc. Mineral. Crist.*, **83**, 48.

Hafner, St. and Laves, F. (1957). Ordnung/Unordnung und Ultrarotabsorption. II Variation der Lage und Intensität einiger Absorptionen von Feldspäten. Zur Struktur von Orthoklas und Adular. *Z. Krist.*, **109**, 204.

Hahn, Th. (1962). Verfeinerung zweier Feldspatstrukturen. *Fortschr. Mineral.*, **40**, 54.

Hall, K. M. and Quareni, S. (1967). A note on monalbite. *Mineral. Mag.*, **36**, 78.

Hart, S. R. (1964). The petrology and isotopic-mineral age relations of a contact zone in the Front Range, Colorado. *J. Geol.*, **72**, 493.

Heier, K. S. (1961). The amphibolite–granulite facies transition reflected in the mineralogy of potassium feldspar. *Inst. "Lucas Mallada", Curs. Conf.*, **VIII** (Feldspar Symp., 1960).

Hewlett, C. G. (1959). Optical properties of potassium feldspars. *Bull. Geol. Soc. Am.*, **70**, 511.

Ito, T. I. (1939). The existence of a monoclinic soda feldspar. *Z. Krist.*, **100**, 297.

Jones, J. B. (1966). Order in alkali feldspars. *Nature*, **210**, 1352.

Jones, J. B. (1968). Al-O and Si-O tetrahedral distances in alumosilicate framework structures. *Acta Cryst.*, **B24**, 355.

Jones, J. B. and Taylor, W. H. (1961). The structure of orthoclase. *Acta Cryst.*, **14**, 443.

Kempster, C. J. E., Megaw, H. D. and Radoslovich, E. W. (1961). The structure of anorthite. *Inst. "Lucas Mallada" Curs. Conf.*, **VIII**, 139.

Kempster, C. J. E., Megaw, H. D. and Radoslovich, E. W. (1962). The structure of anorthite, I. *Acta Cryst.*, **15**, 1005.

Korekawa, M. and Jagodzinski, H. (1967). Die Satelliten des Labradorits. *Schweiz. Mineral. Petrog. Mitt.*, **47**, 269.

Kracek, F. C. and Neuvonen, K. J. (1952). Thermochemistry of plagioclase and alkali feldspars. *Am. J. Sci.* (Bowen Vol.), 293.

Laves, F. (1950). The lattice and twinning of microcline and other potash feldspars. *J. Geol.*, **58**, 548.

Laves, F. (1951). Artificial preparation of microcline. *J. Geol.*, **59**, 511.

Laves, F. (1952). Phase relations of the alkali feldspars. *J. Geol.*, **60**, 436, 549.

Laves, F. (1960). Al/Si-Verteilungen, Phasen-Transformätionen und Namen der Alkalifeldspäte. *Z. Krist.*, **113** (Laue Vol., II), 265.

Laves, F. and Goldsmith, J. R. (1954). Long-range–short-range order in calcic plagioclases as a continuous and reversible function of temperature. *Acta Cryst.*, **7**, 465.

Laves, F. and Goldsmith, J. R. (1961). Comments on the anorthite papers by Megaw and coworkers presented in this symposium. *Inst. "Lucas Mallada" Curs. Conf.*, **VIII**, 155.

Laves, F. (1965). The correlation of optics and lattice geometry of microcline. *Am. Mineralogist*, **50**, 509.

Loewenstein, W. (1954). The distribution of aluminium in the tetrahedra of silicates and aluminates. *Am. Mineralogist*, **39**, 92.

Luth, W. C. and Tuttle, O. F. (1966). The alkali feldspar solvus in the system $Na_2O-K_2O-Al_2O_3-SiO_2-H_2O$. *Am. Mineralogist*, **51**, 1359.

McConnell, J. D. C. and McKie, D. (1960). The kinetics of the ordering process in triclinic $NaAlSi_3O_8$. *Mineral. Mag.*, **32**, 436.

Machatschki, F. (1928). Zur Frage der Struktur und Konstitution der Feldspäte. *Centralbl. Mineral., etc., Abt.* A., 97.

MacKenzie, W. S. (1952). The effect of temperature on the symmetry of high-temperature soda-rich feldspars. *Am. J. Sci.* (Bowen Vol.), 319.

MacKenzie, W. S. (1954). The orthoclase–microcline inversion. *Mineral. Mag.*, **30**, 354.

MacKenzie, W. S. (1957). The crystalline modifications of $NaAlSi_3O_8$. *Am. J. Sci.*, **255**, 481.

MacKenzie, W. S. and Smith, J. V. (1959). Charge balance and stability of alkali feldspars. *Acta Cryst.*, **12**, 73.

MacKenzie, W. S. and Smith, J. V. (1961). Experimental and geological evidence for the stability of alkali feldspars. *Inst. "Lucas Mallada," Curs. Conf.*, **VIII**, 53.

Mallard, F. (1876). Explications des phénomènes optiques anomaux, qui présent un grand nombre de substances cristallisée. *Ann. Mines*, **10**, 187.

Marfunin, A. (1961). The relation between structure and optical orientation in potash–soda feldspars. *Inst. "Lucas Mallada," Curs. Conf.*, **VII**, 97.

Marfunin, A. (1966). *The Feldspars*. (Transl. from Russian, 1962) (Israel Sci. Transl., Jerusalem, 1966).

Marmo, V., Hytönen, K. and Vorma, A. (1963). The occurrence of potash feldspars of inferior triclinicity within the Precambrian rocks in Finland. *Compt. Rend. Soc. Geol. Finlande*, **35**, 51.

Martin, R. F. (1967). The synthesis of low albite (Abstract). *Trans. Am. Geophys. Union*, **48**, 225.

Megaw, H. D. (1956). Notation for feldspar structures. *Acta Cryst.*, **9**, 56.

Megaw, H. D. (1959). Order and disorder in feldspars, I. *Mineral. Mag.*, **32**, 226.

Megaw, H. D. (1960). Order and disorder: I.Theory of stacking faults and diffraction maxima. II. Theory of diffraction effects in the intermediate plagioclase feldspars. III. The structure of the intermediate plagioclase feldspars. *Proc. Roy. Soc.* **A259**, 59, 159, 184.

Megaw, H. D. (1961). Structure of the intermediate plagioclase feldspars. Effect of temperature and composition in the plagioclase feldspars. *Inst. "Lucas Mallada" Curs. Conf.*, **VIII**, 143, 149.

Megaw, H. D. (1962). Order and disorder in feldspars. *Norsk Geol. Tidsskr.*, **42**, II (Feldspar Vol.), 104.

Megaw, H. D., Kempster, C. J. E. and Radoslovich, E. W. (1962). The structure of anorthite, $CaAl_2Si_2O_8$. *Acta Cryst.*, **15**, 1017.

Merwin, H. E. (1911). The temperature, stability ranges, density, chemical composition and optical and crystallographic properties of the alkali feldspars. *J. Wash. Acad. Sci.*, **1**, 59.

Niggli, A. (1967). Die Ordnungsmöglichkeiten der Si–Al-Verteilung in Plagioklasen. *Schweiz. Mineral. Petrog. Mitt.*, **47**, 279.

Nissen, H.-U. (1967). Direct electron-microscopic proof of domain texture in orthoclase. *Contr. Mineral. Petrol.*, **16**, 354.

Nowakowski, A. (1959). On the adularized dyke rock in the vicinity of Klimontow. *Bull. Acad. Polon. Sci., Ser. Sci. Geol. Geograph.*, *VII*, **10**, 751.

Ohta, Y. and Kizaki, K. (1966a). Optical characteristics of the potash feldspars. *JARE Sci. Rept. Geol., Ser. C*, No. **5**, 10 (Tokyo).

Ohta, Y. and Kizaki, K. (1966b). X-ray research on the potash feldspars. *JARE Sci. Rept. Geol., Ser. C*, No. **5**, 22 (Tokyo).

Onorato, E., Penta, M. and Sgarlata, F. (1963). Struttura del sanidino. *Periodico Mineral.* (*Rome*), **32**, 1.

Orville, P. M. (1963). Alkali ion exchange between vapor and feldspar phases. *Am. J. Sci.*, **261**, 201.

Orville, P. M. (1967). Unit cell parameters of the microcline–low albite and the sanidine–high albite solid solution series. *Am. Mineralogist*, **52**, 55.

Ribbe, P. H. (1963). A refinement of the crystal structure of sanidinized orthoclase. *Acta Cryst.*, **16**, 426.

Ribbe. P. H., Ferguson, R. B. and Taylor, W. H. (1962). A three-dimensional refinement of the structure of low albite. *Norsk Geol. Tidsskr.*, **42**, II (Feldspar Vol.), 152.

Ribbe, P. H. and Gibbs, G. V. (1967). *Trans. Amer. Geophys. Union.*, **48**, 229.

Ribbe, P. H. and Megaw, H. D. (1962). The structure of transitional anorthite: A comparison with primitive anorthite. *Norsk Geol. Tidsskr.*, **42**, II (Feldspar Vol.), 158.

Schiebold, E. (1928). Über den Feinbau der Feldspäte. *Z. Krist.*, **85**, 425.

Schiebold, E. (1931). Über die Isomorphie der Feldspatminerale. *Neues Jahrb. Mineral. Geol. Palaeontol., Abt. A*, **64**.

Schneider, T. R. and Laves, F. (1957). Barbierit oder Monalbit? *Z. Krist.*, **109**, 241.

Smith, J. V. and Bailey, S. W. (1963). Second review of Al—O and Si—O tetrahedral distances. *Acta Cryst.*, **16**, 801.

Smith, J. V. and MacKenzie, W. S. (1961). Atomic, chemical and physical factors that control the stability of alkali feldspars. *Inst. "Lucas Mallada," Curs. Conf.*, **VIII**, 39.

Smithson, S. B. (1962). Symmetry relations in alkali feldspars of some amphibolite facies rocks from the southern Norwegian Precambrian. *Norsk Geol. Tidsskr.*, **42**, II (Feldspar Vol.), 586.

Sörum, H. (1951). Studies on the structures of plagioclase feldspars. *Kgl. Norske Videnskab. Selskabs., Skrifter*, **3**.

Sörum, H. (1953). The structures of plagioclase feldspars II. *Acta Cryst.*, **6**, 413.

Spencer, E. (1937). The potash–soda feldspars I. *Mineral. Mag.*, **24**, 453.

Steiger, R. H. and Hart, S. R. (1967). The microcline–orthoclase transition within a contact aureole. *Am. Mineralogist*, **52**, 87.

Stewart, D. B. and Limbach, D. von. (1964). Thermal expansion of $NaAlSi_3O_8$ and calcic labradorite (Abstract). *Trans. Am. Geophys. Union*, **45**, 126.

Stewart, D. B. and Limbach, D. von. (1967). Thermal expansion of low and high albite. *Am. Mineralogist*, **52**, 389.

Takéuchi, Y. and Donnay, G. (1959). The crystal structure of hexagonal $CaAl_2Si_2O_8$. *Acta Cryst.*, **12**, 465.

Feldspars

Taylor, W. H. (1933). The structure of sanidine and other feldspars. *Z. Krist.*, **85,** 425.

Taylor, W. H. (1962). The structures of the principal feldspars. *Norsk Geol. Tidsskr.*, **42,** II (Feldspar Vol.), 1.

Taylor, W. H. (1965). Framework silicates: The feldspars. In Bragg, L. W. (Ed.), *Crystal Structure of Minerals*. Bell, London.

Taylor, W. H., Darbyshire, J. A. and Strunz, H. (1934). An x-ray investigation of the feldspars. *Z. Krist.*, **87,** 464.

Tomisaka, T. (1962). On order–disorder transformation and stability range of microcline under high water vapour pressure. *Mineral. J.* (*Tokyo*), **3,** 261.

Tuttle, O. F. and Bowen, N. L. (1950). High-temperature albite and contiguous feldspars. *J. Geol.*, **58,** 572.

Williams, P. P. and Megaw, H. D. (1964). The crystal structure of low and high albites at −180°c. *Acta Cryst.*, **17,** 882.

Wright, T. L. (1964). Exsolution and inversion history of the Tatoosh perthites. *Am. Mineralogist.*, **49,** 715.

Wright, T. L. (1967). The microcline–orthoclase transformation in the contact aureole of the Eldorado stock, Colorado. *Am. Mineralogist*, **52,** 117.

Yoder, H. S., Stewart, D. B. and Smith, J. R. (1957). Ternary feldspars. *Ann. Rept. Geophys. Lab., Carnegie Inst. Wash., Yearbook*, **56,** 206.

4

Physical Properties of Feldspars

4.1 HARDNESS

Hardness, H, in terms of the old Mohs scale is currently used in the mineralogical literature.

Orthoclase	6–$6\frac{1}{2}$	Albite	6–$6\frac{1}{2}$
Sanidine	6	Oligoclase	6–$6\frac{1}{2}$
Adularia	6–$6\frac{1}{2}$	Andesine	6
Microcline	6–$6\frac{1}{2}$	Labradorite	6
Anorthoclase	6	Bytownite	6
		Anorthite	6–$6\frac{1}{2}$

The relation between Mohs hardness numbers and the indentation hardnesses is shown in figure 4.1.

An atomistic expression of hardness is the volumetric cohesive energy, U/V, whose dimension is cal/cm³ (Plendl and Gielisse, 1963). It has a non-linear relation to the Mohs numbers:

$$U/V = \tfrac{1}{2}H^3 \text{ kcal/cm}^3, \text{ when } H < 4$$

For greater hardnesses the relation is linear:

$$U/V = 48(H - 4) + 36 \text{ for most minerals}$$

Relative Schleifhärte is measured against quartz on (0001) which is put equal to 100; according to Rosiwall (quoted by Kleber, 1963) the values for orthoclase are:

$$\text{on (001)} = 17\cdot2, \text{ on (010)} = 25\cdot7, \text{ on (001)} = 27\cdot7$$

Abrasion hardness, H_S, is the *Schleifhärte* measured by Holmquist (1914). If by grinding with carborundum under standard conditions a volume V of feldspar is worn away, compared to a volume V^0 of quartz ground on the (0001) face, then $H_S = 1000 \, V^0/V$.

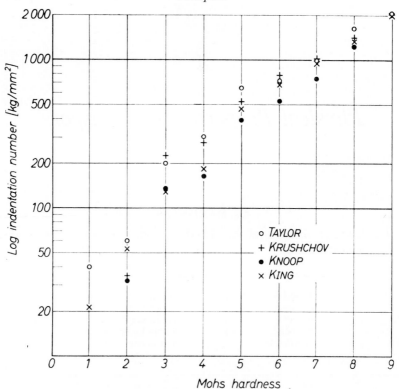

FIGURE 4.1 Mohs' hardness scale versus log average indentation hardness. (After Plendl and Gielisse, 1963). 1 = talc, 2 = gypsum, 3 = calcite, 4 = fluorite, 5 = apatite, 6 = orthoclase, 7 = quartz, 8 = topaz, 9 = corundum (the Mohs' hardness number 10 (diamond) is abnormally high and not plotted in this diagram)

Vicker's microhardness, H_V, of the plagioclases was measured by Mookherjee and Sahu (1960), with a Leitz 'Durimet' microhardness tester. Each sample was tested with 7 different working loads from 15 to 500 grams; the averages of each series of 7 for each of the 6 plagioclases investigated are shown in table 4.2.

The hardness data indicate:

(1) All feldspars exhibit maximum hardness on the face (100); this is obviously related to the crystal structure: the SiO_4–AlO_4 chains run zig-zagwise parallel to the direction [100].

(2) The perthites tend to be slightly harder than either of the two components of which they are mixtures, but sanidine which is a homogeneous mixed crystal of Or and Ab is decidedly less hard than either.

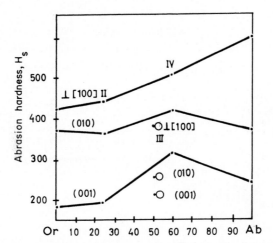

FIGURE 4.2 Abrasion hardness of alkali feldspars. Dots connected by curves refer to perthites, open circles refer to homogeneous sanidine. Roman numerals as in table 4.1. (Data of Holmquist, 1914)

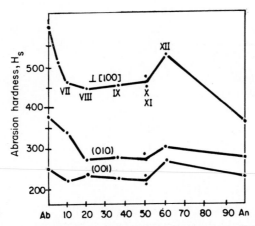

FIGURE 4.3 Abrasion hardness of plagioclases. Roman numerals as in table 4.1. (Data of Holmquist, 1914)

TABLE 4.1

Abrasion hardness

Feldspar[a]		Composition	$H_S \perp [100]$	H_S on (001)	H_S on (010)
I	Adularia	Or_{100}	433	193	380
II	Microcline perthite	Or_{75}, Ab_{25}	454	206	374
III	Sanidine	Or_{50}, Ab_{50}	388	219	265
IV	Orthoclase perthite	Or_{40}, Ab_{60}	521	328	431
V	Albite	Ab_{100}	614	251	380
VI	Albite	Ab_{95}, An_5	513	—	$(304)^b$
VII	Oligoclase–albite	Ab_{90}, An_{10}	466	219	338
VIII	Oligoclase	Ab_{80}, An_{20}	450	234	275
IX	Andesine	Ab_{64}, An_{36}	458	224	279
X	Labradorite	Ab_{50}, An_{50}	455	213	264
XI	Labradorite	Ab_{50}, An_{50}	486	232	285
XII	Labradorite	Ab_{40}, An_{60}	535	270	302
XIII	Anorthite	An_{100}	367	225	276

[a] Localities: I unknown; II Ytterby, Sweden; III Drachenfels, Germany; IV Frederiksværn, Norway; V Ruschuna, Switzerland; VI Gellivara, Sweden; VII Tammela, Finland; VIII Bamble, Norway; IX Tvedestrand, Norway; X Sokndal, Norway; XI unknown; XII Tscherkassy, South Russia; XIII Miakijima, Japan.

[b] Only two measurements.

TABLE 4.2

Vicker's microhardness

Feldspar	An content	H_V (kg/mm^2)
Albite, Norway	5	1677
Oligoclase, Tvedestrand, Norway	25	969
Andesine, Estérel, France	40	1043
Labradorite, Finland	52	1053
Bytownite, Bengal	75	470
Bytownite, Grass Valley, Calif.	85	127
Adularia[a]		1850

[a] After von Engelhardt and Haussühl (1965).

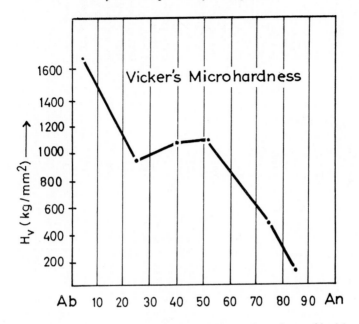

FIGURE 4.4 Indentation hardness of plagioclases. Data from table 4.1.
(After Mookherjee and Sahu, 1960)

(3) In the plagioclase series, there is a noteworthy decrease in the hardness of the intermediate members approximately in the range An_{30}–An_{70}; this applies for both abrasion hardness and microhardness. It seems significant that structural breaks take place in the plagioclase series at compositions of about An_{30} and An_{70}, see p. 161.

4.2 DENSITY OF CRYSTALS AND GLASSES

In handbooks on mineralogy the densities of the feldspar minerals are given as shown in the following table.

Orthoclase	2·5 –2·62	Albite	2·57–2·69
Adularia	2·56	Oligoclase	2·62–2·67
Sanidine	2·57–2·58	Andesine	2·65–2·69
Microcline	2·54–2·57	Labradorite	2·69–2·72
Anorthoclase	2·56–2·65	Bytownite	2·72–2·75
		Anorthite	2·75–2·77

TABLE 4.3 K-feldspars and Na-feldspars

Feldspar	Reference[f]	Composition			Mole weight	Cell vol. (Å³)	Density (g/cm³)	Order index (S)	Remarks
		Or	Ab	An					
Microcline: No. 9	1	—	—	—	278·19	721·8	2·560	—	[a]
Pontiskalk	2	99	1	0	278·19	721·3	2·562	86	Homogeneous
Pellotsalo	3	86	13	1	278·03	720·0	2·564	92	Perthitic[b]
Spencer U	4	99·5	0·3	0·2	278·03	720·0	2·564	61	Perthitic
Synthetic	10	—	—	—	278·30	722·5	2·558	—	Homogeneous
'Adularia': No. 8	1	89	11	0	278·35 / 276·59	719·9	2·568 / 2·552	—	[c]
Orthoclase: Spencer C	5	91	6·5	2·5	277·71	719·3	2·564	19	Perthitic[d]
Sanidinized: Spencer C	2	91	6·5	2·5	277·31	719·6	2·559	5	Homogeneous
Synth. sanidine	6	100	0	0	278·35	(723·7)	(2·554)	—	Homogeneous
Synth. sanidine	10	100	0	0	278·35	722·6	2·560	—	Homogeneous
Low albite: Spencer T	7	1·4	98·2	0·4	262·54	664·2	2·625	—	Glass clear
Ramona	8	1	98·5	0·5	262·48	664·2	2·6245	92	Homogeneous
Synthetic	10	1·0	98·8	0·2	262·43	663·4	2·627	—	Homogeneous
Amelia	9	0·7	97·7	1·6	262·61	665·0	2·623	—	Translucent[e]
Amelia	1	0·7	97·7	1·6	262·61	665·6	2·620	—	Translucent
Heated albite: Amelia	8	0·7	97·7	1·6	262·61	666·7	2·616	9	Homogeneous
Heated albite: Amelia	9	0·7	97·7	1·6	262·61	667·6	2·612	—	Homogeneous
Synthetic albite (high)	9	0	100	0	262·24	668·0	2·607	—	Homogeneous
Synthetic albite (high)	6	0	100	0	262·24	(669·7)	(2·600)	—	Homogeneous
Synthetic albite (high)	10	0	100	0	262·24	666·1	2·615	—	Homogeneous

[a] No data on composition; it is assumed that 1% Ab is in solid solution.

[b] Coarsely perthitic with areas of homogeneous M-twinned microcline which probably contains ca. 2% Ab in solid solution.

[c] The adularia is truly monoclinic, it contains 11% Ab. Two density values are calculated: the high value corresponding to the assumption that the adularia is inhomogeneous with all Ab exsolved as cryptoperthite, the lower value to the assumption that Ab exists as solid solution in the microcline lattice.

[d] The homogeneous orthoclase substance may contain 4% Ab in solid solution.

[e] Chemical analysis by Weibel (1958).

[f] 1 Laves (1952); 2 Finney and Bailey (1964); 3 Brown and Bailey (1964); 4 Bailey and Taylor (1955); 5 Jones and Taylor (1961); 6 Donnay and Donnay (1952); 7 Cole and others (1951); 8 Ferguson and others (1958); 9 Smith (1956); 10 Orville (1967).

For pure microcline, Rottenbach (1936) gave an extrapolated value of 2·559. Other extrapolated and interpolated values are shown graphically in figure 4.5. However, these old values are not accurate, partly because the effects of crypto- or microperthitic inclusions were difficult to assess, mostly because the existence of high- and low-temperature modifications was unknown. It is now realized that both the chemical composition and the structural state of the feldspars affect the density. The best values are probably calculated from the volume of the unit cell and the chemical composition. The relation between density D, molecular weight M and the volume of the unit cell V (expressed in Å^3) is:

$$D = \frac{v \cdot M}{N \cdot V}$$

where v is the number of molecules in the unit cell ($v = 4$ for feldspars), N is Avogadro's number $= 6·0226 \times 10^{23}$ g mole^{-1}.

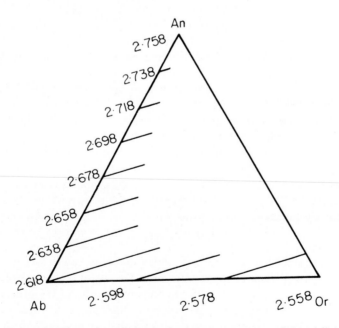

FIGURE 4.5 Lines of equal density in the ternary system of the triclinic feldspars. (After Chudoba, 1936). Averaged values of natural feldspars are used; high- and low-temperature modifications are not distinguished

The refractive index, n, is in some ways a measure of the actual mass contained in the unit cell. It is directly related to the density through the equation of Gladstone and Dale

$$D = \frac{1}{k}(n - 1)$$

it follows that

$$V = \frac{k \cdot M \cdot v}{N(n - 1)}$$

where k is the specific refractive energy. This energy can be calculated from the constituent oxides (Larsen and Berman, 1934) and for the feldspar compounds it is:

$KAlSi_3O_8$–0·2054, $NaAlSi_3O_8$–0·2031, $CaAl_2Si_2O_8$–0·2174 (see below).

The specific refractive energy can also be determined by measuring n and D of the various feldspars. For ordered and disordered variants of albite, k is in the range 0·203–0·204. For glass of albite composition, $k = 0·205$. The same holds for the crystalline variants of $KAlSi_3O_8$, $k = 0·203$–0·204. For glass of $KAlSi_3O_8$ exact data are lacking, but because of the close analogy with albite the same value, $k = 0·205$, is supposed to hold for $KAlSi_3O_8$ glass also.

By combining and critically examining the available data, new density values for the feldspar minerals are obtained and offered for consideration.

4.21 Alkali feldspars

Pure potassium feldspar has a cell volume of 721·6 ± 2Å³ (adjusted cell, see below) regardless of its structural state. There is probably some difference in volume between orthoclase and microcline, but it cannot be determined from the present material. Note that the correct volume of Donnay's synthetic sanidine listed in table 4.3 is probably close to 721·7 Å³ (instead of 723·7 Å³) (see below). Similarly, the density is practically the same for all pure potassium feldspars:

$$D = 2·562 ± 0·007 \text{ g/cm}^3$$

It follows that the average refractive index should be same.

Pure sodium feldspar behaves differently. The cell of the disordered form —high albite—is noticeably inflated compared to that of the ordered low albite. To get an accurate figure for pure $NaAlSi_3O_8$ it is necessary to adjust for the small amounts of K and Ca that slightly expand the low-albite lattice. The adjusted cell volumes computed from the five low-albite crystals listed in table 4.3 by extrapolation to 100% Ab come out as:

663·4, 663·6, 662·8, 664·5, 665·1 Å³; average 663·8 Å³. The corresponding density is $D = 2·624$ g/cm³. For high albite the values calculated from Smith's synthetic crystals (1956) are accepted.

The best values for sodium feldspars are:

	Vol. (Å³)	D (g/cm³)
Low albite	663·8	2·624
High albite	668·0	2·607

The alkali feldspar series shows interesting volume relations (see Barth, 1965), and is well known from the studies of Donnay and Donnay (1952) and of Orville (1967) who determined the accurate unit-cell dimensions on synthetic samples ranging from monoclinic KAlSi₃O₈ to triclinic NaAlSi₃O₈, and calculated the corresponding densities and cell volumes, see table 4.4 and figure 4.6.

Smith (1956) pointed out that there is probably a small, systematic error in Donnay's determinations, and later measurements by other authors

TABLE 4.4

Density of the synthetic alkali feldspar series

Ab (wt. %)	Or	Donnay and Donnay (1952)[a]		Orville (1967)	
		Density (g/cm³)	Cell vol. (Å³)	Cell vol. (Å³)	Density (g/cm³)
0	100	2·553	723·7	722·6	2·558
20	80	2·545	717·3	715·1	2·555
40	60	2·551	707·1	704·9	2·562
50	50	2·557	701·1	699·7	2·566
60	40	2·566	694·5	693·6	2·573
65	35	2·570	691·5	—	—
70	30	2·579	687·1	687·2	2·581
80	20	2·585	681·5	679·6	2·594
90	10	2·597	674·3	672·7	2·610
100	0	2·600	669·7	666·1	2·615

[a] The cell volumes of Donnay and Donnay are probably about 2 Å³ too high, accordingly the correct density values are obtained by adding 0·008 g/cm, see text. A recent determination on albite synthesized at 925°c and 250 bar H₂O pressure gave $V = 667·0$ Å³ (Stewart and von Limbach, 1967a).

TABLE 4.5

Natural alkali feldspars

No.	Or	Ab (mole %)	An	Cn	Vol. (Å³)	$D_{\text{x-ray}}$ (g/cm³)	$D_{\text{pycn.}}$ (obs)
145	36·8	62·7	0·0	0·5	689·3	2·584	2·591
161	17·1	67·3	15·3	0·3	677·3	2·623	2·631
173	23·4	70·0	6·1	0·5	682·5	2·600	2·615
183	19·7	68·6	11·5	0·2	679·4	2·613	2·622
195	37·6	61·4	1·0	−0	691·6	2·565	2·583
200	43·8	55·4	0·0	0·8	693·3	2·581	2·578

Alkali feldspar phenocrysts in trachyte (nos. 161–183), phonolite (nos. 145 and 200) and tuff (no. 195) from Kenya and Northern Tanganyika (from Häkli, 1960).

seem to verify that the cell volumes and densities as given in table 4.4 and figure 4.6 are about 2 Å³ too high and 0·007 g/cm³ too low, respectively. This would slightly displace the curves of the figure but would not alter the shape.

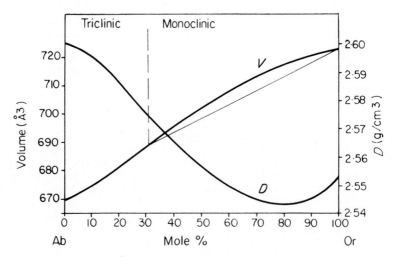

FIGURE 4.6 The volume of the unit cell and the density of the high-temperature alkali feldspar mixed-crystal series. (Donnay and Donnay, 1952)

A refinement of the data of the Donnays is recently reported by Wright (1964), see also Stewart and von Limbach (1967).

The unit volumes and density of the mixed crystals, when plotted against composition, give lines of peculiar curvature. At the transition point, see figure 4.6, the volume itself is continuous but shows a discontinuity in its first derivative. Evidently, anomalous changes in chemical activity and

TABLE 4.6

Natural plagioclases

No.	Or	Ab (Wt. %)	An	Mole weight	Cell vol. (Å^3)	Density (g/cm^3)	Type
Amelia	0·7	97·7	1·6	262·59	665·0	2·623	Pegmatite
BM 1940, 27	2·6	86·5	10·9	264·29	666·0	2·636	Pegmatite
81822	1·3	81·0	17·1	265·135	666·4	2·6425	Pegmatite
103086	3·5	74·4	22·1	266·16	667·6	2·648	Pegmatite
97 490	3·6	66·5	29·9	267·39	668·4	2·657	Pegmatite
152(6)	1·5	62·6	35·9	268·00	667·4	2·667	Gneissoid
64(7)	3·2	60·7	36·1	268·30	668·1	2·667	Dacite
144(8)	2·0	60·0	38·0	268·41	667·9	2·669	Granodiorite
24(9)	3·8	47·2	49·0	270·45	669·4	2·683	Anorthosite
Cole (1951)	1·4	42·1	56·5	271·26	667·6	2·699	Anorthosite
Wenk (1966)	0·9	33·7	65·4	272·62	671·0	2·699	Lava, Surtsey
Stewart and others (1966)	1·3	31·5	67·2	273·19	669·5	2·710	Lava, Lake Co.
Stewart and others (1966)[a]	1·3	31·5	67·2	273·19	669·7	2·709	—
Cole and others (1951) (Prim. An[b])	—	—	97·0	277·00	669·4	2·748	Vesuvius
Ribbe and Megaw (1962) (Trans. An) Srinivasan and Ribbe (1965)	—	—	99·1	278·08	670·0	2·757	Lava, Miyake
Fleet and others (1966)	—	—	80·0	275·02	669·76	2·727	St. Louis Co., Minn.

[a] After heating to 1141°c. The composition of this feldspar is given in mole per cent.

[b] The difference in dimensions between primitive and transitional anorthite is supposed to be non-significant.

Smith (1956) determined the lattice parameters of the first nine plagioclases in the list, the numbers are those of Smith. The three lava feldspars are high-temperature plagioclases, all the others are supposed to be low-temperature forms.

in crystal structure take place, see Barth (1967). At a composition of about Or_{80}, Ab_{20} the density has a minimum

$$D_{min} \simeq 2 \cdot 550$$

being appreciably less than in either component. This composition corresponds approximately to that of a common sanidine, which thus represents the lightest variety of a feldspar mineral. Upon unmixing the density increases about $0 \cdot 8 \%$.

4.22 Plagioclases

Plagioclase feldspars show marked volume differences between high and low (disordered and ordered) modifications. This is particularly noticeable in the sodic part of the series. The calcic plagioclases seem to have a fairly ordered lattice at all temperatures, and the differences between high and low forms vanish. In anorthite it has not been possible to demonstrate any change in the geometric lattice parameters after heating. The natural plagioclases usually have some potassium in solid solution. The amounts— given in table 4.6—affect the cell volumes, and in order to compare the potassian species with the pure plagioclases, adjustments in the volumes have to be made. It is assumed that the effect is proportional to the amount of potassium. The projection points plotted into figures 4.7 and 4.8 have been thus adjusted. But it should be remembered that the potassium content nonetheless introduces an additional uncertainty into the values of the cell volumes.

Figure 4.7 demonstrates peculiar differences between the high- and the low-plagioclase series. The curves are constructed from the data of tables 4.6 and 4.7.

High plagioclases come from synthetic material and from heated natural material. As the natural plagioclases—as explained above—have some potassium in solid solution, and as heated material has a tendency to yield slightly lower values than synthetic material, it would be misleading to draw an average curve fitting a maximum number of points. The curves for high plagioclase in figure 4.7 have been drawn through the points of the synthetic material of Smith (1956) in the range An_{0-50}. Smith has no measurements on more calcic material than An_{50}. Generally speaking, there are fewer and not such reliable data for the calcic range; the latest measurements are those of Fleet and others (1966) on bytownite. They are very carefully done, but reflect the despairing situation that physicists gladly use 12 years for drawing three-dimensional electron density maps and refining a complicated structure without, however, sacrificing a few weeks' work, to study the mineral itself, chemically, optically and

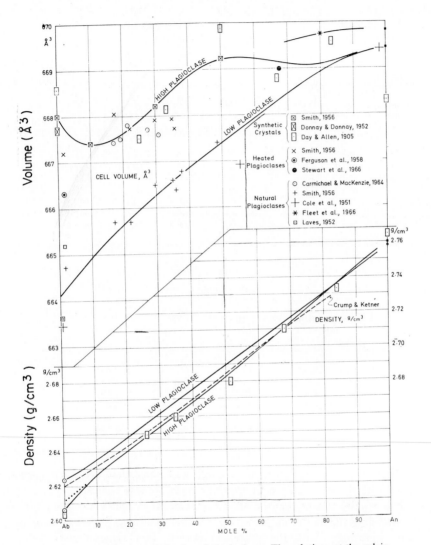

FIGURE 4.7 Volume and density of plagioclases. The relations at the calcic end are uncertain, alternative interpretations are indicated. The stippled line represents the density curve for natural plagioclases, see text

TABLE 4.7(a)

Synthetic plagioclases

Smith (1956)			Day and Allen (1905)				
Crystals			Crystals			Glass	
An (mole %)	Vol. (Å³)	D (g/cm³)	An (mole %)	Vol. (Å³)	D (g/cm³)	Vol. (Å³)	D (g/cm³)
0	668·0	2·607	0	668·6	2·605	731·2	2·382
10	667·4	2·624	25	667·5	2·649	719·4	2·458
30	668·2	2·651	33·3	668·1	2·660	715·7	2·483
50	669·2	2·679	50	669·9	2·679	708·5	2·533
			66·7	668·8	2·710	699·5	2·591
			83·3	669·6	2·733	691·1	2·648
			100	668·3	2·765	684·4	2·700

TABLE 4.7(b)

Heated plagioclases

Nos. as in table 4.6	An (mole %)	Vol. (Å³)	D (g/cm³)
81822	17·0	668·76	2·633
103086	21·8	669·51	2·640
97490	29·7	669·78	2·652
152(6)	35·0	668·70	2·667
64(7)	35·9	669·36	2·662
Stewart	67·2	669·70	2·709

geologically. In this range, an average and somewhat arbitrary curve had to be drawn. Possible alternative curves are also indicated.

It is worthy of note that the old measurements by Day and Allen (1905) —who first succeeded in preparing reliable synthetic materials—are in close agreement with the proposed curves. Few mineralogists today appreciate the colossal initial difficulties, the laborious task and the final tremendous achievement when, for the first time in history, the preparation of the plagioclase feldspars in dry fusion succeeded and the melting phenomena could be explained. Writes Becker (1905): 'Except for Dr. Day's resourcefulness and experimental skill, success would not have been achieved, but a road has now been broken out of this ultratropical jungle which will almost certainly lead to further successful exploration.' The synthetic feldspars, being chemically pure and homogeneous, gave a perfectly definite density that Day and Allen could determine with great accuracy if the specimens were completely crystallized. Their density data—also recalculated into cell volumes—have been plotted onto figure 4.7. They herald the general results of the much later x-ray data.

A comparison between high and low plagioclases shows that the volume relations of the high plagioclases are most complicated. This is related to the fact that, particularly in the compositional ranges An_{2-20} and An_{45-55}, the mix-crystals are on the verge of unmixing. In the range An_{2-20} the

TABLE 4.8

Preferred density values for the plagioclases

Feldspar	An (mole %)					
	0	10	$33\frac{1}{3}$	50	$66\frac{2}{3}$	100
Glass	2·382	2·412	2·483	2·533	2·591	2·700
Δ Crystal–glass	0·225	0·214	0·176	0·149	0·117	0·060
High plag.	2·607	2·626	2·659	2·682	2·708	2·760
Δ Low–high crystals	0·016	0·009	0·008	0·007	0·004	0
Low plag.	2·623	2·635	2·667	2·689	2·712	2·760

mix-crystals contract and, so to speak, prepare themselves for breaking up into peristerites; in the range An_{45-55} the lattice is expanded and has a tendency to separate into extremely thin lamellae responsible for the schiller effect of the labradorites, see figure 4.8.

The low-plagioclase series is in many respects very complicated. The relation between An content and various crystallographic parameters is not linear. A number of discontinuities were also discovered. Brown (1960) first pointed out that the Si/Al ratio, rather than the An content, is the deciding factor. The several discontinuities in the angle γ^*, as demonstrated by Doman and others (1965), are shown in figure 4.8. In this connexion, it is worthy of note that no discontinuities are apparent in either the cell volume or density. Both these parameters actually change remarkably regularly with the An content. It seems that the pronounced flexures and irregularities exhibited in the corresponding curves of the high-plagioclase mix-crystals are completely eliminated. The internal tension present in the true mixed crystals at room temperature and

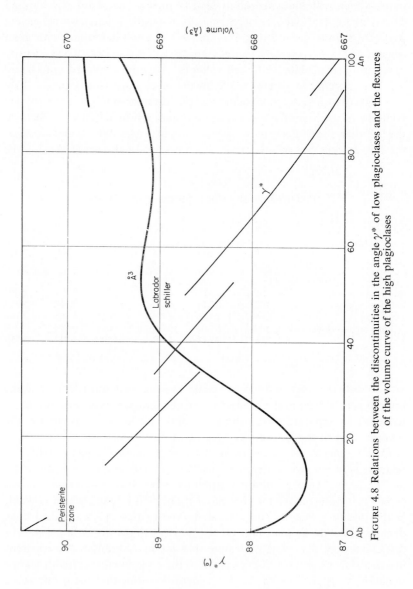

FIGURE 4.8 Relations between the discontinuities in the angle γ* of low plagioclases and the flexures of the volume curve of the high plagioclases

responsible for their deformation is released by unmixing or internal ordering; the resulting crystals (composite on a submicroscopic scale)' will behave as ultra-fine mechanical mixtures yielding an 'average, x-ray pattern.

4.23 Ternary feldspars

Ternary feldspars have recently been investigated by various authors. Of special interest for the present study are the x-ray data by Carmichael and MacKenzie (1964). Cell volumes and densities are listed in table 4.9. A few additional data come from table 4.5. All samples are of natural feldspars from volcanic rocks, and presumably of high-temperature structure. This is supported by the fact that heat treatment for 28 days at

TABLE 4.9

Ternary feldspars

No.[a]	Or	Ab	An	Cn	Mole weight	Cell vol. ($Å^3$)	Density (g/cm^3)
1	11·8	76·8	10·7	0·6	266·45	674·9	2·622
2	14·0	77·4	7·8	0·8	266·23	675·9	2·616
3	17·8	74·1	6·9	0·3	268·74	679·6	2·626
4	18·7	71·1	8·9	0·4	269·28	680·4	2·629
5	18·8	79·1	1·1	0·7	266·67	681·0	2·601
6	21·2	75·6	2·1	0·6	267·67	682·2	2·606
9	23·0	69·3	7·4	0·3	267·17	681·6	2·603
12	24·0	65·9	10·1	0·0	267·51	686·8	2·587
14	32·5	61·4	6·1	0·0	268·23	686·9	2·594
1'	3·3	65·6	31·1	—	267·53	669·1	2·656
1"	3·3	65·6	31·1	—	267·53	669·3	2·655
2'	5·4	68·0	26·6	—	267·16	670·4	2·647
3'	6·7	72·2	20·6	—	267·79	671·1	2·650
4'	5·0	75·9	19·1	—	265·93	670·0	2·636
4"	5·0	75·9	19·1	—	265·93	669·4	2·6385
5'	5·0	77·9	17·1	—	265·62	669·9	2·6335

Composition (wt. %)

[a] Composition and cell volume after Carmichael and MacKenzie (1964); nos. 1–14 are phenocrysts from volcanic rocks and described in tables I and III of these authors. They are anorthoclases and triclinic at ordinary temperature, monoclinic at elevated temperature.

The primed numbers are potassic plagioclases, they are triclinic at all temperatures. They are listed in table IV of the above authors.

Doubled primed numbers (1" and 4") are nos. 1' and 4' respectively heated for 28 days at 1100°c.

1100°C of two samples did not produce significant changes in the lattice constants. Many of these feldspars have a relatively high content of barium (given as weight per cent celsian, Cn, in the tables) which has a large effect on the cell volume.

All volumes plotted in the triangular diagram of figure 4.9 have been adjusted accordingly, assuming that the effect of barium is proportional to its concentration. The curves for equal volume differ only slightly from those given by Carmichael and MacKenzie (1964); they are roughly parallel to the Or content. The curves for equal density are rather regular. They should be compared to the dashed lines indicating the pattern that would emerge if the density were an additive function of the components. Except for the potash-rich members, the actual densities of the ternary feldspars are rather close to the values thus calculated. Evidently, this was the assumption on which the old density data from 1936 were computed, see figure 4.5.

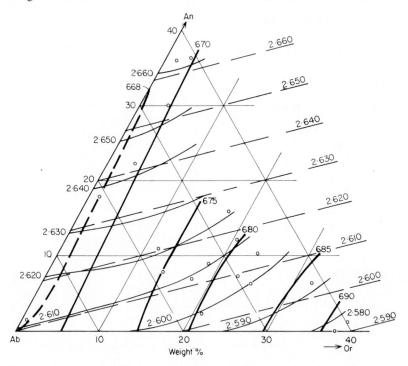

FIGURE 4.9 Cell volume and density of ternary feldspars. Thin dashed lines indicate the density relations if density had been an additive function of the three components. The old density values of 1936—see figure 4.5—were evidently computed under this assumption

4.24 Feldspar glasses

The entropy of fusion of the feldspars is not high, so that no major changes in structure are to be expected on melting. On general grounds one would, therefore, expect the liquid structure to resemble the solid. Feldspar melts possess an ionic constitution in analogy with the solid phase. Typical cations are Na^+, K^+, Ca^{2+} which occupy no fixed position in the melt but exhibit a high degree of mobility. The anions are polymerized Si–Al–oxygen tetrahedra linked together to three-dimensional networks similar to those found in the crystalline feldspars but more irregular, see figure 4.10. The effect of this network is the characteristic

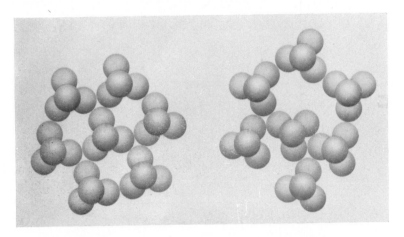

FIGURE 4.10 Left: the regular pattern of the three-dimensional network of $(SiO_4)^{4-}$ tetrahedra in crystals (cristobalite structure) Right: the irregular pattern of the $(SiO_4)^{4-}$ tetrahedra in silica glass. (Photo Carl Zeiss)

TABLE 4.10

Volume, density and indices of refraction of the three feldspar end members

	Volume (Å³)			Density (g/cm³)			Refractive index		
	K-f[a]	Ab	An	K-f[a]	Ab	An	K-f[a]	Ab	An
Glass	779	731	684·4	2·375	2·382	2·700	1·487	1·488	1·577
High crystals	721	668	669·4	2·56	2·607	2·760	1·521	1·532	1·582
Low crystals	722	664	669·4	2·56	2·623	2·760	1·522	1·533	1·582

[a] K-f = K-feldspar.

12

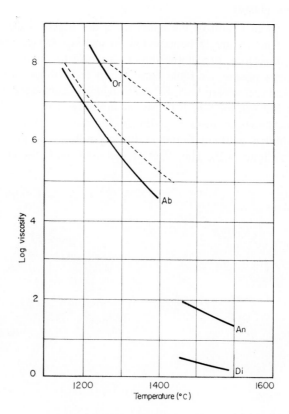

FIGURE 4.11 Viscosity–temperature relations for molten feldspars. Di = diopside is given for comparison. Viscosity in poises. (Data of Bowen, 1934; dashed lines after Kani, 1935)

high viscosity of the feldspar melts, see figure 4.11. Polymerization is favoured by weakly polarizing ions, like K^+ and Na^+, whereas the presence of Ca^{2+} lowers the viscosity by making the macroions break up into smaller units.

The high viscosity of the melt inhibits crystallization; undercooling with the formation of metastable glass at room temperature is, therefore, a common phenomenon. Since the structure of the glass is similar to that of the crystals, one may, for comparative purposes, define the unit cell of the glass as a volume, analogous to the crystal unit cell, containing on an average four feldspar 'molecules'.

TABLE 4.11

Refractive indices for plagioclases and their glasses

	An (mole %)						
	0·2	21·6	44·2	51·8	62·5	80	100
Glass	1·4881	1·5043	1·5241	1·5311	1·5410	1·5568	1·575
Δ	0·0440	0·0385	0·0317	0·0270	0·0231	0·0149	0·007
High crystals	1·5325	1·5428	1·5558	1·5581	1·5641	1·5717	1·5822
Δ	0·0008	0·0001	0·0007	0·0000	0·0003	0·0009	0·0000
Low crystals	1·5333	1·5429	1·5551	1·5581	1·5644	1·5726	1·5822

Except for albite there is no synthetic or analysed material of alkali feldspar the density of which has been determined both in the crystalline and glassy state. Unanalysed material of sanidine (from Ischia) and of adularia from St. Gotthard show on vitrification a decrease in density of 7·6% (Douglas, 1907). Furthermore, the index of refraction, n, is known for pure $KAlSi_3O_8$ in the crystalline and vitreous state. The refractive indices of the alkali feldspar mixed crystals are moderately well known, see table 4.12.

Density data for albite and anorthite, and for the corresponding glasses are directly available. In tables 4.10 and 4.11 the refractive indices are taken from Schairer and Bowen (1955, 1956), Schairer and others (1956) and from J. R. Smith (1958). The mean index $\alpha + \beta + \gamma/3$ is always given.

Volume and density data are listed in tables 4.6, 4.7 and 4.8. The relations are graphically exhibited in figures 4.12, 4.13, 4.14 and 4.15.

The difference in volume between microcline and orthoclase is insignificant, but between low and high albite there is a 0·6% change in volume. Upon melting, both K and Na feldspar show a considerable expansion amounting to 7·9% for K feldspar, and to 9·5% for albite (and 10·1% for low albite). In contrast, the expansion anorthite → glass is only 2·2%. This reflects the presence of the long and stiff polymerized Si–Al–oxygen chains in the alkali feldspar glasses, and the partly destroyed and broken chains in the calcium feldspar glasses.

It is worth mentioning that the albite glass is so viscous that it fails to crystallize even after several years when held in the range of 100°c below

TABLE 4.12 Volume, density and refractive indices of alkali feldspar glasses

Wt. %	Or Ab	0 100	10 90	20 80	30 70	50 50	60 40	80 20	100 0
Volume ($\mathring{A}^3$)		731·2	733·6	737·0	742·0	752·4	757·7	768·3	778·5
Density (g/cm³)		2·382	2·388	2·391	2·389	2·384	2·3815	2·377	2·375
Index, n		1·4880	1·4895	1·4901	1·4897	1·4887	1·4882	1·4874	1·4868

The indices of refraction of the glasses are taken (partly by interpolation) from Kani (1935) and from Franco and Schairer (1951). Volume and density are calculated under the assumption that the specific refractive energy of all glasses is $k = 0.205$.

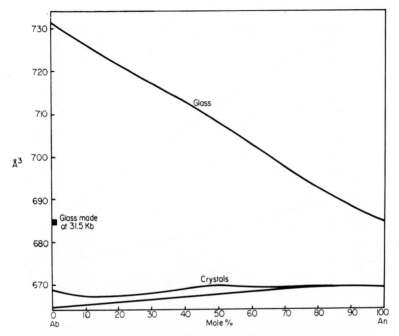

FIGURE 4.12 The volume of the unit cell for plagioclases and for their glasses. Note that albite, which of all plagioclases has the smallest unit cell in the crystalline state, possesses the largest unit cell in the glassy state; by pressure the large cell is strongly compressed

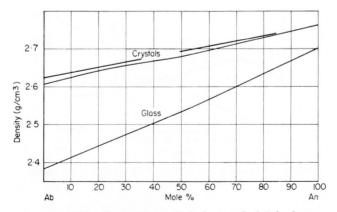

FIGURE 4.13 The density of the plagioclases and of their glasses

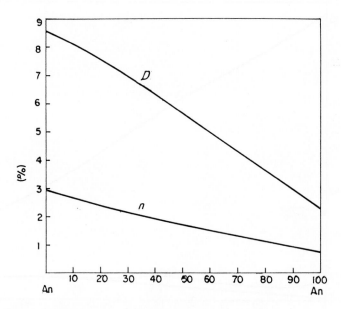

FIGURE 4.14 Decrease on vitrification of density, *D*, and of refractive index, *n*, in the plagioclase series

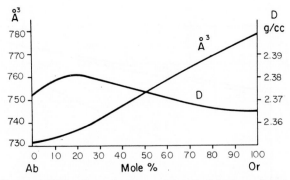

FIGURE 4.15 Density and volume of the alkali feldspar glasses

the melting point (Schairer and Bowen, 1956). However, when albite glass prepared at high temperatures was 'acclimated' (annealed at successively lower temperatures for long periods of time) it developed crystals of albite within a few hours at 1050°C. Schairer and Bowen think that, in addition to the heterogeneous equilibrium between albite crystals and liquid at the melting point, there may be a homogeneous equilibrium involving changes in structure or configuration in the liquid phase, and that this homogeneous equilibrium shifts slowly with temperature.

Boyd and England (1963) found that glasses of albitic composition quenched from above the liquidus at high pressure exhibit indices of refraction markedly higher than the normal values. Moreover, the indices of the glasses formed in high-pressure runs are proportional to the pressure of the runs. The index of albite glass increased linearly from 1·488 at atmospheric pressure to 1·519 at 31·5 kilobars. Recalculated as previously explained, this corresponds to a 6% increase in density, from 2·382 to 2·532 g/cm³, or a decrease in volume from 731·2 to 687·9 Å³, as marked in figure 4.12. This is a tremendous compression and illustrates that the Si–Al–oxygen chains, like fibres, can be permanently compacted by pressure into a small volume.

4.3 THERMAL EXPANSION

The linear coefficients of thermal expansion are designated $\alpha_1 > \alpha_2 > \alpha_3$. The cubic coefficient of expansion is $\beta = \alpha_1 + \alpha_2 + \alpha_3$. Inscribed in the crystal is a sphere of radius $= 1$; by a temperature increase of ΔT it becomes an ellipsoid with semi-axes $(1 + \alpha_1\Delta T), (1 + \alpha_2\Delta T); (1 + \alpha_3\Delta T)$. This is the ellipsoid of thermal expansion. (This ellipsoid is *not* a quadric representative of the tensor of expansion whose equation is $\alpha_{ij}x_ix_j = 1$.)

Adularia is the only feldspar for which the shape and orientation of the ellipsoid is known, see table 4.13 and figure 4.16.

Adularia is monoclinic (or pseudomonoclinic); one of the axes of the ellipsoid of expansion must coincide with the crystallographic b axis, this is α_3, the axis of minimum expansion. The other two principal axes lie in (010); α_1, the axis of maximum expansion, is normal to ($\bar{8}$01); α_2 forms an angle of about 7° with the crystallographic c axis, and has a value very close to α_3. This illustrates the extreme anisotropism of the expansion. In the case of adularia with one axis of the ellipsoid remaining parallel to the binary b axis, a rotation of the ellipsoid should be expected with increasing temperature around this axis. But in the temperature range of investigation no such rotation has been observed. There is an indication that the *b* axis in certain adularias at room temperature corresponds to the mean axis of expansion (i.e. α_2 instead of α_3), but at elevated temperatures the

TABLE 4.13

Adularia: coefficients of thermal expansion ($\times\ 10^{-6}$)

Orientation		Fizeau (1868)[a]	Saucier and Saplewitch (1962)[b]	Orientation	Kozu and Saiki (1926)[a]
α_1	[$\bar{8}$01]	+19·07	+18·7	[100]	+17·8
α_2	[$\bar{1}$08]	− 1·48	− 1·3	[001]	+ 0·22
α_3	[010]	− 2·00	− 1·6	[010]	+ 0·95

[a] From St Gotthard.
[b] From Göschenen.

TABLE 4.14

Coefficients of thermal expansion $\times\ 10^6$

	Microcline		Adularia
Orientation	0–200(°C)	0–800(°C)	0–200(°C)
[100]	16·19	17·09	16·63
[001]	0·45	1·22	0·46
[010]	0·23	0·18	0·27

direction of the *b* axis always becomes negative (i.e. there is actually a contraction) and always corresponds to the minimum axis of expansion.

Microcline has been investigated by Rosenholtz and Smith (1941), (1942), and the results are entered in table 4.14.

At elevated temperatures there is an increase in the coefficients for microcline; but the coefficients for adularia decrease, and α_3 becomes negative. A large number of sudden changes in volume were recorded between 0 and 1000°C.

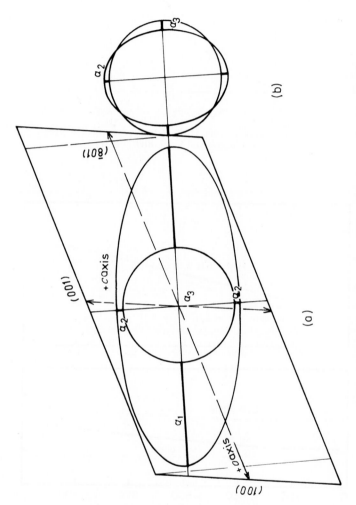

FIGURE 4.16 The ellipsoid of thermal expansion in adularia. (a) Projection on (010); (b) Projection on ($\bar{8}$01). The distances marked in the crystal is shown. The distances marked α_1, α_2, α_3 are proportional to the linear coefficients of the unit sphere over a temperature interval of 1000°c

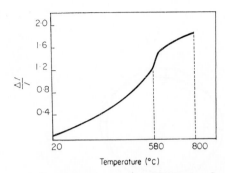

FIGURE 4.17 Thermal expansion along [100] of orthoclase perthite from Andlau, Vosges. (Saucier and Saplewitch, 1962)

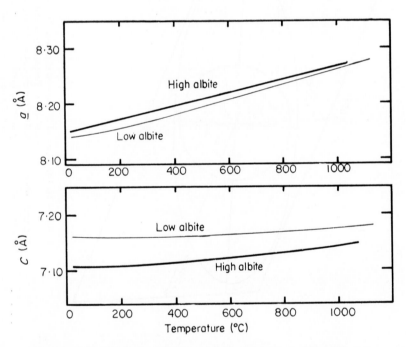

FIGURE 4.18 The change of the crystallographic axes *a* and *c* with temperature in low albite and in high albite. (Stewart and von Limbach, 1967)

Perthites were investigated by Saucier and Saplewitch (1962). In ortho-clase perthite from Andlau, Vosges, France, the thermal expansion along [100] shows a sudden jump at 580–600°C ascribed to release of stress generally present in perthites. These stresses arise from the discrepancy between cell dimensions in albite and orthoclase. It is significant that no such change occurs in peristerites.

Albite was investigated by Stewart and von Limbach (1964, 1967b) who measured the thermal expansion with a heating stage for x-ray powder diffractometry, using a computer programme to process the data gathered. In addition to freedom from the requirement of suitable single crystals, the x-ray method of measuring thermal expansion yields the true crystallo-graphic parameters. With the abundant indexed data on hand it will be possible to study the change of the orientation of the principal axes of thermal expansion with respect to the crystallographic axes, though this has not yet been attempted.

Some results for low albite from Amelia, and synthetic high albite made at 925°C are graphically presented in figures 4.18–4.20. Within a few per cent of the volume per cent expansion they agree with those that were measured with a dilatometer by Kozu and Ueda (1933) on a single crystal of low albite from Alp Rischuna, see table 4.15.

TABLE 4.15

Coefficients of linear expansion of the plagioclases. (Kozu and Ueda, 1933)

Composition	Mean value × 10^6 from 20 to 200°C			Mean value × 10^6 from 20 to 800°C		
	[100]	⊥ (010)	⊥ (001)	[100]	⊥ (010)	⊥ (001)
Albite (An_1)	12	3·3	4·4	17	5·5	6·0
An_{23}	6·7	2·2	3·9	9·2	4·0	5·7
An_{38}	4·4	3·9	5·0	5·5	5·0	6·5
An_{44}	6·1	3·9	3·3	8·8	4·2	3·8
An_{95}	7·8	2·2	8·3	5·9	2·4	5·8

The directions used are approximate.

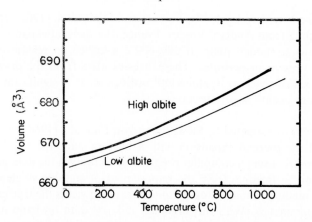

FIGURE 4.19 Thermal volume expansion of low albite and of high albite. (Stewart and von Limbach, 1967)

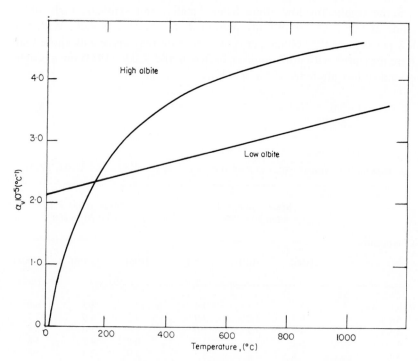

FIGURE 4.20 Thermal expansion of low and high albite, $\alpha_v = \left(\dfrac{\mathrm{d}V}{\mathrm{d}T}\right) \cdot \dfrac{1}{V}$. (Stewart and von Limbach, 1967)

Anorthite, from Vesuvius was heated between 20 and 200°c by Beckenkamp (1881). By measuring the change in various interfacial angles, he was able to locate the axes of expansion. An appreciable rotation of the ellipsoid occurs with rising temperature, see figure 4.21.

Plagioclases do not have a fixed ellipsoid of thermal expansion; the position changes appreciably with the temperature. By measuring the coefficients of expansion of six plagioclases, including one albite and one anorthite, in three perpendicular directions, Kozu and Ueda (1933) were able to calculate the volume expansion, see table 4.15.

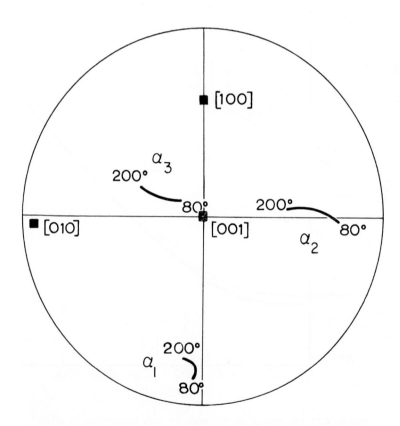

FIGURE 4.21 Anorthite. Stereographic projection normal to [001]. The migration of the axes of the ellipsoid of thermal expansion in the range 80–200°c is illustrated. (Measurements of Beckenkamp, 1881, recalculated by Saucier and Saplewitch, 1962)

On oligoclase, Offret (1890) measured the expansion along the axes of the optical indicatrix, and found a much larger expansion in the direction of the fast ray than in the directions of the other two axes. This indicates that the axis of maximum expansion is in the neighbourhood of [100] as in adularia.

Rinne (1914, 1916), using a heating goniometer, measured the change of the angle (001):(010) in the temperature range −200 to +600°c on crystals of albite, labradorite and anorthite. He noted that labradorite does not give values intermediate between those of albite and anorthite. Much

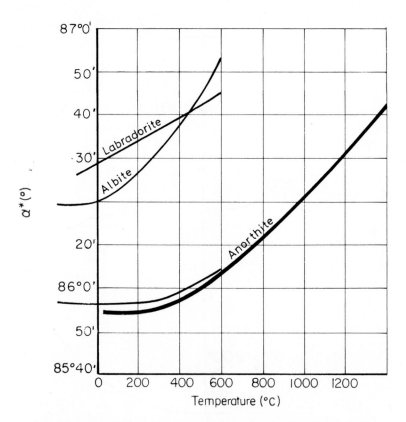

FIGURE 4.22 The change of the angle α^* with temperature in albite, labradorite and anorthite. Heavy curve for anorthite from Vesuvius. (Gubser and others, 1963); Thin curves: anorthite from Vesuvius, labradorite from Labrador, albite from Dissentes, Switzerland. (Rinne, 1914, 1916)

later, Gubser and others (1963), using an x-ray precession camera equipped with a heating device, extended the measurements (for anorthite) to 1400°c, see figure 4.22.

Stewart and others (1966) measured the thermal expansion of labradorite ($An_{67.2}$), with an x-ray diffractometer and a heating stage. They gave the values for a_0, b_0, c_0 and α, β, γ in the range 26–1141°c. The volume expansion is shown graphically in figure 4.23. The observations indicate a step on the volume curve from 650 to 1050°c, but further work is needed to confirm the reality of this irregularity—a smooth curve can actually be drawn without coming outside the interval of standard error for the observations.

New and more complete data are now given by Grundy and Brown (1967) who measured the reciprocal angles of six plagioclases up to 1200°c; see figure 4.24.

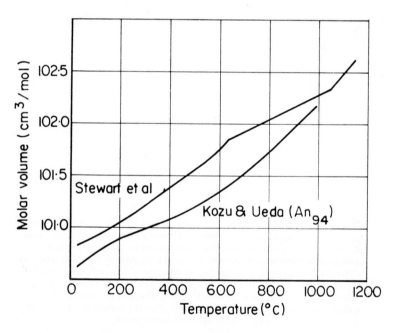

FIGURE 4.23 Molar volume of labradorite ($An_{67.2}$) from Lake Co. measured by Stewart and others (1966) at various temperatures. The curve for anorthite (An_{94}) from Miyake measured by Kozu and Ueda (1933) is approximate and is displaced by -0.2 cm^3/mole in order to separate it from the curve for labradorite

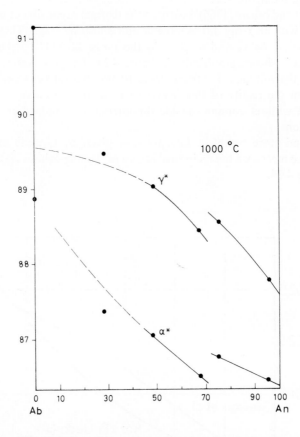

FIGURE 4.24 Variation of the reciprocal angles α^* and γ^* against com-position for plagioclases at 1000°c. Constructed after Grundy and Brown (1967); but the oligoclase and albite used by them are original low-temperature minerals and do not fit into the series with the calcic plagio-clases which represent original high-temperature materials. The stippled curves in the oligoclase–albite range are taken by extrapolation of the values of Stewart and von Limbach (1967). The discontinuity at An_{70-75} is clearly seen. Compare figure 1.21 which gives the variations in the inter-axial angles at room temperature

4.4 ELASTIC CONSTANTS

4.41 Compressibility

Compressibility can be calculated using the following equations:

$$(V_0 - V)/V_0 = aP - bP^2, P \text{ in megabars}$$

TABLE 4.16

Data for compressibility

Feldspar	$a \times 10^6$	$b \times 10^{12}$
Sanidine	1·78	4·2
Orthoclase	2·123	14·5
linear, a axis	1·013	4·8
linear, a^* axis	1·097	6·9
linear, b axis	0·559	4·9
linear, c axis	0·468	1·3
Microcline	1·92	13
Albite	2·02	21·6
Oligoclase, An_{22}	1·79 / 1·74	13·4 / 9·1
Andesine, An_{48}	1·39	3·1
Labradorite, An_{52}	1·50	9·8

TABLE 4.17

Data for compressibility above 12 kbar $(V_0 - V)/V_0$ or $(L_0 - L)/L_0$

	$P(kg/cm^2)$			
	10,000	20,000	30,000	40,000
Orthoclase, volume				
Madagascar	0·0171	0·0333	0·0488	0·0634
Spain	0·0175	0·0335	0·0484	0·0625
Labradorite, volume	0·0133	0·0260	0·0381	0·0495

Measurements of the linear constants for orthoclase demonstrate that maximum compressibility is approximately along the a axis, which is the direction of the silicon–aluminium–oxygen chains. This indicates that the chains are able to stretch and shorten like an accordion. The same behaviour is found if sodium replaces potassium. But if calcium substitutes for the alkalis the concentration of aluminium will increase in the chains and the movements of the accordion will become more difficult.

4.42 Elastic constants

The quantities C_{ij} are known as elastic constants or stiffness coefficients, the S_{ij} as elastic moduli or compliances. Their relations to stress and strain are as follows:

Stress requires for its specification six independent parameters, *the components of stress,*

$$T_i = \sum_{j=1}^{6} C_{ij} e_j.$$

Similarly, *the components of pure strain* are:

$$e_i = \sum_{j=1}^{6} S_{ij} T_j.$$

TABLE 4.18

Elastic constants. (From *Handbook of Physical Constants*, 1965)

ij	Microcline Karelia, USSR $Or_{78.5}Ab_{10.4}An_{2.1}$ $\rho = 2.56$		Oligoclase Chupa, White Sea An_{15-16} $\rho = 2.64$		Labradorite Golorino, Ukraine An_{57-60} $\rho = 2.68$	
	C_{ij}	S_{ij}	C_{ij}	S_{ij}	C_{ij}	S_{ij}
11	0·664	1·9531	0·806	2·3538	1·010	1·4888
22	1·710	0·7396	1·630	0·7421	1·582	0·8426
33	1·215	0·9491	1·242	1·3739	1·510	0·7978
44	0·143	7·0236	0·177	5·6585	0·214	4·8656
55	0·238	4·6946	0·274	5·0934	0·335	3·0976
66	0·361	2·7822	0·362	2·7667	0·370	2·8142
12	0·438	−0·4790	0·417	−0·1990	0·617	−0·5175
13	0·259	−0·3652	0·538	−1·0516	0·480	−0·3841
23	0·192	0·0294	0·374	−0·1605	0·260	0·0071
15	−0·033	−0·2281	0·161	−1·5429	−0·003	−0·0002
25	−0·148	0·4097	0·171	−0·3895	−0·080	0·1946
35	−0·131	0·4900	−0·074	1·0891	0·096	−0·2304
46	−0·015	0·2918	0·010	−0·1563	−0·056	0·7364

C_{ij} in megabars; S_{ij} in reciprocal megabars.

TABLE 4.19

Elastic constants for twinned plagioclase crystals (treated as monoclinic).
(From *Handbook of Physical Constants*, 1965)

$\%$ An $\rho =$	9 2·61		24 2·64		29 2·64		53 2·68		56 2·69	
ij	C_{ij}	S_{ij}	C_{ij}	S_{ij}	C_{ij}	S_{ij}	C_{ij}	S_{ij}	C_{ij}	S_{ij}
11	0·749	1·719	0·818	1·588	0·845	1·546	0·970	1·380	0·989	1·336
22	1·375	0·852	1·449	0·806	1·505	0·779	1·629	0·742	1·720	0·699
33	1·289	0·983	1·328	0·953	1·325	0·952	1·410	0·863	1·414	0·881
44	0·172	5·84	0·177	5·65	0·185	5·41	0·196	5·13	0·199	5·05
55	0·303	3·69	0·312	3·52	0·314	3·49	0·330	3·22	0·341	3·18
66	0·311	3·23	0·333	3·01	0·343	2·92	0·370	2·72	0·376	2·68
12	0·363	−0·35	0·393	−0·33	0·417	−0·34	0·507	−0·35	0·521	−0·33
13	0·376	−0·39	0·407	−0·38	0·409	−0·37	0·442	−0·32	0·441	−0·32
23	0·326	−0·09	0·341	−0·10	0·330	−0·09	0·370	−0·09	0·366	−0·08
15	−0·091	−0·15	−0·09	0·15	−0·087	0·134	−0·096	0·20	−0·081	0·09
25	−0·104	−0·13	−0·079	−0·05	−0·069	−0·03	−0·051	−0·03	−0·051	−0·02
35	−0·191	0·47	−0·185	0·43	−0·185	0·44	−0·150	0·29	−0·191	0·41
46	−0·013	0·24	−0·008	0·14	−0·011	0·17	−0·016	0·22	−0·019	0·26

C_{ij} in megabars; S_{ij} in reciprocal megabars.

4.43 Tensile strength

Tensile strength of potassium feldspar is shown in the table.

	Tensile strength (kg/cm²)
Maximum $\perp$ ($\bar{8}01$)	50–90
Mean $\quad\perp$ (010)	20–30
Minimum $\perp$ (001)	10–20

Estimates of O. Andersen (1928).

4.44 Shear strength

The shear strength of labradorite is 13·15 kbars according to Riecker and Seifert (1964).

4.45 Velocities of compressional waves

Velocities of compressional waves, V_p, in various minerals were measured by Simmons (1964) at pressures up to 10 kbar.

TABLE 4.20

Compressional velocities in microcline as a function of pressure at room temperature (km/sec)

P (bar)	⊥(001)	‖[010]	⊥(100)	Mean
30	6·43	7·67	4·65	6·25
100	6·73	7·82	4·83	6·49
200	6·91	8·00	4·98	6·63
400	7·16	8·15	5·09	6·80
600	7·28	8·21	5·12	6·87
800	7·36	8·23	5·15	6·91
1000	7·43	8·25	5·18	6·95
2000	7·53	8·29	5·22	7·01
4000	7·58	8·33	5·28	7·06
6000	7·60	8·37	5·31	7·09
8000	7.60	8·40	5·35	7·12
10,000	7·62	8·45	5·38	7·15

TABLE 4.21

Percentage gain along axes

Pressure (kbar)	a^*	b^*	c^*	Mean
0–1	11·4	7·5	15·5	11·2
1–10	3·9	2·4	2·6	2·9

TABLE 4.22

Compressional velocity of plagioclases at 10 kbar

An (mole %)	Velocity (km/sec)
3	6·52
12	6·67
49	6·92
50	6·86
88	7·07
100	7·20

TABLE 4.23

V_s, shear velocity

P (bar)	Shear velocity (km/sec)	
	Albitite	Anorthosite
000	3·43	3·56
500	3·54	3·65
1000	3·57	3·69
2000	3·61	3·72
4000	3·65	3·76
6000	3·68	3·77
10,000	3·73	3·81
$\Delta V =$	0·30	0·25
$\Delta V =$	9%	7%

4.46 Viscosity

Viscosity is defined as the ratio of the shearing stress to the rate of shear. If the stress is measured in dynes per centimetre per centimetre (dyn/cm²), and the rate of shear per second, the viscosity is given in dyn sec cm^{-2}, or equivalently in g/cm sec. This unit (η) is called the poise, and is used in table 4.24.

TABLE 4.24

Feldspar melts. (According to Kani, 1935)

Temperature (°c)	Or 100 Ab 0	80 20	60 40	40 60	20 80	0 100
1300	—	—	—	—	—	$1·1 \times 10^6$
1350	—	—	$2·0 \times 10^6$	$1·5 \times 10^6$	10^6	$4·3 \times 10^5$
1400	—	$1·7 \times 10^6$	$7·6 \times 10^5$	$6·4 \times 10^5$	$4·5 \times 10^5$	$1·8 \times 10^5$
1450	4×10^6	7×10^5	$3·2 \times 10^5$	$2·5 \times 10^5$	$1·8 \times 10^5$	—

Temperature (°c)	Ab — An —	80 20	60 40	40 60	20 80	0 100
1300		$3·2 \times 10^5$	$4·7 \times 10^4$	—	—	—
1400		$4·3 \times 10^4$	$7·8 \times 10^3$	$(2·5 \times 10^3)$	—	—
1500		—	—	460	190	—
1555		—	—	—	130	110

Bowen (1934) measured the viscosity of various silicate melts. His results for feldspars and for diopside are presented in figure 4.11 and compared with Kani's data for orthoclase and albite.

REFERENCES

Andersen, O. (1928). Genesis of some types of feldspar from granite pegmatites. *Norsk. Geol. Tidsskr.*, **10**, 116.

Bailey, S. W. and Taylor, W. H. (1955). The structure of triclinic potassium feldspar. *Acta Cryst.*, **8**, 621.

Barth, T. F. W. (1965). On the constitution of the alkali feldspars. *Tschermaks Mineral. Petrog. Mitt.* [3], **10** (Machatschki Vol.), 14.

Barth, T. F. W. (1967). Structure and volume relations of the alkali feldspar mixed crystals. *Schweiz. Mineral. Petrog. Mitt.*, **47**, 121.

Beckenkamp, J. (1881). Ueber die Ausdehnung monosymmetrischer und asymmetrischer Krystalle durch die Wärme. *Z. Krist.*, **5**, 436.

Becker, G. F. (1905). Introduction. In Day, A. L. and Allen, E. T. The isomorphism and thermal properties of the feldspars. *Carnegie Inst. Wash. Publ.*, **31**.

Bowen, N. L. (1934). Viscosity data for silicate melts. *Trans. Am. Geophys. Union, 15th Ann. Meeting.*

Boyd, F. R. and England, J. L. (1963). Effect of pressure on the melting of diopside and albite in the range up to 50 kilobars. *J. Geophys. Res.*, **68**, 311.

Brace, W. F. (1964). Indentation hardness of minerals and rocks. *Neues Jahrb. Mineral., Monatsh.*, **9–11**, 257–269.

Brown, B. E. and Bailey, S. W. (1964). The structure of maximum microcline. *Acta Cryst.*, **17**, 1319.

Brown, W. L. (1960). Lattice changes in heat-treated plagioclases. The existence of monalbite at room temperature. *Z. Krist.*, **113**, 297.

Carmichael, I. S. E. and MacKenzie, W. S. (1964). The lattice parameters of high-temperature triclinic sodic feldspars. *Mineral. Mag.*, **33**, 949.

Chudoba, K. (1936). Dichte und chemische Zusammensetzung der Plagioklase auf ternärer Grundlage. *Zentr. Mineral., Abt. A*, 1.

Cole, W. F., Sörum, H. and Taylor, W. H. (1951). The structure of the plagioclase feldspars. *Acta Cryst.*, **4**, 20.

Crump, R. M. and Ketner, K. B. (1953). Feldspar optics. *Geol. Soc. Am., Mem.*, **52** (Ed. R. C. Emmons), 23.

Day, A. L. and Allen, E. T. (1905). The isomorphism and thermal properties of the feldspars. *Carnegie Inst. Wash. Publ.*, **31**.

Doman, R. C., Cinnamon, C. G. and Bailey, S. W. (1965). Structural discontinuities in the plagioclase feldspar series. *Am. Mineralogist*, **50**, 145.

Donnay, G. and Donnay, J. D. H. (1952). The symmetry changes in the high temperature alkali-feldspar series. *Am. J. Sci.* (Bowen Vol.), 115.

Douglas, J. A. (1907). On changes of physical constants which take place in certain minerals and igneous rocks, on the passage from crystalline to glassy state. *Quart. J. Geol. Soc. London*, **63**, 145.

Engelhardt, W. von and Haussühl, S. (1965). Festigkeit und Härte von Kristallen. *Fortschr. Mineral.*, **42** (1), 5–49.

Ferguson, R. B., Traill, R. J. and Taylor, W. H. (1958). The crystal structure of low-temperature and high-temperature albites. *Acta Cryst.*, **11**, 331.

Finney, J. J. and Bailey, S. W. (1964). Crystal structure of an authigenic maximum microcline. *Z. Krist.*, **119**, 413.

Fizeau, H. (1868). Sur la dilatation des corps solides par la chaleur (deuxième Mémoire, seconde partie). *Compt. Rend.*, **66**, 1072; *Ann. Phys. Chem.* [5], **15**, 372.

Fleet, S. G., Chandrasekhar, S. and Megaw, H. D. (1966). The structure of bytownite. *Acta Cryst.*, **21**, 782.

Franco, R. R. and Schairer, J. F. (1951). Liquidus temperatures in mixtures of the feldspars of soda, potash and lime. *J. Geol.*, **59**, 259.

Grundy, H. D. and Brown, W. L. (1967). Preliminary single-crystal study of the lattice angles of triclinic feldspars at temperatures up to 1200°c. *Schweiz. Mineral. Petrog. Mitt.*, **47**, 21.

Gubser, R. A., Hoffmann, W. and Nissen, H.-U. (1963). Röntgenaufnahmen mit der Buergerschen Präzessionskamera bei Temperaturen zwischen 1000°c und 2000°c. *Z. Krist.*, **119**, 264.

Häkli, A. (1960). On high-temperature alkali feldspars of some volcanic rocks of Kenya and Northern Tanganyika. *Bull. Comm. Geol. Finlande*, **32**, 99.

Holmquist, P. J. (1914). Die Schleifhärte der Feldspate. *Geol. Foren. Stockholm Forh.*, **36**, 401.

Jones, J. B. and Taylor, W. H. (1961). The structure of orthoclase. *Acta Cryst.*, **14**, 443.

Kani, K. (1935). Viscosity phenomena of the system $KAlSi_3O_8–NaAlSi_3O_8$ and of perthite at high temperature. *Proc. Imp. Acad. Japan*, **11**, 334.

Kleber, W. (1963). Einführung in die Kristallographie V.E.B. Verlag Technik, Berlin.

Kozu, S. and Saiki, S. (1925). The thermal expansion of alkali-feldspars. *Sci. Rept. Tohoku Univ.*, **2**, 203.

Kozu, S. and Ueda, J. (1933). Thermal expansion of plagioclase. *Proc. Imp. Acad. (Tokyo)*, **9**, 262.

Larsen, E. S. and Berman, H. (1934). The microscopic determination of the nonopaque minerals. *U.S. Geol. Surv. Bull.*, **848**, 31.

Laves, F. (1952). Phase relations of the alkali feldspars. *J. Geol.*, **60**, 549.

Mookherjee, A. and Sahu, K. C. (1960). Microhardness of the plagioclase series. *Am. Mineralogist*, **45**, 742.

Offret, A. (1890). De la variation sous l'influence de la chaleur, des indices de refraction de quelques espèces minerales, dans l'etendue du spectre visible. *Bull. Soc. Franc. Mineral. Crist.*, **13**, 405.

Orville, P. H. (1967). Unit-cell parameters of the microcline–low albite and the sanidine–high albite solid solution series. *Am. Mineralogist*, **52**, 55.

Plendl, J. N. and Gielisse, P. J. (1963). Atomic expression of hardness. *Z. Krist.*, **118**, 404–421.

Ribbe, P. H. and Megaw, H. D. (1962). The structure of transitional anorthite: A comparison with primitive anorthite. *Norsk Geol. Tidsskr.*, **42**, II (Feldspar Vol.), 158.

Riecker, R. E. and Seifert, K. E. (1964). Shear deformation of upper-mantle mineral analogues; tests to 50 kilobars at 27°c. *J. Geophys. Res.*, **69**, 3901.

Rinne, F. (1914). Die Kristallwinkelveränderung verwandter Stoffe beim Wechsel der Temperatur I. *Centralbl. Mineral.*, 705.

Rinne, F. (1916). Zur Deformation des Winkels P:M der Plagioklasgestalt durch isomorphe Beimischung. *Centralbl. Mineral.*, 361.

Rosenholtz, J. L. and Smith, D. T. (1941). Linear expansion of adularia. *Am. Mineralogist*, **26**, 991.

Rosenholtz, J. L. and Smith, D. T. (1942). Thermal studies of orthoclase and microcline. *Am. Mineralogist*, **27**, 344.

Rottenbach, E. (1936). Die Dichte der reinen Kalifeldspatanteils im Mikroklin und dessen allgemeine chemische Zusammensetzung. *Zentr. Mineral.*, *Abt. A.*, 231.

Saucier, H. and Saplewitch, A. (1962). La dilatation thermique des feldspaths. *Norsk Geol. Tidsskr.*, **42**, II (Feldspar Vol.).

Schairer, J. F. and Bowen, N. L. (1955). The system $K_2O–Al_2O_3–SiO_2$. *Am. J. Sci.*, **253**, 681.

Schairer, J. F. and Bowen, N. L. (1956). The system $Na_2O–Al_2O_3–SiO_2$. *Am. J. Sci.*, **254**, 129.

Schairer, J. F., Smith, J. R. and Chayes, F. (1956). Refractive indices of plagioclase glasses. *Ann. Rept. Geophys. Lab.*, *Carnegie Inst. Wash.*, *Yearbook*, **55**, 195.

Simmons, G. (1964). Velocity of compressional waves in various minerals at pressures to 10 kilobars. *J. Geophys. Res.*, **69**, 1117; Velocity of shear waves in rocks at pressures to 10 kilobars. *J. Geophys. Res.*, **69**, 1123.

Smith, J. R. (1958). The optical properties of heated plagioclases. *Am. Mineralogist*, **43**, 1179.

Smith, J. V. (1956). The powder patterns and lattice parameters of plagioclase feldspars, I: The soda-rich plagioclases. *Mineral. Mag.*, **31**, 47.

Srimivasan, R. and Ribbe, H. P. (1965). Some statistical investigations of feldspar structures. *Z. Krist.*, **121**, 21.

Stewart, D. B. and Limbach, D. von. (1964). Thermal expansion of $NaAlSi_3O_8$ and calcic labradorite (Abstract). *Trans. Am. Geophys. Union*, **45**, 126.

Stewart, D. B. and Limbach, D. von. (1967). Thermal expansion of low and high albite. *Am. Mineralogist*, **52**, 399.

Stewart, D. B., Walker, G. W., Wright, T. L. and Fahey, J. J. (1966). Physical properties of calcic labradorite from Lake County, Oregon. *Am. Mineralogist*, **51**, 177.

Tabor, D. (1954). Mohs's hardness scale—A physical interpretation. *Proc. Phys. Soc. (London)*, *B*, **67**, 249.

Taylor, E. W. (1949). Correlation of the Mohs's scale of hardness with the Vickers's hardness numbers. *Mineral. Mag.*, **28**, 718.

Taylor, W. H. (1962). The structures of the principal feldspars. *Norsk Geol. Tidsskr.*, **42**, II (Feldspar Vol.), 1.

Weibel, M. (1958). Chemische Untersuchungen an Albiten aus den Schweizer Alpen. *Schweiz. Mineral. Petrog. Mitt.*, **38**, 61.

Wenk, H. R. (1966). Labradorite from Surtsey, Iceland. *Schweiz. Mineral. Petrog. Mitt.*, **46**, 81.

Winchell, H. (1945). The Knoop microhardness tester as a mineralogical tool. *Am. Mineralogist*, **30**, 583.

Wright, T. L. (1964). X-ray determination of composition and structural state of alkali feldspar (Abstract). *Trans. Am. Geophys. Union*, **45**, 127.

5

Thermodynamic Properties of Feldspars

5.1 THERMOCHEMICAL DATA

The total structure energy or lattice energy, U, of an ionic crystal is the difference of energy between two states, viz. (1) that of the dispersed state: the ions being so far apart that they do not influence each other, and (2) that of the crystalline state: all ions being concentrated in a crystal lattice. Let us first suppose that the ions are very far apart. As they approach each other to form a crystalline lattice, potential energy will be liberated until other forces come into play and exercise a repulsion which prevents a closer approach of the ions. In the majority of silicates, it is too complicated to calculate this difference between the loss of potential energy and the gain of repulsive energy when the crystal lattice is formed in this way.

Born and Landé gave the original equation (for a binary compound):

$$U = \frac{A z^2 e^2 N}{R} \left(1 - \frac{1}{m} \right)$$

in which R is the distance between a positive and a negative ion in the crystal, z is the valence, e is the electron charge, N is Avogadro's number, A is the Madelung constant (which is different for each structure type), m is a constant calculated from the compressibility.

A simplification was introduced by Kapustinsky (1933) in what he calls the 'second principle of crystallochemistry.' His principle correlates the number of ions (Σn), the ionic radii (r_a, r_c) and valences (z_a, z_c). He found a way of eliminating both the Madelung constant, A, and m; thus arriving at the following equation:

$$U = 287 \cdot 2 \sum n \frac{z_a \cdot z_c}{r_a \cdot r_c} \left(1 - \frac{0 \cdot 345}{r_a + r_c} \right)$$

Using this equation, Tauson (1950) published a table of structure energies of rock-forming silicates which was reproduced by Eitel (1952).

Born (1919) and Haber (1919) independently showed an alternative way of calculation. The energy balance of the formation of an ionic compound is made up of a series of positive and negative contributions that can be put together in a cycle. The following diagram shows this for potassium feldspar.

$$[K] + [Al] + 3[Si] + 4(O_2) \xrightarrow{\ -\Sigma L\ } (K) + (Al) + 3(Si) + 4(O_2)$$

with vertical contributions $-\Delta H$, $-\Sigma I$, $-4D$, $+8E$, $|8\,O|$, and

$$[KAlSi_3O_8] \xleftarrow{\quad U \quad} K^+ + Al^{3+} + 3Si^{4+} + 8O^{2-}$$

We start in the upper left corner with one mole each of crystalline potassium and aluminium, three moles of crystalline silica, and four moles of gaseous oxygen. The metals and silicon are evaporated by use of the respective heats of sublimation, L, then they are ionized by use of the energy of ionization, I, while oxygen is dissociated by use of the heat of dissociation D; oxygen captures the liberated electrons and recovers the electron affinity, E.

The lattice energy U is obtained by letting the free ions condense into a feldspar lattice. Consequently:

$$U = \Delta H + \Sigma L + \Sigma I + 4D - 8E$$

The true lattice energy U_0 at $T = 0$ is larger than that which may be calculated from the following data, which have not been reduced to the temperature of absolute zero: $4D = 710$, $8E = 380$ kcal. Values for ΔH are given in the following tables.

Values in kcal per mole for heat of sublimation, L, and for energy of ionization, I, are given in the table for the ions in question.

	Na	K	Ca	Al	Si
L	30	27	40	60	92
I	117	100	413	1220	2350

The heat of formation $-\Delta H$ can be measured calorimetrically, or it may be calculated (or estimated) from known values of other silicates and from the component oxides. The following heats of formation from the elements are given by Rossini and others (1952): SiO_2 (quartz) $-$ 205·4; Al_2O_3 $-$ 399·1; CaO $-$ 151·9; Na_2O $-$ 99·4; K_2O $-$ 86·4.

The heat of fusion ΔH_f has been calculated from the melting point lowering in the system Ab–An (Bowen, 1913), and from differential heats of solution data (Kelley, 1960).

Heat content and entropy can be measured calorimetrically. The heat capacity, C_p, equals the sum of the atomic heats of the constituent atoms. According to the rule of Dulong and Petit the atomic heat of most elements is about 6·4; exceptions are Si = 3·8, O = 4·0 (rule of Neumann–Kopp).

$T =$ absolute temperature measured in degrees Kelvin ($°K$)
$H_T =$ heat at absolute temperature T
$H^0 =$ heat at standard temperature, i.e. 25°C = 298·16°K
Analogously the entropy is given as S_T and S^0
$C_p =$ heat capacity at constant pressure
1 calorie = 4·1840 absolute joules.

All energy values given in this section and unlabelled with regard to units are in terms of calories per mole.

Whereas the molar weights and volumes are accurately known, the values of the thermodynamic properties are not. This will be evident from

TABLE 5.1

Selected values of some thermodynamic constants

	Formula weight (g/mole)	Molar vol. (cm³)	Entropy $\left(\dfrac{cal/mole}{deg}\right)$	ΔH_{298} (cal/mole)	$\Delta F_{298.15}$ (cal/mole)	Log K_f
Anorthite	278·22	100·79	48·45	−21·810	−23·900	17·518
Albite	262·24	{100·58 / 99·99	50·20	−35·900	−37·530	27·509
Orthoclase	278·35	108·65	52·47	−51·030		
Hexagonal anorthite	278·22		45·84	−16·920	−18·230	13·36

The entropy values, $\Delta H =$ heat of formation from oxides, and $\Delta F =$ free energy of formation from oxides are taken from Robie (1966); the molar volumes are adjusted to the results presented in this book. For albite, two values are given corresponding to high albite and low albite respectively.

the following sections, in which detailed measurements on the various feldspars are compiled and discussed.

Waldbaum (1968) determined the heat of transition (at 49·7°C) for

$$\begin{aligned}
\text{microcline} &\rightarrow \text{sanidine} &=& \quad 1890 \pm 440 \text{ cal/mole} \\
\text{sanidine} &\rightarrow \text{glass} &=& \; 11{,}100 \pm 370 \text{ cal/mole} \\
\text{low albite} &\rightarrow \text{high albite} &=& \quad 2630 \pm 280 \text{ cal/mole} \\
\text{high albite} &\rightarrow \text{glass} &=& \; 11{,}890 \pm 400 \text{ cal/mole}
\end{aligned}$$

and derived new values for the standard heats of formation of the alkali feldspars. The reader is referred to his paper. The values came too late to receive consideration in the following tables but are to be preferred inasmuch as the compositions and x-ray crystallographic properties of the samples are accurately known.

5.11 Data for $KAlSi_3O_8$ (Mol. wt. 278·35)

(a) Total structure energy $U = 12{,}350{,}000$ (Eitel, 1952).
   Calculated from the Born–Haber cycle, $U = 9{,}992{,}000$.

(b) Heat of formation from the elements at 18°C.

Feldspar	Bichowsky and Rossini (1936)	Rossini and others (1952)	Schiebold (1931)	Ramberg (1953)
Glass	873,500	890,000	—	—
Adularia	905,300	921,000	865,000	—
Microcline	892,200	908,000	—	996,000

(b′) Heat of formation from the oxides, selected values.

Feldspar	Rossini and others (1952)	Selby (1962)	Sommerfeld (1967)
Glass	41,000	—	—
Adularia	62,000	—	—
Orthoclase	—	56,300	52,900
Microcline	49,000	—	—

(c) Heat of fusion (Mulert, 1912):

Microcline	(at 20°c)	27,800
Adularia	(at 20°c)	23,200
Sanidine	(at 47·9°c)	11,000 (Waldbaum, 1968)

(c′) Heat of inversion microcline → sanidine is 1890 ± 440 (Waldbaum, 1968).

(d) Entropy at 25°c:

Adularia $S^0 = 51·4$ (Eitel, 1952); $S^0 = 52·5$ (Kelley and others, 1953); Orthoclase 52·47.

TABLE 5.2

Heat content and entropy at various temperatures. (Kelley, 1960)

T	H_T-H^0		S_T-S^0	
	K-feldspar	Glass	K-feldspar	Glass
400	5500	5700	15·81	16·40
600	17,950	18,650	40·94	42·53
800	32,000	32,750	61·11	62·77
1000	46,900	48,050	77·72	79·81
1200	62,200	63,950	91·67	94·30
1400	77,900	80,550	103·76	107·08

Heat content of crystals:

$$H_T - H^0 = 63·83T + 6·45 \times 10^{-3}T^2 + 17·05 \times 10^5T^{-1} - 25,323$$

Heat capacity:

$$C_p = 63·83 + 12·90 \times 10^{-3}T - 17·05 \times 10^5T^{-2}$$

Heat content of glass:

$$H_T - H^0 = 61·96T + 8·58 \times 10^{-3}T^2 + 14·29 \times 10^5T^{-1} - 24,029$$

Heat capacity:

$$C_p = 61·96 + 17·16 \times 10^{-3}T - 14·29 \times 10^5T^{-2}$$

At room temperature the above equation yields for K-feldspar, $C_p = 48.7$. The rule of Neumann–Kopp yields:

$$C_p = 6·4 + 6·4 + 3 \times 3·8 + 8 \times 4 = 56·2$$

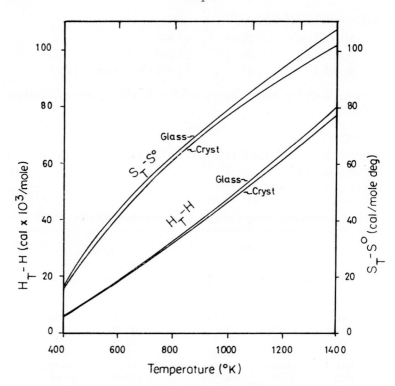

FIGURE 5.1 Heat content and entropy of glass and crystals of
KAlSi$_3$O$_8$. (After Kelley, 1960)

5.12 Data for NaAlSi$_3$O$_8$ (Mol. wt. 262·24)

(a)   Albite: Total structure energy $U = 12,400,000$ (Eitel, 1952).
       Calculated from the Born–Haber Cycle $U = 9,985,000$.

(b)   Heat of formation from the oxides:

	Selby (1962)	Ramberg (1953)	Schiebold (1931)
Low albite	41,200	99,000	29,500
High albite	39,000		

Heat of formation from the elements is obtained by adding 866,000 to the above
figures.

(c)   Heat of fusion and entropy of fusion at 1105°c.

	$-\Delta H_f$	ΔS_f	Reference
High albite	12,740	9·2	Bowen (1913)
High albite	12,900	9·3	Kracek and
Natural albite	16,300	11·7	Neuvonen (1952)

(c′) Heat of inversion low albite → high albite is about 3400 (Kracek and Neuvonen, 1952), or 2630 (Waldbaum, 1968).

(c″) The activation energy E (a measure of the energy barrier involved in the disordering process) low → high albite:

$E = 96,000 \pm 11,000$ for Schmirntal albite; $E = 74,300 \pm 1400$ for Amelia albite (McKie and McConnell, 1963); $E = 60,000 \pm 200$ for synthetic $NaAlSi_3O_8$ (McConnell and McKie, 1960).

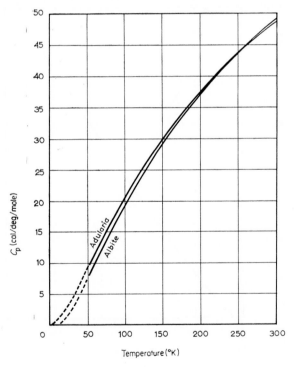

FIGURE 5.2 Heat capacities of adularia and of albite.
(After Kelley and others, 1953)

(d) Entropy at 25°C:

$S^0 = 49.2$ (Eitel, 1952); $S^0 = 50.2$ (Kelley and others, 1953).

TABLE 5.3

Heat content and entropy at various temperatures. (Kelley, 1960)

T	H_T-H^0		S_T-S^0	
	Albite	Glass	Albite	Glass
400	5410	5540	15·55	15·93
600	17,900	18,220	40·73	41·48
800	31,690	32,360	60·54	61·78
1000	46,220	47,220	76·74	78·34
1200	61,340	63,380	90·51	93·05
1400	76,860	—	102·47	—

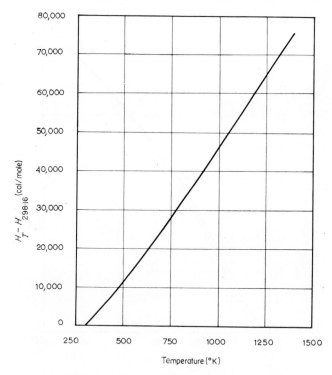

FIGURE 5.3 Heat content of albite at high temperatures.
(After Kelley and others, 1953)

Heat content of crystals:

$$H_T - H^0 = 61 \cdot 70T + 6 \cdot 95 \times 10^{-3}T^2 + 15 \cdot 01 \times 10^5 T^{-1} - 24{,}048$$

Heat capacity:

$$C_p = 61 \cdot 70 + 13 \cdot 90 \times 10^{-3}T - 15 \cdot 01 \times 10^5 T^{-2}$$

Heat content of glass:

$$H_T - H^0 = 61 \cdot 31T + 9 \cdot 00 \times 10^{-3}T^2 + 16 \cdot 16 \times 10^5 T^{-1} - 24{,}500$$

Heat capacity:

$$C_p = 61 \cdot 31 + 18 \cdot 00 \times 10^{-3}T - 16 \cdot 16 \times 10^5 T^{-2}$$

At room temperature the above equation yields for albite, $C_p = 49 \cdot 2$. The rule of Neumann–Kopp yields:

$$C_p = 6 \cdot 4 + 6 \cdot 4 + 3 \times 3 \cdot 8 + 4 \times 8 = 56 \cdot 2$$

5.13 Data for $CaAl_2Si_2O_8$ (Mol. wt. 278·22)

(a) Anorthite: Total structure energy $U = 11{,}550{,}000$ (Eitel, 1952). Calculated from the Born–Haber cycle $U = 8{,}834{,}000$.

(b) Heat of formation

	$-\Delta H$ from oxides	From elements	Reference
Anorthite	59,000	1,020,800	Ramberg (1953)
Anorthite	61,000	—	Schiebold (1931)
Natural anorthite	30,100	—	Sommerfeld (1967)
Synthetic anorthite	28,900	—	Kracek and Neuvonen (1952)

(c) Heat of fusion and entropy of fusion

	ΔH_f	ΔS_f	Reference
Natural anorthite	19,500	10·7	Kracek and
Natural anorthite	18,200	10·0	Neuvonen
Synthetic anorthite	17,700	9·7	(1952)
Synthetic anorthite	27,800	15·3	Vogt (1904)
Synthetic anorthite	29,400	16·1	Bowen (1913)

(c′) Heat of transition low → high anorthite is about 500 cal/mol according to Kracek and Neuvonen (1952).

TABLE 5.4

Heat content and entropy at various temperatures. (Kelley, 1960)

T	$H_T - H^0$		$S_T - S^0$	
	Anorthite	Glass	Anorthite	Glass
400	5570	5590	16·02	16·07
600	18,450	18,590	41·99	42·27
800	32,570	32,870	52·27	62·77
1000	47,430	47,750	78·83	79·36
1200	62,970	—	92·99	—
1400	79,050	—	105·37	—
1600	96,170	—	116·79	—
1700	105,230	—	122·28	—

Heat content of crystals:

$$H_T - H^0 = 64 \cdot 42T + 6 \cdot 85 \times 10^{-3}T^2 + 16 \cdot 89 \times 10^5 T^{-1} - 25{,}481$$

Heat capacity:

$$C_p = 64 \cdot 42 + 13 \cdot 70 \times 10^{-3}T - 16 \cdot 89 \times 10^5 T^{-2}$$

Heat content of glass:

$$H_T - H^0 = 66 \cdot 46T + 5 \cdot 92 \times 10^{-3}T^2 + 18 \cdot 22 \times 10^5 T^{-1} - 26{,}452$$

Heat capacity:

$$C_p = 66 \cdot 46 + 11 \cdot 84 \times 10^{-3}T - 18 \cdot 22 \times 10^5 T^{-2}$$

At room temperature the above equation yields for anorthite $C_p = 49 \cdot 7$. The rule of Neumann–Kopp yields:

$$C_p = 6 \cdot 4 + 2 \times 6 \cdot 4 + 2 \times 3 \cdot 8 + 4 \times 8 = 58 \cdot 8$$

The heat of formation (from the oxides) of various feldspars was estimated by Ramberg (1953)

Feldspar	Formula	$-\Delta H \times 10^{-3}$	Feldspar	Formula	$-\Delta H \times 10^{-3}$
Li–f	$LiAlSi_3O_8$	53	Mg–f	$MgAl_2Si_2O_8$	30
Ab	$NaAlSi_3O_8$	99	An	$CaAl_2Si_2O_8$	59
Or	$KAlSi_3O_8$	137	Sr–f	$SrAl_2Si_2O_8$	78
Rb–f	$RbAlSi_3O_8$	140	Ba–f	$BaAl_2Si_2O_8$	93
Cs–f	$CsAlSi_3O_8$	142	Ra–f	$RaAl_2Si_2O_8$	(106)[a]

[a] Not given by Ramberg.

Lithium and magnesium feldspars do not exist, the (negative) heat of formation is smaller than in any of the stable feldspars. Schiebold (1931) in an earlier estimate indicated heats of formation of opposite sign for these unstable compounds.

5.14 The alkali feldspar series $NaAlSi_3O_8$–$KAlSi_3O_8$ solid solutions

The molar heats of formation of solid solution for the alkali feldspar series are small, the experimental scatter is rather large, and the results are therefore not wholly conclusive. It is clearly evident that this heat of formation is positive, but the actual course of the curve is uncertain, see figure 5.4.

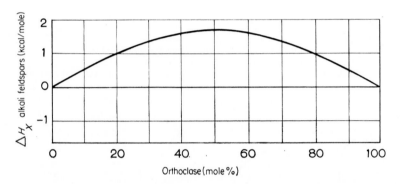

FIGURE 5.4 Molar heats of formation of solid solution for alkali feldspars from high albite and orthoclase. (Kracek and Neuvonen, 1952)

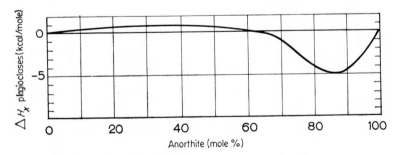

FIGURE 5.5 Molar heats of formation of solid solution for plagioclases from natural albite and synthetic anorthite. (Kracek and Neuvonen, 1952)

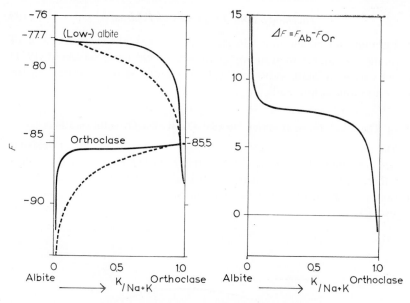

FIGURE 5.6 Partial molar free energy at 700°c
(from $Na_{(liquid)}$, $K_{(liquid)}$, $\frac{1}{4}O_2, \frac{1}{2}Al_2O_3, 3SiO_2$)
The dashed lines give the curves for an ideal mixed crystal. The actual
curves indicate by their nearly horizontal slopes in the range $x = 0\cdot20{-}0\cdot70$
the proximity of a miscibility gap at lower temperatures

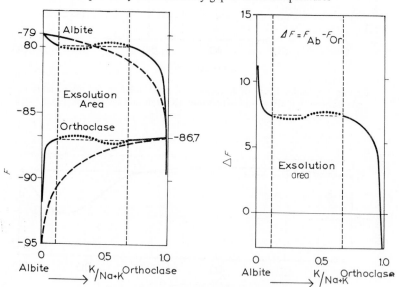

FIGURE 5.7 Partial molar free energy at 600°c
In the region of the miscibility gap the curves are dotted, because these
values cannot be realized in nature

5.15 The plagioclase series $NaAlSi_3O_8$–$CaAl_2Si_2O_8$ solid solutions

Bowen (1913) concluded from his work on the melting phenomena of the plagioclases that albite and anorthite form ideal solid solutions at the liquidus temperatures. At lower temperatures the relationship is much more complicated. The molar heats of formation of plagioclase solid solutions are small, and the data are inconclusive. The molar heats, ΔH_x are probably very close to zero from pure albite up to some point above 60% anorthite. From An_{60} to An_{100} the plagioclases are characterized by a slightly negative ΔH_x attaining -200 to -500 cal/mole in the range An_{80-90}.

Data for *andesine* $Ab_{60}An_{40}$ (Mol. wt. 268·35), (White, 1919).

Heat capacity for crystals:

$$C_p = 63\cdot62 + 12\cdot84 \times 10^{-3}T - 16\cdot37 \times 10^5 T^{-1}$$

Heat capacity for glass:

$$C_p = 65\cdot22 + 13\cdot21 \times 10^{-3}T - 17\cdot83 \times 10^5 T^{-1}$$

5.16 The partial free energy of albite and orthoclase in alkali feldspar

From Orville's data (1963) on the alkali ion exchange between vapour and alkali feldspars, the partial molar free energy of the pure components in the mix-crystal region was calculated by Allmann and Hellner (1962). The results are given in figures 5.6 and 5.7.

5.2 SOLUBILITY AND ALTERATION OF FELDSPARS

In cold water the feldspars are hydrolysed:

$$2KAlSi_3O_8 + nH_2O = Al_2Si_2O_5(OH)_4 + 4SiO_2 + 2K^+ + 2(OH)^-$$

$$CaAl_2Si_2O_8 + nH_2O = Al_2Si_2O_5(OH)_4 + Ca^{2+} + 2(OH)^-$$

Bondam (1967) demonstrated an iso-structural exchange of K^+ by $(H_3O)^+$ in the lattice of adularia exposed to hydrolytic conditions, resulting in an expanded lattice and the formation of hydrogen bonds having a colinear arrangement with the existing bonds in the feldspar.

Manus (1967) found on the feldspar surfaces a residue product which slows down the rate of leaching; it develops by three successive stages: (1) stripping of loosely held ions from the fresh feldspar surface,

(2) disorganization and expansion of the surface feldspar lattice and development of a residue product capable of retarding the loss of K^+, (3) further development of the residue material into a more stable product. Albite behaves analogously to potassium feldspar.

These equations describe only the initial stage; by prolonged action aluminium ions (and ion complexes) are liberated (Barnes, 1965; Correns, 1962; Garrels and Howard, 1959; Hemley, 1959; Hemley and Jones, 1964; Hess, 1966; Lagache, 1965; Lagache and others, 1961; Wollast, 1967).

At higher temperatures and pressures the feldspars go into true solution (Morey and Chen, 1955).

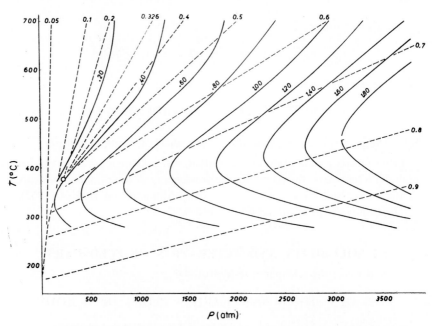

FIGURE 5.8 Solubility of orthoclase in pure H_2O. Full curves = isolytes. Dashed curves = vapour tension of pure water with the corresponding isochores. Open circle = the critical point of water. (After Schloemer, 1962)

The solubility relations of potassium feldspar are displayed in figure 5.8. The solubility of sodium feldspar as determined by Burnham and Jahns (1962) emerges from table 5.5.

TABLE 5.5

The solubility of sodium feldspar

Dissolved albite (%)	Temp. (°c)	Pressure (bar)
4·2	655	1000
4·2	930	1000
6·6	635	2000
6·4	850	2000
11·2	650	5000
9·9	750	5000
20	675	10,000
16·8	700	10,000

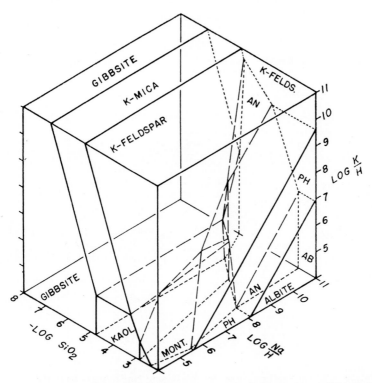

FIGURE 5.9 Phase diagram for the system K_2O–Na_2O–Al_2O_3–SiO_2–H_2O at 25°c and 1 atmosphere. Kaol = kaolinite, Mont = montmorillonite, Ph = phillipsite, An = analcite, Ab = albite. (After Hess, 1966)

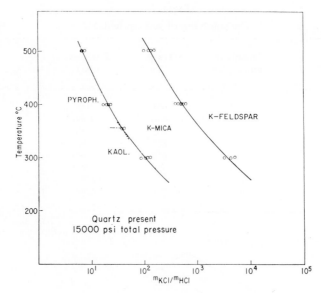

FIGURE 5.10 (a) Reaction curves for the system: K_2O–Al_2O_3–SiO_2–H_2O

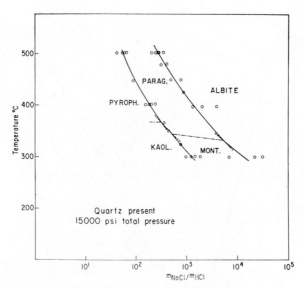

FIGURE 5.10 (b) Reaction curves for the system: Na_2O–Al_2O_3–SiO_2–H_2O.
(After Hemley and Jones, 1964)

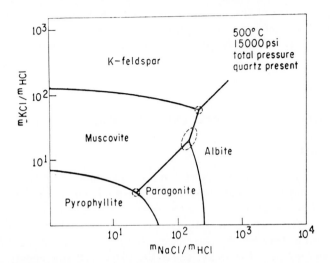

FIGURE 5.11 Mineral stability relations in the system $K_2O–Na_2O–Al_2O_3–SiO_2–H_2O$ at 500°c and 15,000 lb/in² total pressure. (After Hemley and Jones, 1964)

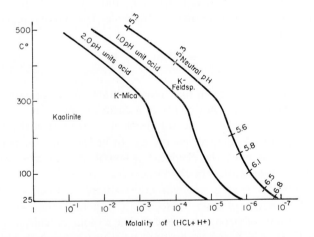

FIGURE 5.12 Phase relations in the K-feldspar–H_2O–H^+ system in equilibrium with (KCl) + (K^+) at a total concentration of 1·0 molal, and with quartz at 1·0 kbar. Observe that the values for neutral pH vary with temperature and are given numerically. (After Barnes, 1965)

A rapid survey of the phases of the system K_2O–Na_2O–Al_2O_3–SiO_2–H_2O at 25°c and one atmosphere is afforded by figure 5.9. The phase relations at various pH values are shown in figures 5.10, 5.11 and 5.12.

5.3 PHASE EQUILIBRIA AND MELTING IN FELDSPARS

5.31 General

Melting and polymorphic phase transformations occur reversibly at constant temperature and pressure. A thermodynamic consequence is that the Gibbs free energy must be the same for both phases in equilibrium. On the other hand, at a temperature and pressure which do not correspond to equilibrium between the two phases, the free energy will be different for the two phases. The stable phase has the lowest free energy. If the system is found in the phase of higher free energy, it will be unstable and irreversibly change to the other phase.

The free energy may be applied to a pure substance or to a specified component, i, in a solution. The solution may be either solid or liquid. The free energy of i is often denoted by F_i and is called the partial molal free energy, or the chemical potential per mole. The activity, a_i, is defined by the relation

$$F_i = RT \ln a_i + F_i^0$$

where F_i^0 is the free energy in the 'standard state', R the gas constant and T absolute temperature. The activity of a chemical species is proportional to its vapour tension. In dilute solutions, it is proportional also to its concentration. Just as the free energy has to be the same for two phases in equilibrium, so must the chemical potential and, in most cases, the activity and vapour tension be the same.

Molten silicates possess an *ionic* constitution by analogy with solid silicates. The extent of ionic dissociation is comparable with that of aqueous solutions of strong electrolytes. The cations in feldspar melts are Na^+, K^+, Ca^{2+}, which occupy no fixed positions in the melt but exhibit a high degree of mobility.

The anions are silicon–oxygen tetrahedra linked together by oxygen bridges to one-, two- or three-dimensional networks. The network is similar to that found in crystalline silicates, but more irregular, see figure 4.10.

The bonds between the central silicon ion and the oxygens at the corners of the tetrahedra are mainly covalent, but may also be regarded as largely polarized ionic links.

Support for the existence of a polymerized silica network is the high viscosity of silicate melts. The viscosity increases with increasing SiO_2 content. The viscosity is found also to increase upon adding Al_2O_3. This shows that Al can replace Si in the polymerized anion, as it does in crystalline feldspars.

In addition to the anions mentioned above, the melt contains small amounts of free oxygen ions, O^{2-}, the amount of which is determined by the following reactions:

$$(SiO_4)^{4-} \rightleftharpoons (SiO_{3\cdot5})^{3-} + \tfrac{1}{2}O^{2-}$$

$$(SiO_{3\cdot5})^{3-} \rightleftharpoons (SiO_3)^{2+} + \tfrac{1}{2}O^{2-}$$

$$(SiO_3)^{2-} \rightleftharpoons (SiO_{2\cdot5})^{1-} + \tfrac{1}{2}O^{2-}$$

$$(SiO_{2\cdot5})^{1-} \rightleftharpoons (SiO_2) + \tfrac{1}{2}O^{2-}$$

For each reaction we can write the corresponding equilibrium equation, for example:

$$\frac{[SiO_{2\cdot5}] \cdot [O^-]^{\frac{1}{2}}}{[SiO_3]} = K$$

where the square brackets indicate the activity of the components, and K is the equilibrium constant.

The activity of the oxygen ion may be taken to be proportional to its concentration, and it is readily seen that a large oxygen ion concentration shifts the reactions to the left, i.e. the oxygen ion concentration increases with increasing basicity of the melt. It becomes appreciable in melts of composition more basic than that corresponding to an orthosilicate. Thus the 'pO value' is a measure of the basicity of the silicate melt. In formal analogy with the symbol pH, the oxygen ion activity is indicated by its negative logarithm and denoted by the symbol pO.

The degree of polymerization is markedly influenced by the nature of the cations present. This means that the nature of the cation influences the activity coefficient of the different types of macroions. The effect is that at constant basicity the formation of oxygen bridges is favoured by a weakly polarizing ion, such as K^+, and decreases in the sequence K^+–Na^+–Li^+.

At a certain basicity where the K silicates contain anions with 2·5 oxygen/ Si the Na silicates have 3 oxygen/Si and the Li silicates 4 oxygen/Si. This is in agreement with the fact that in the alkali silicate melts the viscosity decreases in the sequence K–Na–Li, i.e. with the polarizing power of the cation.

When H_2O is dissolved in the melt the following reaction takes place

$$H_2O + O^{2-} \rightleftharpoons 2(OH)^-$$

in harmony with the fact that $(OH)^-$ is an individual building brick in the crystal structure of many silicate minerals.

The structural configurations in silicate liquids and glasses have a bearing on the interpretation of phase diagrams, particularly with regard to the relationships to be expected in magmas at depth. Clearly in phase studies the liquid phase must be considered as well as the crystalline phases.

In the hydrothermal melting of basalt the plagioclase liquidus is depressed drastically compared with the other silicate phases at increasing water pressure. The explanation lies in the structural position of aluminium in the melt. In plagioclase Al is four coordinated, as it is in the liquid at low pressures. However, Al may go into sixfold coordination in the melt at high pressures if the demand for oxygen is met. This is easily accomplished by the addition of water reducing the negative charge excess around the Al ions from 9 (all oxygens) to 3 (if all hydroxyles). The higher the water pressure the more readily would Al go into sixfold coordination, and the more difficult the crystallization of four-coordinated-Al plagioclases from a melt containing close-packed six-coordinated-Al.

Lacy (1967) stressed that entry of Al into sixfold coordination is only possible in anhydrous melts having the glassformer ratio

$$\frac{O}{Al + Si} > 2·0$$

As the glassformer ratio approaches 2·0 (e.g. granites, feldspar and feldspathoidal melts), Al cannot be forced into six-coordination since the demand for oxygen cannot be met. Then the liquidus temperatures of feldspars, etc., increase with pressure in a similar manner to other silicates.

The free energy of silicate melts reflects its compressibility and the extent of depolymerization due to water. The compressibility has two components: (1) the general deformations of atoms and (2) change of equilibrium structure with change of pressure. The rise with pressure of the liquidus temperature of feldspars thus depend upon the equilibrated melt. The changes appear largely to be complete at pressures of 30 kbar, see next section.

5.32 The temperature of melting

In order to study the relations of the *temperature of crystallization*, we may first consider a pure solvent, e.g. water. At the freezing point (= melting point) ice and water are in equilibrium, which implies that the activity of $[H_2O]_{ice}$ = activity of $[H_2O]_{water}$. By adding a soluble substance (e.g. NaCl) to the water one obtains a solution in which water is 'diluted' with NaCl. This causes the activity of $[H_2O]$ to drop below the value of the activity in pure water. Consequently, activity of $[H_2O]_{ice}$ > activity of $[H_2O]_{solution}$, i.e. the temperature of crystallization has decreased.

Thermodynamic equations relate the depression of the point of crystallization with the heat of melting.

For ideal solutions equation (5.1) is valid:

$$\Delta t = \frac{RT^2}{Q} \cdot X_2 \qquad (5.1)$$

It is seen that the depression of the melting point, Δt, is proportional to the amount of the dissolved substance, X_2, and inversely proportional to the heat of melting, Q. It should be noted, however, that this simple equation is only valid for systems in which no mixed crystals or solid solutions occur.

The relation between melting point and pressure is expressed by the Clausius equation:

$$\frac{dt}{dP} = \frac{T\Delta V}{Q}$$

where ΔV is the difference in specific volume between melt and crystal; it is positive for practically all silicates.

The melting diagrams presented in figures 5.13–5.55 are ordinary equilibrium diagrams commonly regarded as freezing-point diagrams. They are at the same time solubility diagrams giving the solubility relations of any phase with temperature. According to equation (5.1), the change of the freezing point with composition depends upon the heat effect involved in solution, and the diagrams contain complete information on this effect. Thus Bowen (1915) from his melting equilibrium diagram of the plagioclase feldspar (figure 5.17) calculated the latent heat of melting of albite and anorthite (16,300 and 29,400 cal/mole respectively, see section 5.1).

The diagrams are collected in blocks dispersed through the text which follows and are intended in this way to give a rapid and convenient survey of the melting phenomena, and the phase relations of the feldspar minerals. For this purpose the diagrams are fully adequate. Some of them have been strongly reduced, and it goes without saying that anyone who wants to make a detailed study of any of the thermodynamic properties of the feldspars must consult the original literature as given in the figure captions.

Mixed-crystal series are very common in feldspars. The activity of an end member will vary continuously throughout the series, although not in direct proportion to its molecular concentration (p. 201). Depending upon the relative variations of the activities in the solid solution and in the liquid solution (= the melt), the melting curves will assume different shapes.

The melting curve of orthoclase in the system $KAlSi_3O_8$–H_2O (figure 5.50) is of considerable interest. High partial pressures of water have effects of opposite sign on the melting point of silicates. At successively higher pressures more water tends to be dissolved in a silicate liquid and thus its temperature of melting decreases. However, when the limit of solubility of water in silicate melt is reached, or nearly reached, then the effect of increasing pressure of water is to increase the melting point of the silicate. In this particular instance, the dramatic change in the slope of the melting curve takes place as orthoclase reacts to muscovite and is the result of the very substantial density differences between the orthoclase and muscovite phases. Thus, the slope of the melting curve of muscovite with increasing fluid pressure is strongly positive, whereas the slope of the melting curve of orthoclase is negative. Unfortunately, the detailed relations of the slopes of the curve in the region of the triple point as shown in figure 5.50 are not accurately determined. A remarkable similarity is displayed by the melting curve of the albite–nepheline mixture in the system $NaAlSi_2O_6$–H_2O as shown in figure 5.46, inset. Here the change in the slope of the curve is introduced as nepheline + albite react to analcite.

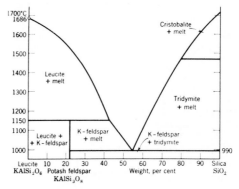

FIGURE 5.13 Equilibrium diagram of the binary system leucite–silica. (Schairer and Bowen, 1938)

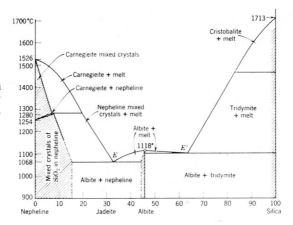

FIGURE 5.14 Equilibrium diagram of the binary system nepheline–silica. (Greig and Barth, 1938)

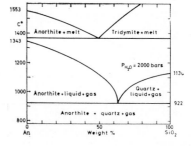

FIGURE 5.15 Upper part: Melting equilibrium diagram of anorthite SiO₂. Lower part: melting at 2 kbar H₂O pressure (Schairer and Bowen, 1947)

Feldspars

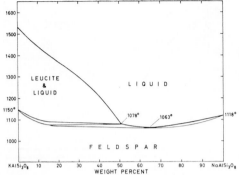

FIGURE 5.16 The alkali feldspar join in the system albite–potassium feldspar–quartz. Heavy curves refer to binary equilibrium and light curves to ternary equilibrium. (Schairer, 1950)

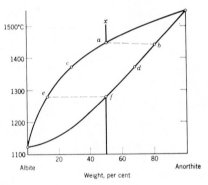

FIGURE 5.17 Melting equilibrium diagram of the plagioclase feldspars. (Bowen, 1915)

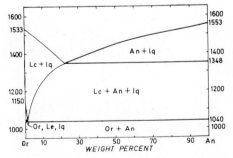

FIGURE 5.18 The orthoclase–anorthite join in the system anorthite–leucite–silica. Heavy curves refer to binary equilibrium and light curves to ternary equilibrium. (Schairer and Bowen, 1947)

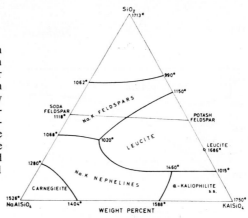

FIGURE 5.19 Melting equilibrium diagram of the ternary system NaAlSiO$_4$–KAlSiO$_4$–SiO$_2$. (After Schairer, 1950). The minimum temperature on the boundary curve feldspar–silica is approximately 960°C. Incumbent pressures of water vapour will displace the boundary curve toward the feldspar field. (After Tuttle and Bowen, 1958), see also figure 5.31

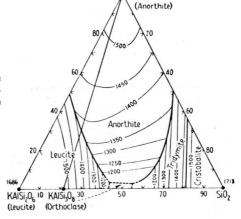

FIGURE 5.20 Melting diagram of the ternary system anorthite–leucite–silica. (Schairer and Bowen, 1947)

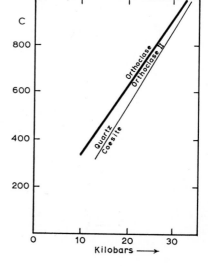

FIGURE 5.21 The field of stability of orthoclase II, a high-pressure variant of the sanidine structure. (Kennedy, 1961)

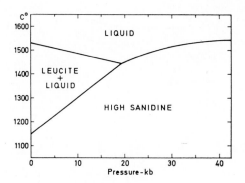

FIGURE 5.22 Melting relations of KAlSi$_3$O$_8$: effect of pressure up to 40 kbar. (Lindsley, 1967)

FIGURE 5.23 Effect of pressure on the melting albite. Light curve after Birch and LeComte (1960) and heavy curve after Boyd and England (1963). The curvature found by Boyd and England is unexpectedly large. The experimentally determined slope at 30–35 kbar is only about half the initial slope. If the curvature persists to higher pressures, as predicted by the Simon equation, its slope would decrease to a value within the range shown by metals. The effect would seem to be a 'warning' of the approaching breakdown into jadeite, see figure 5.24

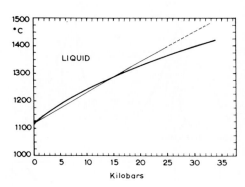

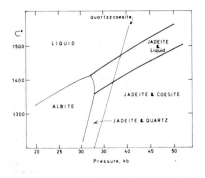

FIGURE 5.24 Phase diagram for albite composition in the system nepheline–silica. (Bell and Roseboom, 1965)

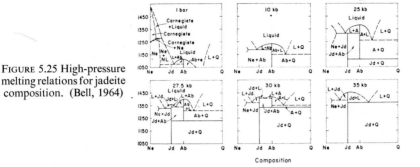

FIGURE 5.25 High-pressure melting relations for jadeite composition. (Bell, 1964)

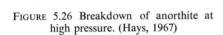

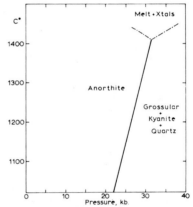

FIGURE 5.26 Breakdown of anorthite at high pressure. (Hays, 1967)

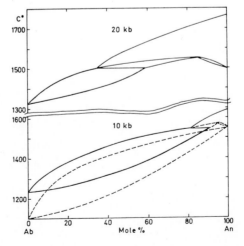

FIGURE 5.27 Melting relations of the plagioclase feldspars at 1 atmosphere (dashed lines), 10 kbar and 20 kbar. (Lindsley, 1967)

15A

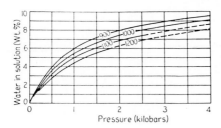

FIGURE 5.28 Solubility of water in albite melts. (Goranson, 1938)

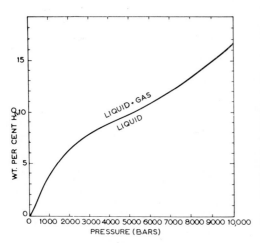

FIGURE 5.29 The solubility of water in albite melt as a function of pressure at temperatures slightly above those of the water-saturated liquidus. The temperature decreases regularly from 870°c at 2000 bar to 690°c at 10,000 bar. The solubilities here determined are in disagreement, especially at pressures below 4000 bar, with those earlier obtained by Goranson (figure 5.28). This suggests that the maximum amounts of water that can be held in solution by melts of granitic composition are considerably *less* than those indicated by the results of earlier experimental work at pressures up to about 4000 bar. On the other hand, amounts of water substantially in excess of 10% can be held in solution by such melts at pressures greater than 5000 bar, or at depths of 20 km or more beneath the earth's surface. (Burnham and Jahns, 1962)

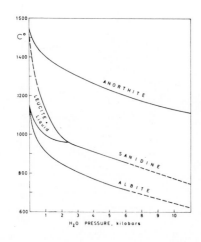

FIGURE 5.30 Melting curves of feldspars under high H_2O pressure. (Yoder, 1958)

FIGURE 5.31 Pressure–temperature projection showing the effect of water vapour pressure on the liquidus of albite, the albite–orthoclase minimum, the quartz–albite euctecti and the ternary minimum in the system $NaAlSi_3O_8$–$KAlSi_3O_8$–SiO_2. (Tuttle and Bowen, 1958)

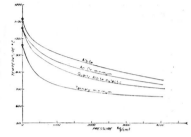

FIGURE 5.32 Comparison of the depression of melting temperature of synthetic feldspars under pressure of a mixture of water vapour and carbon dioxide (unlabelled curves), and under pressure of water vapour alone. (Wyllie and Tuttle, 1959)

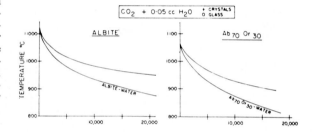

FIGURE 5.33 Isobaric equilibrium relations in the system $NaAlSi_3O_8$–$KAlSi_3O_8$–H_2O projected onto the Ab–Or face of the temperature–composition prism. (Tuttle and Bowen, 1958)

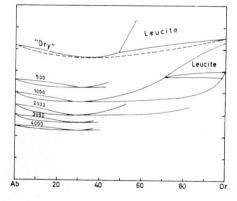

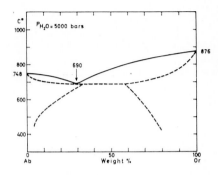

FIGURE 5.34 Projection of the ternary system $NaAlSi_3O_8$–$KAlSi_3O_8$–H_2O at 5000 bar H_2O pressure. Note that the solvus is transected by the solidus. The maximum of the solvus is actually at 715°c and Ab_{55}, but does not appear on this *projection*, since only those assemblages in equilibrium with vapour are indicated. (Yoder and others, 1957)

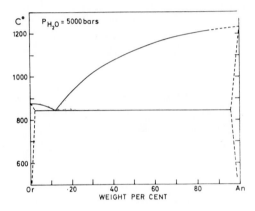

FIGURE 5.35 Projection of the ternary system potassium feldspar–anorthite–H_2O at 5000 bar H_2O pressure. (Yoder and others, 1957)

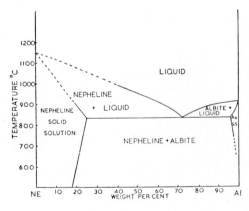

FIGURE 5.36 Phase–equilibrium relations in the system nepheline–albite–water at $P_{H_2O} = 1000$ atm. (Edgar, 1964). Morey (1957) has discussed the possible P–T curves and invariant points in this system

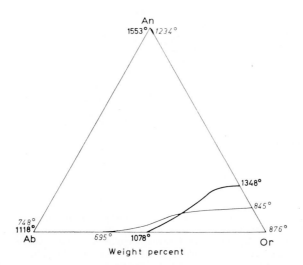

FIGURE 5.37 Projection of the quaternary system Ab–Or–An–H₂O at 5000 bar H₂O pressure superimposed on the ternary melting diagram of the dry system Ab–Or–An. Heavy curves and bold face temperature values refer to the 'dry' system, light curves and italicized temperature values refer to the 'wet' system. (After Yoder and others, 1957; Franco and Schairer, 1951)

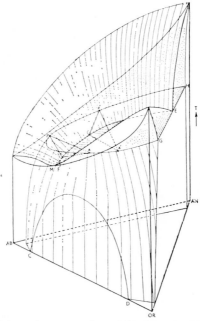

FIGURE 5.38 Schematic presentation of the general relationships in the ternary feldspar system at moderate water vapour pressures. Three main surfaces are depicted within the triangular temperature–composition prism: the liquidus, the solidus and the solvus. The liquidus surface is represented by curved parallel lines dipping down from the melting temperatures of anorthite, albite and orthoclase to intersect in the field boundary EF which separates the field of plagioclase from that of potassium feldspar over most of the area of the triangle

The solidus surface (stippled) meets the liquidus at four points: the melting temperatures of anorthite, albite and orthoclase, and the minimum melting composition in the alkali feldspar system M. The solvus is a dome-shaped surface truncated by two vertical planes: the anorthite–orthoclase join and the alkali feldspar solvus CD. The top of the solvus intersects the solidus along HP′PAA′GE

The field boundary intersects the underlying solvus dome only at E (the anorthite–potassium feldspar eutectic) and thereafter with falling temperature runs towards the alkali feldspar minimum M, which, however, it does not reach, fading out just before at F. This field boundary represents compositions of liquids in equilibrium with two feldspars, a plagioclase (or anorthoclase) and a sanidine. Two hypothetical three-phase triangles (at two different temperatures) are shown, L′P′A′ and LPA, where L represents the composition of the liquid, P the plagioclase feldspar, and A the sanidine; these triangles are parallel to the base of the prism. The coexisting feldspars lie on the intersection of the feldspar solidus (stippled) with the underlying solvus, and the complete trace of this intersection is represented by HP′PAA′G. The truncated solvus dome dips towards the sides of the TX prism and portrays the progressive decrease of ternary solid solution with decrease in temperature. (After Carmichael, 1963)

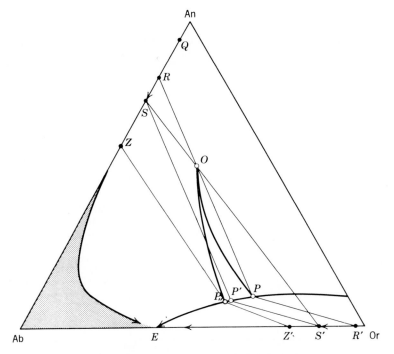

FIGURE 5.39 Schematic illustration of crystallization of feldspars from a deep-seated hydrated magma. (1) Equilibrium is maintained during the crystallization: from the initial liquid O, a plagioclase of composition Q begins to separate. In the course of crystallization the composition of the crystals changes from Q to R, while the melt migrates from O to P in such a way that O always remains on the tie-line between the crystal and the co-existing melt at any one time. At P the boundary curve is reached, and a simultaneous crystallization of plagioclase R and alkali feldspar R′ begins. Thereby the liquid is pushed from P to P′, the crystalline phases simultaneously changing from R to S in the plagioclase series, and from R′ to S′ in the alkali feldspar series. The last vanishing amount of liquid will be at P′, and the now completely solid material will be a mixture of S and S′ in the proportion (O–S′):(O–S). (2) By fractional crystallization the early formed crystals are prevented from reacting completely with the liquid: again the first plagioclase to crystallize has the composition Q. As the crystallizing material changes from Q to Z, Q and other early crystals will not be resorbed; the melt therefore migrates from O to P″ in such a way that the tie-line between crystal and melt at any one time is the tangent to O–P″. At P″ an alkali feldspar of composition Z′ joins, thus the liquid will be pushed to point E where it congeals to a crystal of the same composition. The completely solid material will now be a mixture of plagioclases ranging from Q over Z to E, and of alkali feldspars ranging from Z′ to E. In the Ab corner there are ternary solid solutions that complicate the path of crystallization, but do not affect the principle that by fractional crystallization point E is always reached regardless of the initial position of point O

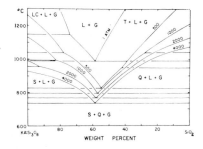

FIGURE 5.40 The effect of H₂O pressure on the melting phenomena in the system KAlSi₃O₈–SiO₂. Melting curves for 1, 500, 1000, 2000 and 4000 bar are shown. (Shaw, 1963)

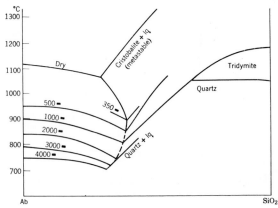

FIGURE 5.41 The effect of H₂O pressure on the melting relations of the system albite–silica. Melting curves for 1, 500, 1000, 2000, 3000 and 4000 bar are shown. (Tuttle and Bowen, 1958)

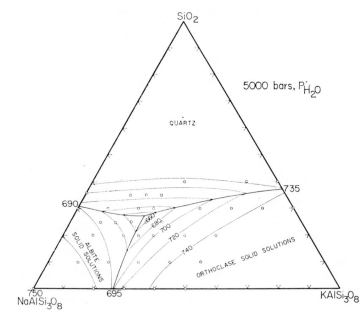

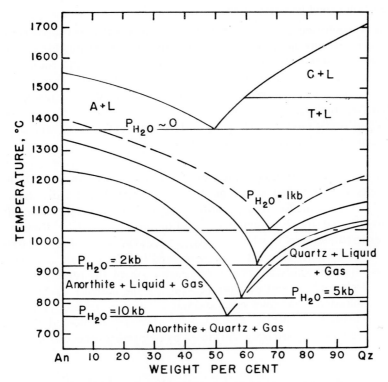

FIGURE 5.43 Projections of the liquidus for water-saturated melts at 0, 1, 2, 5 and 10 kbar in the system anorthite–quartz–water. (Stewart, 1967)

FIGURE 5.42 The 5 kbar equilibrium diagram for the 'granite system', showing the compositions of water-saturated liquids projected onto the anhydrous base of the tetrahedron. This figure differs drastically from comparable isobaric diagrams for the same system at pressures of 3 kbar and less (Tuttle and Bowen, 1958). At 5 kbar the feldspar solvus on the $NaAlSi_3O_8$–$KAlSi_3O_8$ sideline is intersected (in projection), and three primary fields appear on the liquidus: albite solid solution, orthoclase solid solution and quartz. (After Luth, Jahns and Tuttle, 1964)

5.33 Solid–solid transformations

It is mentioned in the introduction to chapter 3 that the fundamental unit of structure in feldspars is the positive Si ion surrounded by four oxygens in tetrahedral coordination (figure 3.1), and furthermore that Machatschki 50 years ago presented the feldspar structures as essentially silica frameworks in which one-quarter to one-half of the tetravalent Si atoms are replaced by trivalent Al.

Transformations in the feldspar structures involve rearrangements of the oxygen tetrahedra. They may result from:

1. Changes in the effective ionic radii of the large cations (K, Na, Ca, Ba) outside the tetrahedra. This mechanism can operate in the dry state.
2. Changes in the Si–Al distribution pattern. The size of the tetrahedra is affected by the aluminium substitution (see p. 102). Therefore, ordered feldspars in which the oxygen tetrahedra are of different size are structurally different from disordered feldspars of the same composition in which all oxygen tetrahedra are of the same size. This order/disorder transformation depends on the mobility of Al and Si by diffusion in the solid state, and water is a necessary catalyst for this mechanism to operate. Donnay and others (1959) showed that the tetrahedra are pried open and closed by diffusing protons and hydroxyl ions.

Such differences in the feldspar structures as, for example, the monoclinic symmetry of Ba-feldspars and of some K-feldspars in contrast to the pronounced triclinic symmetry of the plagioclases—or the displacive transformation monoclinic/triclinic in the high-temperature K–Na feldspar mix-crystal series—correlate with the *effective* radii of the large cations (see p. 127), which through their push slightly rearrange the oxygen tetrahedra. This effect is immediate and independent of catalysts.

On the other hand, structural differences induced by increase in disorder of the Al/Si distribution (and a consequent slight rearrangement of the four oxygen tetrahedra) are, for example: the transitions microcline → orthoclase → sanidine, see figure 3.11; low–high albite, figure 3.17; or the monotropic changes of the hexagonal and orthorhombic forms of $CaAl_2Si_2O_8$ into anorthite. For these transitions, catalysts (protons) are necessary. Davis and Tuttle (1952, p. 113) observed: 'in the presence of water vapour at 1000 kg/cm^2, both forms invert to anorthite at temperatures well below (700°c) those at which no change can be detected when heated in the absence of water'.

Changes at high pressure

All silica frameworks are open structures—the ions are loosely packed and they tend to be unstable at high pressure.

An interesting consequence was just recently understood: the partial

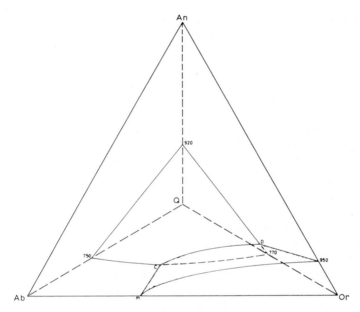

FIGURE 5.44 Schematic isobaric section at 2000 bar vapour pressure of the quinary system $NaAlSi_3O_8$–$CaAl_2Si_2O_8$–$KAlSi_3O_8$–SiO_2–H_2O (albite–anorthite–orthoclase–quartz–water). (After Barth, 1966)

The crystallization process is graphically described by two boundary surfaces dividing the tetrahedron into three regions. The surface 770–920–750 separates liquids (melts) precipitating feldspar (the regions in front of the plane) from those liquids that precipitate quartz (behind the plane).

The plane 950–D–C–m divides the feldspar region into two by separating liquids that precipitate plagioclase (above the plane) from those liquids that precipitate alkali feldspar (below the plane). The line of intersection, C–D, is a cotectic line, and from liquids on this line quartz, plagioclase and alkali feldspar are simultaneously precipitated.

At elevated temperatures (low vapour pressure) the crystallization process becomes more complicated due to the formation of ternary mixed crystals, particularly interesting are compositions close to the base area Ab–m–C–750, see Carmichael (1963) and figure 5.38

and complete vitrification without melting caused by shock waves from meteorite impacts. Feldspars are most susceptible to this type of transformation; next comes quartz, whereas the non-framework silicates (biotite, hornblende, pyroxene, olivine) are unaffected. Von Engelhardt and Stöffler (1966) referred to these semivitreous products as: *diaplectic glasses*. In the meteorite from Shergotty, Tschermak (1872) found a glass of labradoritic composition and called it *maskelynite*; a diaplectic glass.

Low to moderate shocks, giving peak temperatures around 600°c and transient peak pressure in the range 250–500 kbar in a span of time from several microseconds to seconds, are able to partly transform feldspars and quartz to diaplectic glasses in the zone of impact metamorphism. The transformation is highly selective; the original structure of the wall rock is preserved. The transformed feldspars represent pseudomorphs exhibiting the grain boundaries, cleavages and twin lamellae of the primary feldspars.

Characteristic of this stage are deformation bands or platelets of many different orientations. The most prominent and broadest bands—in plagioclases of shocked rocks from Ries Crater (Chao, 1967, Stöffler, 1967)—are 1 to 17 microns wide, they are parallel to (100) (010) and (001). The widths of the bands of the other sets range from less than 0·5 to 3·5 μ and are with decreasing frequency parallel to $(1\bar{2}0)$, (012), (130), (201), $(\bar{1}01)$, $(1\bar{1}0)$, (102). A total of 124 poles (89% of all lamellae) gave 24 different directions of low indices.

Physical properties of diaplectic plagioclase glasses from suevite breccia, Ries Crater, were determined by von Engelhardt and others (1967),

TABLE 5.6

Density and refractivity of plagioclase substances of the same chemical composition[a]

	Density (g/cm³)	Refractive index
Normal plagioclase glass	2·431	1·522
Range of diaplectic plagioclase glasses	2·448– 2·557	1·524– 1·533
Crystalline plagioclase	2·654	1·550

[a] The composition corresponds to Or_8, Ab_{53}, An_{39}. (After von Engelhardt and others, 1967)

and are partly reproduced in table 5.6. It is evident that the diaplectic glasses are physically different from normal glasses and represent transitional states of order between crystalline phases and normal glasses.

FIGURE 5.45 Fields of solid solubility in feldspars at various temperatures (Barth, 1962a). The tie-lines indicate the composition of the coexisting phases. The slope of the tie-lines, expressed by

$$\frac{\text{Mol \% Ab in alkali feldspar}}{\text{Mol \% Ab in coexisting plagioclase}} = k$$

depends upon temperature and is the basis for the two-feldspar thermometer (see Barth, 1962b, 1968). Further data on the solvus and on the subsolidus relations are given by figures 3.20 and 3.23, see also Iiyama (1966)

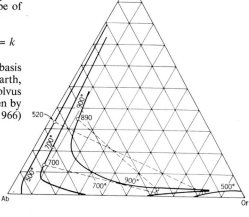

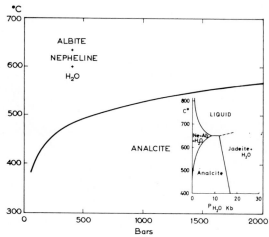

FIGURE 5.46 Stability of albite and nepheline in the presence of water saturated with $NaAlSi_2O_6' H_2O$ (analcite) (Greenwood, 1961). The inset gives the place of the jadeite reaction

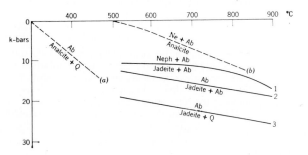

FIGURE 5.47 Phase relations of nepheline, albite and jadeite in the P–T field. (Kennedy, 1961)

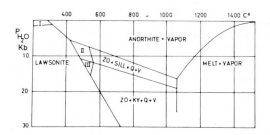

FIGURE 5.48 Equilibrium diagram of the system anorthite–water. Zo = zoisite, Sill = sillimanite, Q = quartz, Ky = kyanite, V = vapour.

I = field of thomsonite,
II = field of pyrophyllite + zoisite + sillimanite + vapour,
III = field of pyrophyllite + zoisite + kyanite + vapour.
(Newton and Kennedy, 1963)

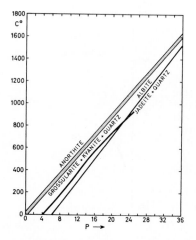

FIGURE 5.49 Feldspar breakdown curves in the P–T field. The straight line for the reaction:

$$NaAlSi_3O_8 \rightarrow NaAlSi_2O_6 + SiO_2$$
$$\text{Albite} \rightarrow \text{Jadeite} + \text{Quartz}$$

represents the earlier results of Birch and LeComte (1960). Newton and Smith (1967) presented an improved equilibrium curve for this reaction based on new experiments and taking account of the entropy change of disordering of albite. The curve, denoted by a heavy line, falls about 2 kbar lower in the 200°c range than the curve of earlier investigations.

The location of the equilibrium curve for the reaction:

$$3\ CaAl_2Si_2O_8 \rightarrow Ca_3Al_2Si_3O_{12} + 2\ Al_2SiO_5 + SiO_2$$
$$15\ \text{An} \rightarrow 8\ \text{Grossularite} + 6\ \text{Kyanite} + \text{Quartz}$$

has an uncertainty indicated by the stippled field. (After Newton, 1966)

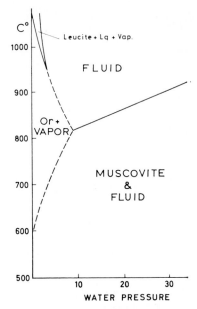

FIGURE 5.50 Melting relations in the system $KAlSi_3O_8-H_2O$. (Seki and Kennedy, 1965)

FIGURE 5.51 The fields of stability of leucite, sanidine + hexagonal kalsilite, and $KAlSi_3O_8 \cdot H_2O$ + hexagonal kalsilite. Full curves after Seki and Kennedy (1964a), dashed curve after Scarfe and others (1965) and Lindsley (1967). There is a discrepancy in the location of the 'pseudoleucite reaction' curve (Lc = Or + Ks). Seki and Kennedy's curve which was determined hydrothermally is displaced to higher pressures; Scarfe and others and Lindsley experimented with water pressure and dry pressure respectively, and agree on the location as given in the diagram

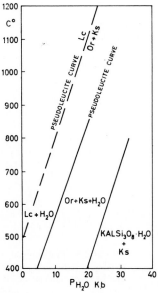

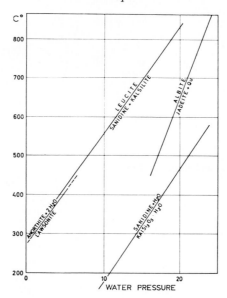

FIGURE 5.52 Comparative representation of phase boundaries of
$KAlSi_3O_8 \cdot H_2O \rightleftharpoons$ sanidine $+ H_2O$, jadeite $+$ quartz $\rightleftharpoons$ albite, sanidine
$+$ hexagonal kalsilite $\rightleftharpoons$ leucite, and lawsonite $\rightleftharpoons$ anorthite $+ 2H_2O$.
(Seki and Kennedy, 1964b)

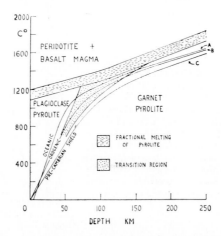

FIGURE 5.53 Petrological model for the upper mantle, showing the locale
in which plagioclase is stable. Potassium feldspar may be stable to greater
depths. The curves A, B and C indicate characteristic geotherms as
labelled. (Ringwood, 1962)

Moderate to high shocks, up to 1000 kbar, first cause selective melting of feldspar grains with formation of normal glasses with vesicles and streaks. Eventually the residual temperature rises to values sufficient to effect total rock melting.

Other consequences of the open structure of feldspars and feldspathoids are:

Nepheline ($NaAlSiO_4$) dissociates at elevated pressure into two phases, jadeite ($NaAlSi_2O_6$) and sodium aluminate, $Na_2O \cdot Al_2O_3$ with 10–20% SiO_2 in solid solution:

$$2\,NaAlSiO_4 \rightarrow \left(\frac{2-4x}{2-3x}\right) NaAlSi_2O_6 + \left(\frac{2}{2-3x}\right) Na_{1-x}Al_{1-x}Si_xO_2$$

The existence of this solid solution was long known, it has the structure of carnegieite (= high-temperature nepheline) with all the extra holes in the lattice stuffed with Na ions (Barth, 1935). But the above reaction of dissociation was first demonstrated by Neuhaus and others (1965). Ringwood and Major (1967), whose experiments invited the same conclusion, did not however favour the explanation. They were apparently not aware of the earlier literature.

The formation of jadeite is of great petrological importance, and has been investigated repeatedly (see figures 5.23–5.25, 5.47, 5.49, 5.52. The latest contribution is by Boettcher and Wyllie, 1967). The thermochemistry of the following reactions has been investigated:

$$NaAlSi_3O_8 + NaAlSiO_4 \rightarrow 2\,NaAlSi_2O_6 \qquad (1)$$
Albite + Nepheline → Jadeite

and

$$2\,NaAlSi_3O_8 \qquad\qquad \rightarrow 2\,NaAlSi_2O_6 + 2\,SiO_2 \qquad (2)$$
Albite → Jadeite + Quartz

For (1):

$\Delta S^0 = -14\cdot6, \quad \Delta H^0 = -6670, \quad \Delta V = -33\cdot6, \quad \Delta G_{298} = -2300\,\text{cal/mol.}$

For (2):

$\Delta S^0 = -14\cdot8, \quad \Delta H^0 = -1230, \quad \Delta V = -34\cdot6, \quad \Delta G_{298} = +3200\,\text{cal/mol.}$

However, Kennedy (1961) found mutual solid solutions between nepheline and albite. His diagram is given in figure 5.47.

A high-pressure variant of the orthoclase structure was suggested by Kennedy's (1961) experiments, see figure 5.21. However, neither the potassium feldspar ($KAlSi_3O_8$) structures, nor the variants of the $KAlSiO_4$ structure show any dissociation at high pressure (up to 55 kbar at 1000°c).

Nor do any major transitions in the structure patterns take place. Crystallochemically this is explained by the larger K ions which more effectively fill the interstices of the skeleton lattice. K-feldspar melts incongruently at 1 atmosphere to leucite + liquid. Goranson (1938) showed that the temperatures of initial and of complete melting are depressed by increasing water pressure, the field leucite + liquid becomes narrower until, at 2·6 kbar water pressure, K-feldspar melts congruently to a water-saturated liquid. Thus for water pressures above 2 kbar the field of leucite in the 'granite system' $NaAlSi_3O_8$–$KAlSi_3O_8$–SiO_2–H_2O becomes negligible (figures 5.19, 5.33 and 5.34).

But leucite, $KAlSi_2O_6$ (density $= 2·47$), which in the equilibrium diagram lies between $KAlSiO_4$ (density $= 2·59$) and $KAlSi_3O_8$ (density $= 2·56$), splits at elevated pressure into the two denser phases (see figure 5.51), the pseudoleucite reaction:

$$2\ KAlSi_2O_6 \rightarrow KAlSi_3O_8 + KAlSiO_4 \qquad (3)$$
$$\text{Leucite} \quad \rightarrow \quad \text{Pseudoleucite}$$

This reaction describes the most important mechanism by which pseudoleucite is formed in some igneous rocks. Leucite breaks down into a mixture of sanidine and hexagonal kalsilite–nepheline solid solutions caused by falling temperature under substantial pressure of water.

Anorthite ($CaAl_2Si_2O_8$) dissociates into grossularite, kyanite and quartz at pressures in the range 20–30 kbar (Hays, 1967), see figure 5.26:

$$3\ CaAl_2Si_2O_8 \rightarrow Ca_3Al_2Si_3O_{12} + 2\ Al_2SiO_5 + SiO_2 \qquad (4)$$

Thermochemical properties of the crystalline phases, $298·15°$k, 1 atm are given in table 5.7.

Plagioclases are mixed crystals of albite and anorthite. The two end members have different breakdown relations, but their breakdown temperatures are rather similar, see figure 5.27. At a given temperature,

TABLE 5.7

Thermochemical data for anorthite and its breakdown products

	Mole V (cal/bar)	Mole S (cal/deg)	ΔH_f^0 (cal)	ΔG_f^0 (cal)
Anorthite	2·408	48·45	−21,810	−23,902
Grossularite	2·996	57·73	−79,673	−75,922
Kyanite	1·054	20·02	−1880	−1275
Quartz	0·542	9·88	0	0

increasing pressure will first affect anorthite, later albite. At, say, 800°c the breakdown pressures are about 18 and 23 kbar respectively. This means that a plagioclase will break down differentially, the last feldspar to disappear will be albitic in composition.

Note that these values cannot be generally used for rock-forming plagioclases in the crust or upper mantle, for the chemical environment exerts great influence. If, for example, nepheline is present, albite will go into jadeite at lower pressures, see reaction (1) and figure 5.47. But under such conditions anorthite also may dissociate at lower pressures according to various relations (see Hays, 1967). A simple possibility is:

$$CaAl_2Si_2O_8 \rightarrow CaAl_2SiO_6 \qquad + SiO_2 \qquad (5)$$
$$\text{Anorthite} \quad \rightarrow \text{Tschermak mol} + \text{Quartz}$$

Here the 'Tschermak mol' together with jadeite from reactions (1) or (2) may enter into omphacitic pyroxenes of the eclogite facies.

There are, at present, no exact data for reaction (5), but Ringwood (1962) estimated the stability region of plagioclase in the crust and upper mantle as shown in figure 5.53.

Reactions between the feldspar minerals and the surrounding rock are of primary importance in petrology. It is now generally recognized that the anorthite content of plagioclase in plagioclase–epidote assemblages increases with increasing metamorphic grade. The possibility of using this relationship as a relative geologic thermometer and facies marker has aroused much discussion.

Kretz (1963) investigated six equilibria relations of this kind, utilizing thereby the Gibbs phase rule and the concept of minimum Gibbs free energy.

The following mineral molecules were used:

8 Ep	$= Ca_2Al_3Si_3O_{12}(OH)$	5 An	$= CaAl_2Si_2O_8$
7 Mu	$= KAl_3Si_3O_{10}(OH)_2$	5 Or	$= KAlSi_3O_8$
10 Chl	$= (Fe,Mg)_5Al_2Si_3O_{10}(OH)_8$	3 Ky	$= Al_2SiO_5$
15 Act	$= Ca_2(Fe,Mg)_5Si_8O_{22}(OH)_2$	4 Px	$= Ca(Fe,Mg)Si_2O_6$
8 Gross	$= Ca_3Al_2Si_3O_{12}$	2 Cc	$= CaCO_3$
		1 Q	$= SiO_2$

The six relations are as follows:

$$16\ Ep + 7\ Mu + 2\ Q = 20\ An + 5\ Or + 2\ H_2O \qquad (6)$$
$$16\ Ep + 3\ Ky + Q = 20\ An + H_2O \qquad (7)$$
$$16\ Ep + CO_2 = 15\ An + 2\ Cc + H_2O \qquad (8)$$
$$48\ Ep + 10\ Chl + 7\ Q = 50\ An + 15\ Act + 6\ H_2O \qquad (9)$$
$$48\ Ep + 15\ Act + 2\ Q = 45\ An + 20\ Px + 4\ H_2O \qquad (10)$$
$$32\ Ep + Q = 25\ An + 8\ Gross + 2\ H_2O \qquad (11)$$

The reader is referred to Kretz's paper for derivations of equations interrelating the composition of plagioclase, temperature, pressure, chemical potential of H_2O and the composition of other solid solutions which take part in the equilibria.

REFERENCES

Allman, R. and Hellner, E. (1962). Indirect calculation of the partial free energy of albite and orthoclase in alkali feldspar. *Norsk Geol. Tidsskr.*, **42**, II (Feldspar Vol.).

Barnes, H. L. (1965). Environmental limitations to mechanics of ore transport. In *Problems of Postmagmatic Ore Deposition*, Vol. II. Prague. p. 316.

Barth, T. F. W. (1935). Non-silicates with cristobalite-like structure. *J. Chem. Phys.*, **3**, 323.

Barth, T. F. W. (1962a). Feldspar solid solutions. *Chem. Erde*, **22**, 31.

Barth, T. F. W. (1962b). The feldspar geologic thermometer. *Norsk Geol. Tidsskr.*, **42**, II (Feldspar Vol.), 330.

Barth, T. F. W. (1966). Aspects of the crystallization of quartzo-feldspathic plutonic rocks. *Tschermaks Mineral. Petrog. Mitt.*, **11**, 209.

Barth, T. F. W. (1968). Additional data for the two-feldspar geothermometer. *Lithos*, **1**, 348.

Bell, P. M. (1964). High-pressure melting relations for jadeite composition. *Carnegie Inst. Wash., Yearbook*, **63**, 179.

Bell, P. M. and Roseboom, E. H. (1965). Phasediagram for the system nepheline–quartz. *Carnegie Inst. Wash., Yearbook*, **64**, 139.

Bichowsky, F. R. and Rossini, F. D. (1936). *Thermochemistry of Chemical Substances*. New York.

Birch, F. and LeComte, P. (1960). Temperature–pressure plane for albite composition. *Am. J. Sci.*, **258**, 209.

Boettcher, A. L. and Wyllie, P. J. (1967). Hydrothermal melting reactions in the system $NaAlSiO_4$–SiO_2–H_2O at pressures above 10 kbar: Jadeite stability (Abstract). Program. *Ann. Meeting Geol. Soc. Am.*, 17.

Bondam, J. (1967). Structural changes in adularia in hydrolytic environments. *Medd. Dansk Geol. Forh.* (*Bull. Geol. Soc. Denmark*), **17**, 358.

Born, M. (1919). Eine thermochemische Anwendung der Gittertheorie. *Verhandl. Deut. Phys. Ges.*, **21**, 13, 679.

Bowen, N. L. (1913). The melting phenomena of plagioclase feldspars. *Am. J. Sci.*, **35**, 577.

Bowen, N. L. and Tuttle, O. F. (1950). The system $NaAlSi_3O_8$–$KAlSi_3O_8$–H_2O. *J. Geol.*, **58**, 489.

Boyd, F. R. and England, J. L. (1961). Melting of silicates at high pressure. *Carnegie Inst. Wash., Yearbook*, **60**, 118.

Boyd, F. R. and England, J. L. (1963). Effect of pressure on the melting of diopside $CaMgSi_2O_6$, and albite, $NaAlSi_3O_8$ in the range up to 50 kilobars. *J. Geophys. Res.*, **68**, 311.

Burnham, C. W. and Jahns, R. H. (1962). A method for determining the solubility of water in silicate melts. *Am. J. Sci.*, **260**, 721.

Campbell, A. S. and Fyfe, W. S. (1965). Analcime–albite equilibria. *Am. J. Sci.*, **263**, 807.

Carmichael, I. S. E. (1963). The crystallization of feldspar in volcanic acid liquids. *Quart. J. Geol. Soc. London*, **119**, 95.

Chao, E. C. T. (1967). Shock effects in certain rock-forming minerals. *Science*, **156**, No. 3772, 192.

Correns, C. W. (1962). Über die chemische Verwitterung von Feldspäten. *Norsk Geol. Tidsskr.*, **42**, II (Feldspar Vol.), 272.

Davis, G. L. and Tuttle, O. F. (1952). Two new crystalline phases of the anorthite composition, $CaO \cdot Al_2O_5 \cdot 2SiO_2$. *Am. J. Sci.* (Bowen Vol.), 107.

Donnay, G., Wyart, J. and Sabatier, G. (1959). Structural mechanism of thermal and compositional transformations in silicates. *Z. Krist.*, **112**, 161.

Edgar, A. D. (1964). Phase–equilibrium relations in the system nepheline–albite–water at 1000 kg/cm^2. *J. Geol.*, **72**, 448.

Eitel, W. (1952). *Thermochemical Methods in Silicate Investigation*. Rutgers Univ. Press.

Engelhardt, W. von, Arndt, J., Stöffler, D., Müller, W. F., Jeziorkowski, H. and Gubser, R. A. (1967). Diaplectische Gläser in den Breccien des Ries von Nördlingen als Anzeichen für Stosswellenmetamorphose. *Contrib. Mineral. Petrolog.*, **15**, 93.

Engelhardt, W. von and Stöffler, D. (1966). Stages of shock metamorphism in crystalline rocks of the Ries basin. Conf. on shock metamorphism of natural materials. April 14–16, 1966. Greenbelt, Md., U.S.A.

Franco, R. R. and Schairer, J. F. (1951). Liquidus temperatures in mixtures of the feldspars of soda, potash and lime. *J. Geol.*, **59**, 259.

Garrels, R. M. and Howard, P. (1959). Relations of feldspars and mica with water at low temperature and pressure. *Clays Clay Minerals Monogr.*, **2**.

Goranson, R. W. (1938). Silicate–water systems: Phase equilibria in the $NaAlSi_3O_8$ and $KAlSi_3O_8–H_2O$ systems at high temperatures and pressures. *Am. J. Sci.*, **35A**, 71.

Greenwood, H. J. (1961). The system $NaAlSi_2O_6–H_2O$–argon: Total pressure and water pressure in metamorphism. *J. Geophys. Res.*, **66**, 3923.

Greig, J. W. and Barth, T. F. W. (1938). The system $Na_2O \cdot Al_2O_3 \cdot 2\ SiO_2$ (nepheline–carnegieite)–$Na_2O \cdot Al_2O_3 \cdot 6\ SiO_2$ (albite). *Am. J. Sci.*, **35A**, 93.

Haber, F. (1919). Betrachtungen zur Theorie der Wärmetönung. *Verhandl. Deut. Phys. Ges.*, **21**, 750.

Hays, J. F. (1967). Lime–alumina–silicates. *Carnegie Inst. Wash.*, *Yearbook*, **65**, 234.

Hemley, J. J. (1959). Mineralogical equilibria in the system $K_2O–Al_2O_3–SiO_2–H_2O$. *Am. J. Sci.*, **257**, 241.

Hemley, J. J. and Jones, W. R. (1964). Chemical aspects of hydrothermal alteration with emphasis on hydrogen metasomatism. *Econ. Geol.*, **59**, 538.

Hess, P. C. (1966). Phase equilibria of some minerals in the $K_2O–Na_2O–Al_2O_3–SiO_2–H_2O$ system at 25°c and 1 atmosphere. *Am. J. Sci.*, **264**, 289.

Iiyama, J. T. (1966). Contribution à l'étude des équilibres sub-solidus du système ternaire orthose–albite–anorthite à l'aide des réactions d'échange d'ions Na–K au contact d'une solution hydrothermale. *Bull. Soc. Franc. Mineral. Crist.*, **89**, 442.

Kapustinsky, A. F. (1933). Über das zweite Prinzip der Kristallchemie. *Z. Krist.*, **86**, 359; *Acta Physiochim. USSR*, **38**, 370 (1943).

Kelley, K. K. (1960). Contributions to the data on theoretical metallurgy XIII: High-temperature heat content, heat capacity and entropy data for the elements and inorganic compounds. *U.S. Bur. Mines, Bull.*, **584** (50 Anniversary).

Kelley, K. K., Todd, S. S., Orr, R. L., King, E. G. and Bonnickson, K. R. (1953). Thermodynamic properties of sodium–aluminium and potassium–aluminium silicates. *U.S. Bur. Mines, Rept. Invest.*, No. **4955** (N.G.U.).

Kennedy, G. C. (1961). Phase relations between nepheline, albite, and jadeite in the P–T field. *Advan. Geophys.*, **7**, 303.

Kracek, F. C. and Neuvonen, K. J. (1952). Thermochemistry of plagioclase and alkali feldspars. *Am. J. Sci.* (Bowen Vol.), 293–318.

Kretz, R. (1963). Note on some equilibria in which plagioclase and epidote participate. *Am. J. Sci.*, **261**, 973.

Lacy, E. D. (1967). Silicate melts and volcanic glasses. *Proc. Geol. Soc. London.* No. **1641**, 171.

Lagache, M. (1965). Contribution à l'étude de l'alteration des feldspaths, dans l'eau, entre 100° et 200°c, sous diverses pressions de CO_2, et application à la synthèse des minéraux argileux. *Bull. Soc. Franc. Mineral. Crist.*, **88**, 223.

Lagache, M., Wyart, J. and Sabatier, G. (1961). Mécanisme de la dissolution des feldspaths dans l'eau pure ou chargé de CO_2 à 200°. *Compt. Rend.*, **253**, 2296.

Lindsley, D. H. (1967). Melting relations of potassium feldspar up to 40 kilobars. *Carnegie Inst. Wash., Yearbook*, **65**, 244.

Luth, W. C., Jahns, R. H. and Tuttle, O. F. (1964). The granite system at pressures of 4 to 10 kilobars. *J. Geophys. Res.*, **69**, 759.

Manus, R. W. (1967). Experimental chemical weathering of two alkali feldspars (Abstract). Program. *Ann. Meeting Geol. Soc. Am.*, 139.

McConnell, J. D. C. and McKie, D. (1960). The kinetics of the ordering process in triclinic $NaAlSi_3O_8$. *Mineral. Mag.*, **32**, 436.

McKie, D. and McConnell, J. D. C. (1963). The kinetics of the low–high transformation in albite I. Amelia albite under dry conditions. *Mineral. Mag.*, **33**, 581–588.

Morey, G. W. (1957). The system water–nepheline–albite. *Am. J. Sci.*, **255**, 461.

Morey, G. W. and Chew, W. T. (1955). The action of hot water on some feldspars. *Am. Mineralogist*, **40**, 996.

Mulert, O. (1912). Über die Thermochemie der Kieselsäure und der Silikate. *Z. Anorg. Chem.*, **75**, 198.

Neuhaus, A. and others (1965). Arbeiten und Betrachtungen zur Synthese und Kristallchemie anorganischer Verbindungen bei hohen Drücken und Temperaturen. Landesamt für Forschung, Nordrhein–Westfalen. *Jahrbuch*, 1965, 487.

Newton, R. C. (1966). Some calc-silicate equilibrium relations. *Am. J. Sci.*, **264**, 204.

Newton, R. C. and Kennedy, G. C. (1963). Some equilibrium relations in the join $CaAl_2Si_2O_8–H_2O$. *J. Geophys. Res.*, **68**, 2967.

Newton, R. C. and Smith, J. V. (1967). Investigations concerning the breakdown of albite at depths in the Earth. *J. Geol.*, **75**, 268.

Orville, P. M. (1963). Alkali ion exchange between vapor and feldspar phases. *Am. J. Sci.*, **261**, 201–237.

Ramberg, H. (1953). Relations between heat of reactions among solids and properties of the constituent ions, and some geochemical implications. *J. Geol.*, **61**, 318.

Ringwood, A. E. (1962). A model for the upper mantle. 1 and 2. *J. Geophys. Res.*, **67**, 857, 4473.

Ringwood, A. E. and Major, A. (1967). Some high pressure transformations of geophysical significance. *Earth Planetary Sci. Letters*, **2**, 106.

Robie, R. B. (1966). Thermodynamic properties of minerals. In Clark, S. P. (Ed.), Handbook of Physical Constants (rev. ed.). *Geol. Soc. Am., Mem.*, **97**.

Rossini, F. D., Wagman, D. D., Evans, W. H., Lewine, S. and Jaffe, I. (1952). Selected values of chemical thermodynamic properties. *U.S. Bur. Standards Circular*, **500**.

Sand, L. B., Roy, R. and Osborn, E. F. (1957). Stability relations of some minerals in the $Na_2O-Al_2O_3-SiO_2-H_2O$ system. *Econ. Geol.*, **52**, 169.

Scarfe, C. M., Luth, W. C. and Tuttle, O. F. (1965). An experimental study bearing on the absence of leucite in plutonic rocks (Abstract). Program, 1965. *Ann. Meeting Geol. Soc. Am.*, 144.

Schairer, J. F. (1950). The alkali-feldspar join in the system $NaAlSiO_4-KAlSiO_4-SiO_2$. *J. Geol.*, **58**, 512.

Schairer, J. F. and Bowen, N. L. (1938). The system leucite–diopside–silica. *Am. J. Sci.* [5], **35A**, 293.

Schairer, J. F. and Bowen, N. L. (1947). The system anorthite–leucite–silica. *Bull. Soc. Geol. Finlande*, **20** (Eskola Vol.), 67.

Schairer, J. F. and Bowen, N. L. (1955). The system $K_2O-Al_2O_3-SiO_2$. *Am. J. Sci.*, **253**, 681.

Schairer, J. F. and Bowen, N. L. (1956). The system $Na_2O-Al_2O_3-SiO_2$. *Am. J. Sci.*, **254**, 129.

Schiebold, E. (1931). Über die Isomorphie der Feldspatminerale. *Neues Jahrb. Mineral. Geol. Paleontol., Abt. A.*, **64**, 251.

Schloemer, H. (1962). Hydrothermalsynthetische gemeinsame Kristallisation von Orthoclas und Quarz. *Radex Rundschau*, **1962**, 133 (English transl., *Geochemistry Intern.*, **1964**, 578).

Seki, Y. and Kennedy, G. C. (1964a). An experimental study of the leucite–pseudoleucite problem. *Am. Mineralogist*, **49**, 1267.

Seki, Y. and Kennedy, G. C. (1964b). The breakdown of potassium feldspar at high temperatures and high pressures. *Am. Mineralogist*, **49**, 1688.

Seki, Y. and Kennedy, G. C. (1965). Muscovite and its melting relations in the system $KAlSi_3O_8-H_2O$. *Geochim. Cosmochim. Acta*, **29**, 1077.

Selby, S. M. (1962) Editor. *Handbook of Physics and Chemistry*, 43rd. ed. Chemical Rubber Co., Ohio.

Shaw, H. R. (1963). The four-phase curve sanidine–quartz–liquid–gas between 500 and 4000 bars. *Am. Mineralogist*, **48**, 883.

Shaw, H. R. (1964). Theoretical solubility of H_2O in silicate melts. Quasi-crystalline models. *J. Geol.*, **72**, 601.

Stewart, D. B. (1967). Four-phase curve in the system $CaAl_2Si_2O_8-SiO_2-H_2O$ between 1 and 10 kilobars. *Schweiz. Mineral. Petrog. Mitt.*, **47**, 35.

Stöffler, D. (1967). Deformation und Umwandlung von Plagioklas durch Stosswellen in den Gesteinen des Nördlingen Ries. *Contrib. Mineral. Petrolog.*, **16**, 51.

Tauson, L. V. (1950). *Dokl. Akad. Nauk SSSR*, **72**, No. 2, 347.

Tschermak, G. (1872). Die Meteoriten von Shergotti und Gopalpur. *Sitzber. Akad. Wiss. Wien*, **65**, 122.

Tuttle, O. F. and Bowen, N. L. (1958). Origin of granite in the light of experimental studies in the system $NaAlSi_3O_8-KAlSi_3O_8-SiO_2-H_2O$. *Geol. Soc. Am., Mem.*, **74**, 1.

Vogt, J. H. L. (1904). Die Silikatschmelzlösungen, II. Über die Schmelzpunkterniedrigung bei Silikatschmelzlösungen. *Norske Videnskab.-Akad. Skrifter Mat.-Naturw. Kl.*, No. 1.

Waldbaum, D. R. (1968). High-temperature thermodynamic properties of alkali feldspars. *Contrib. Mineral. Petrolog.*, **17**, 71.

White, W. P. (1919). Silicate heats. *Am. J. Sci.*, **47**, 1–59.

Wollast, R. (1967). Kinetics of the alteration of K-feldspar in buffered solutions at low temperature. *Geochim. Cosmochim. Acta*, **31**, 635.

Wyllie, P. J. and Tuttle, O. F. (1959). Effect of carbon dioxide on the melting of granite and feldspars. *Am. J. Sci.*, **257**, 648.

Yoder, H. S. (1958). Effect of water on the melting of silicates. *Carnegie Inst. Wash., Yearbook*, **57**, 189.

Yoder, H. S., Stewart, D. B. and Smith, J. R. (1956). Ternary feldspars. *Carnegie Inst. Wash., Yearbook*, **55**, 190.

Yoder, H. S., Stewart, D. B. and Smith, J. R. (1957). Ternary feldspars. *Carnegie Inst. Wash., Yearbook*, **56**, 206.

6

Historical Notes and Old Names

Feldspar was introduced as a mineral name by Daniel Tilas of Stockholm (1740):

*) Feltspat kallar jag ben gemene spaten, som allestäbes i Gråberg förefaller och är ofta af ben hårbhet, at stå emot fil, samt slå elb meb som flinta, til åtstilnab ifrån ben åbla och weka spaten, som följer malm= och mineralstref åt.

'Feltspat I call the common spar found everywhere in Graystone and often of such hardness as to resist the file and give fire like flint, as distinct from the noble and soft spar accompanying streaks of ore and minerals.'

Some seventy years later Hoffmann (1812) divided the feldspars into: *Adular, Labradorstein, gemeiner und glasiger Feldspath, dichter Feldspath.* At this time potassium feldspars, including adularia, were loosely defined.

Albite was named by Berzelius and Gahn (1815); *labradorite* and *anorthite* became known through the studies of Rose (1823), eventually *oligoclase* was added by Breithaupt (1826). Also, Berzelius (1824) had recognized oligoclase as a new mineral. He analysed it and announced it worthy of further investigation. Each of these species, more or less poorly defined, was treated as an individual mineral of constant chemical composition.

Mohs' (1839) designation of the chief species is shown below:

Orthotomer Feld-Spath	corresponds to potassium feldspar
Empyrodoxer Feld-Spath	corresponds to sanidine
Heterotomer Feld-Spath	corresponds to albite
Antitomer Feld-Spath	corresponds to oligoclase
Polychromatischer Feld-Spath	corresponds to labradorite
Anorthomer Feld-Spath	corresponds to anorthite

Eventually about forty isolated minerals of the feldspar family were recognized.

Tschermak (1864) was the first to systematize the feldspar minerals. He presented the idea that all feldspars were mixtures of only three molecules: orthoclase, albite and anorthite (see p. 30).

The series listed by Tschermak are as follows:

K–Na–Feldspars
1. Adularia and orthoclase, mainly potassium feldspar
2. Amazonite, with some sodium feldspar
3. Perthite up to equal amounts of Or and Ab
4. Loxoclase, $Or_1 Ab_1$–$Or_1 Ab_4$
5. Albite with maximum $1 \cdot 2 \%$ K_2O

Na–Ca–Feldspars are isomorphic mixtures of Ab and An

Na:Ca	
1:0	Albite, pericline
3:1	. . .
5:3	Oligoclase, sunstone
1:1	Andesine
3:5	. . .
1:3	Labradorite (with schiller)
1:7	Bytownite
0:1	Anorthite

The Na–Ca–feldspars were called *plagioclases* ($\pi\lambda\acute{\alpha}\gamma\iota o\varsigma$ = slanting) although Breithaupt (1847) introduced the term for *all* feldspars having an oblique angle between the two main cleavages.

The relations between chemical composition and optical properties have been intensively studied in the feldspar group, and practical methods have been developed for determination of the feldspars in thin sections. The plagioclases are particularly well suited: they are triclinic, and the optical indicatrix, which is different for different wavelengths of light, may assume any position in relation to the crystallographic axes. Extinction angles on defined crystallographic faces are therefore unique diagnostic parameters.

Among the first to understand the potentialities, explain the methods, measure the constants and prepare determinative tables were Zirkel (1863), Bertrand (1878). Becke (1892) explained the phenomenon of the

'Becke line' and introduced the immersion method for plagioclase determinations. Viola (1899) prepared various graphs and tables. Comprehensive monographs were prepared by Michel-Lévy (1894–1896), Becke (1906), (see also Des Cloizeaux, 1874).

The universal stage method was developed by Fedorov and made available to the western world through the monograph of Duparc and Reinhard (1924).

During the last 50 years the development has been very rapid, there exist hundreds of published papers contributing to the optical and, recently, x-ray determinations of the feldspars. The results have been collected in textbooks, tables and monographs, so there is no reason for going into further details here, see p. VI.

List of special feldspar names

Adularia—see p. 8, was first described by Pater Pini (1783) who named it *adulaire de St. Gotthard*. At this time St. Gotthard was regarded as a part of the Adula Mountains.

Analbite—a name given by Laves (1960) to a triclinic albite with a 'monoclinic' history. But recent information indicates that no such mineral exists, see p. 123.

Andesine—a name given by Abich (1840) to the 'pseudo-albite' of the andesites of the South American Cordilleras.

Anemousite—see p. 13, derived from the ancient Greek name of the island of Linosa.

Anorthoït—anorthite from Sillböle, Finland, said to be optically uniaxial, negative (Wiik, 1884).

Aventurine—see p. 40. The aventurine effect can be obtained in glass by throwing haphazardly (*en jetant à l'aventure*) small chips of copper into molten glass. Mineralogically there are aventurine quartz and aventurine feldspar. The latter is synonymous with *sunstone* (*Sonnenstein, pierre de soleil*): this name derives from the designation used by Delamétherie (1797): *heliolite* (*helios* = sun); similarly *hecatolite* (*hecate* = moon). L'abbé Haüy (1801) mentions that the feldspars are divided according to lustre into three varieties: *aventuré* (sunstone), *nacré* (moonstone, adularia) and *opalin* (*pierre de labrador*); but himself wants 'orthose' for all feldspars. Scheerer (1845) proved that the famous sunstones from Tvedestrand, Norway, were oligoclases. Des Cloizeaux (1876) showed that also potassium feldspars may exhibit aventurine flitter.

Barbierite—a hypothetical monoclinic albite, see pp. 123 and 127. Name proposed by Schaller (1910) for a so-called albite from Kragerö, Norway, investigated by Barbier and Prost (1908). Barth (1929) showed that the crystallographic measurements and the chemical analysis of Barbier and Prost were unreliable and should not be accepted. Laves (1952) reintroduced 'barbierite' as the name of a hypothetical high-temperature monoclinic form of $NaAlSi_3O_8$. This name was later changed to *monalbite* by Schneider and Laves (1957).

Barsowite—massive, white, subtranslucent, similar to anorthite, occurring as the gangue of blue corundum in Barsovskoi, Russia (Rose, 1839). *Indianite* is the gangue of the corundum of the Carnatic of India described by Count Bourn in 1802. *Carnatite* shows the same mode of occurrence and was pronounced by Breithaupt (1832) to be labradorite.

Baulite—see krablite.

Biotine—mineral from Vesuvius named by Monticelli and Covelli (1825). Brooke (1873b) showed it to be anorthite.

Bytownite—Thomson (1836), analysis by Hunt (1855) from Bytown (now Ottawa), in Ontario, Canada.

Carnatite—see barsowite.

Cassinite—dull bluish aventurine feldspar from Media, Pa., Lea (1866).

Chesterlite—K-feldspar from Poorhouse quarry in Chester Co., Pa., U.S.A., named by Seal (1850), analysed by Smith and Brush (1853).

Christianite—from Monte Somma; was named by Monticelli and Covelli (1825) after Prince Christian Frederik of Denmark who explored Vesuvius with them. Breithaupt (1832) declared it to be ordinary anorthite.

Clevelandite—see p. 12, Brooke (1823) writes: 'albite is generally *blue*, sometimes *red*, its name is consequently bad . . . I have preferred adopting the term Clevelandite.'

Cottaite—from Carlsbad is an orthoclase, Breithaupt (1866).

Cyclopite—a calcic plagioclase occurring in small transparent and glassy crystals, tabular parallel to (010), coating cavities in the dolerite of the Cyclopean Islands, off Sicily. Analysed by von Waltershausen (1853) and measured by von Lasaulx (1881).

Delawarite—pearly orthoclase from Delaware Co., Pa., Lea (1866).

Edler Feldspath—labradorite, Hausmann (1813).

Eisspath (= Ice spar)—used by Werner according to Hoffmann (1812), for glassy feldspar from Monte Somma. Haüy (1822) identified it as ordinary orthoclase. Rose (1829) called it *rhyacolite*.

Ersbyite—true ersbyite is according to Wiik (1883) a colourless microcline from Ersby, Finland. It was named by Nordenskiöld (1853), who measured the angle (010):(001) = 90° 22′ before Des Cloizeaux had established microcline as a mineral species. It is associated with a colourless andesine which Rammelsberg (1860) mistook for ersbyite and by analysis determined to be a 'kalk-labrador'.

Erythrite—Thomson (1843), a flesh red variety of orthoclasic feldspar from Kilpatrick in Dunbartonshire, Scotland.

Esmarkite—There are several substances of this name; 'la véritable esmarkite' is according to Des Cloizeaux (1870) an anorthite high in SiO_2 from Bamble, Norway.

Felsit—was proposed by Breithaupt (1830b) to be used instead of feldspath.

Hafnefiordit—a glassy andesine in lava from Hafnarfjördur, Iceland (Forchhammer, 1842).

Hecatolite ($\dot{\epsilon}\kappa\alpha\tau\eta$ = moon)—see moonstone.

Heliolite ($\dot{\eta}\lambda\iota\sigma\varsigma$ = sun)—see aventurine.

Huronite—an impure anorthite-like feldspar. Named by Thomson (1836).

Hyposklerit—feldspar of small hardness ($\dot{\upsilon}\pi\dot{\sigma}$ = under) and of dark green colour from the 'layered formation' of Arendal, Norway. Named by Breithaupt (1830a); analysed by Rammelsberg (1850), who declared it to be albite with the green colour coming from impurities of pyroxene.

Indianite—see barsowite.

Kieselspath—is an albite from Chesterfield, Mass., U.S.A., investigated by Hausmann (1817). Later used synonymously with albite (Hausmann, 1847).

Krablite = Kraflite = Baulite—liparite (ejectementa) from a crater near Krafla, NW Iceland, analysed by Forchhammer (1842) and regarded by him as a special feldspar. This view was adopted by von Waltershausen (1853), but was finally refuted by Flink (1886).

Lasur-Feldspath—Nordenskiöld (1857).

Lennilite—greenish orthoclase from Lenni, Delaware Co., Pa., Lea (1866).

Loxoklas ($\lambda o \xi \acute{o} \varsigma$ = oblique)—(Breithaupt, 1846), analysed by Smith and Brush (1853), alkali feldspars in translucent crystals with calcite and diopside from Hammond, N.Y., U.S.A. It has a green tinge coming from small inclusions of diopside. Tschermak (1864) proposed the loxoclase series: $Or_1 Ab_1$–$Or_1 Ab_4$ with K_2O in the range 7–4%.

Maskelynite—a meteorite mineral first described by Tschermak (1872, 1883); its true nature and genesis was obscure until Milton and De Carli (1963) proved the identity of maskelynite with certain diaplectic glasses in shattered rocks surrounding impact craters of large meteorites. Maskelynite is a diaplectic glass formed by vitrification of plagioclase feldspar in rocks transfigured by shock waves, see section 5.31.

Mauilite, mauite—andesine in basalt of the island of Maui, Hawaii (Thomson, 1836).

Mikroklase—adularia of triclinic habit (Wiik, 1884).

Mikroklin—Breithaupt (1830b) thought that some orthoclases did not cleave at a right angle, and called them therefore mikroklin (micro + -cline). Geometric asymmetry was also observed on adularia, first by Breithaupt (1847) and, in particular, by vom Rath (1868), who, however, in accordance with the ideas of his time, declared: 'ähnliche Abweichungen können unmöglich einen Zweifel an dem monoklinen Character des Feldspathsystems aufkommen lassen'.

Des Cloizeaux (1862–1874) found among the amazonites two varieties, one orthoclasic, the other triclinic, whose cleavage angle differed only 10 to 20 minutes of arc from 90°. This constitutes '*le véritable microcline de Breithaupt*'. Later Des Cloizeaux (1876) found under the microscope that certain 'orthoclases' were built up of innumerable twin lamellae showing triclinic symmetry. Mallard (1876, 1881) and Michel-Lévy (1879) demonstrated mathematically that the monoclinic symmetry and optical properties of orthoclase could be explained on the assumption that it was built up from regular submicroscopic lamellae of microcline that were twinned according to the albite–pericline laws. Thus orthoclase and microcline would be identical minerals, only differing in their twin structure. By studying the twin geometry of such crystals Böggild (1911) succeeded in determining the following crystallographic elements with astonishing accuracy:

$a:b:c = 0.663:1:0.5$; $\alpha = 90° 42'$, $\beta = 115° 50'$, $\gamma = 87° 50'$

(no suitable terminal faces were present for determining c). Following the convention of his time Böggild oriented the crystal by a 180° rotation around the b axis as compared to the present orientation. Böggild's published values for α and γ are therefore the supplements of those given here, see Laves (1952).

Mikrotin—($\mu\iota\kappa\rho\acute{o}\tau\eta\varsigma$ = small) a name for glassy plagioclases, corresponding to sanidine for glassy alkali feldspars. Proposed by Tschermak (1864).

Monalbite—p. 123, see barbierite.

Moonstone—see p. 9. Hausmann (1847) defined it as 'Adular mit blauem Lichtschein'.

Mornite—glassy labradorite from basalt, Antrim, Ireland (Thomson, 1836)—see silicite.

Murchisonite—is a flesh red perthitic feldspar with good cleavage and often gold–yellow reflections in a direction $\perp$ (010) and nearly parallel to ($\bar{8}$01); from Dawlish and Heavitree, Devonshire, England. First described by Levy (1827). Brooke (1837a) proposed that moonstone and the iridescent feldspar from Frederiksværn, Norway, also be called murchisonite.

Necronite—(Hayden, 1819). Mother of pearl blue orthoclase in limestone near Baltimore yielding a fetid smell by hammering. A similar feldspar occurs at Balvraid, Glenelg, Scotland ($\nu\epsilon\kappa\rho o\varsigma$ = corpse), see Heddle (1877).

Olafite—albite from Snarum, Norway. Milky-white translucent with twins of the albite–carlsbad type, or geniculate after (100), Breithaupt (1866), Des Cloizeaux (1876).

Pantellarit—Abich (1849), glassy albite from the island of Pantellaria, south of Sicily.

Paradoxit—Breithaupt (1830b), Adularia from the tin mines near Marienberg.

Parorthoklas—proposed by Zirkel (1893) for anorthoclase.

Pegmatolith—Breithaupt (1830b) = orthoclase.

Pericline—see p. 12. A new 'species' of albite (Breithaupt, 1823). ($\pi\epsilon\rho\iota\kappa\lambda\iota\nu\acute{\eta}\varsigma$ = steep, 'wegen der stärkeren Neigung der terminalen Flächen auf die erste Laterale'.)

Peristerite—see p. 37 (περιστεά a pigeon). The name was first used by Thomson (1843) for an iridescent feldspar from Perth Co. in Canada. But this specimen seems to have been a (crypto) perthite. Later Hunt (1850) analysed an oligoclase from the same locality. Breithaupt (1858) regarded it as an albite. Now used in the sense of Böggild (1924) for unmixed sodic plagioclases.

Perthite—see p. 17, was first described by Thomson (1843) (from Perth Co. in Canada). 'It is very much connected with feldspar in appearance . . . could it be produced in sufficient quantity, it would be an excellent material for the manufacture of porcelain.' His analysis corresponded to a Mg–Al silicate without any alkalis.

Breithaupt's (1861) and Gerhard's (1861) investigations revealed that many feldspars were lamellar intergrowths of orthoclase and albite (or oligoclase). Tschermak (1864) showed that the lamellae were oriented parallel to certain crystallographic directions: (1) parallel to (100), usual in sanidine; (2) parallel to (110) and (1$\bar{1}$0), usually in combinations with lamellae after (100); (3) parallel to (010), rare. In figure 1.15, the original drawings of Tschermak are reproduced.

Radauit—a labradorite supposed to have a high density (Breithaupt, 1866).

Rhyakolith (ῥύαξ = lava), glassy feldspar—see eisspath. Rose (1829, 1833) thought it was different from other glassy feldspars because of a high content of Na_2O. But later (1852) he found many other examples of high soda orthoclases and proposed the name as a synonym for glassy feldspars.

Saccharit—described by Glocker (1844) from a chrysophrase mine at Frankenstein in Silesia as a special feldspar related to andesine. Von Lasaulx (1878) proved it to be a mixture of andesine and alkali feldspar, in places quartz is also present.

Sigterit—from Sigterö near Brevik, Norway, is a mixture of albite and nepheline 1:2, see Tenne (1891).

Silicite—is a labradorite in basalt from Antrim, Ireland (Thomson, 1843)—see mornite.

Sunstone—see aventurine.

Tetartin—a name introduced by Breithaupt (1823) for albite because the tetartohedral symmetry (= triclinic symmetry) was first recognized by the terminal faces of this feldspar.

Thjorsauite--(Genth, 1848) anorthite from Hekla lava at the river Thjorsá, Iceland.

Tschermakit—first used by von Kobell (1873) for a grey-white feldspar containing some magnesium but no calcium from Bamble, Norway, with twin striae on the cleavage plane. According to Des Cloizeaux (1883) it has the optical properties of an albite. Later used by Crustschoff (1894) for a plagioclase (oligoclase) in a variolitic granite from Altai.

Valencianite—adularia from Valenciana Mine, Guanajuato, Mexico. Name proposed by Breithaupt (1830b) because of assumed differences in angles and in the density. According to Des Cloizeaux (1876) it is pure orthoclase without any soda.

Vosgite—a feldspar intermediate between anorthite and labradorite from the porphyry of Ternuay in the Vosges, France (Delesse, 1847).

Weissigit—is a pale red orthoclase in porphyrite from Weissig near Dresden (Jenzsch, 1853).

Zygadite—from Andreasberg in the Harz is translucent or milky albite, twinned according to the pericline law. It occurs in fissures with quartz, stilbite and blende. Named by Breithaupt (1846), recognized as albite by Krenner (1884) ($\zeta v \gamma \alpha \delta \iota v$ = in pairs or twinned).

Pseudomorphs and altered feldspars, particularly altered calcium feldspars are poorly defined substances; they had been given various names: amphodelite, diploite, latrobite, lepolite, lindsayite (linseite), sundvikite, tankite, unionite. Rosellan (roselite, rosite) and polyargite are pinite-like pseudomorphs. They have been investigated by Fischer (1871) and by Des Cloizeaux (1875).

REFERENCES

Abich, H. (1840). Beiträge zur Kentniss des Feldspaths. *Pogg. Ann. Phys. Chem.*, **51**, 519.

Abich, H. (1849). *Berg- Hüttenmänn. Z.*, **19**.

Barbier, P. and Prost, A. (1908). Sur l'existence d'un feldspath sodique mono-clinique isomorphe de l'orthose. *Bull. Soc. Chim.*, **3**, 894.

Barth, T. F. W. (1929). Über den monoklinen Natronfeldspat. *Z. Krist.*, **69**, 476.

Becke, F. (1892). Petrographische Studien, etc.: Mickroskopische Physiographie der Gemengteile. *Sitzber. Akad. Wiss., Wien*, **102**; *Tschermaks Mineral. Petrog. Mitt.*, **13**, 385.

Becke, F. (1906). Die optischen Eigenschaften der Plagioklase. *Tschermaks Mineral. Petrog. Mitt.*, **25** (Tschermak Vol.), 1.

Bertrand, E. (1878). De l'application du microscope a l'étude de la minéralogie. *Bull. Soc. Mineral. France*, **1**, 22.

Berzelius, J. (1824). Nytt mineral i granitbergen kring Stockholm. *Årsberättelse, Kgl. Vetenskap Akad. Stockholm*, 160.

Berzelius, J. and Gahn, J. G. (1815). Undersökning af några i grannskapet af Fahlun funna Fossilier. *Afhandl. Fys. Kemi, Mineral.*, **4**, 180.

Böggild, O. B. (1911). Über die Kristallform des Mikroklins. *Z. Krist.*, **48**, 466.

Böggild, O. B. (1924). On the labradorization of feldspars. *Kgl. Danske Videnskab. Selskab. Medd.*, **6**, Nr. 3.

Breithaupt, A. (1823), (1832). *Vollständige Charakteristik des Mineral Systems*. Arnoldi. Dresden (3rd ed., 1832).

Breithaupt, A. (1826). Bemerkungen über das Geschlecht des Feldspath-Grammits und Beschreibung des Oligoklases, einer neuen Spezies desselben. *Pogg. Ann. Phys. Chem.*, **8**, 238.

Breithaupt, A. (1829). Neu Gewichtbestimmungen verschiedener zum grossen Theil darauf noch gar nicht untersuchten Mineralien. *Schweigger J. Chem. Phys.*, **55**, 246.

Breithaupt, A. (1830a). *Übersicht des Mineral-Systems*. Engelhardt, Freiberg.

Breithaupt, A. (1830b). Über die Felsite und einige neue Specien ihres Geschlechts. *Schweigger J. Chem. Phys.*, **60**, 316.

Breithaupt, A. (1846). Loxoklas (Felsites Loxoclasius), ein neues Glied des Felsit-Genus. *Pogg. Ann. Phys. Chem.*, **67**, 419.

Breithaupt, A. (1846). Neue Mineralien. *Pogg. Ann. Phys. Chem.*, **69**, 441.

Breithaupt, A. (1847). Handbuch Mineralogie, III. Arnold, Leipzig. p. 509.

Breithaupt, A. (1858). Neue Beobachtungen an Felsiten. *Berg- Hüttenmän. Z.*, **17**, 1.

Breithaupt, A. (1861). Über die regelmässige Verwachsung von je zwei Felsit-Specien. *Berg- Hüttenmän. Z.*, **20**, 69.

Breithaupt, A. (1866). Mineralogische Studien. *Berg- Hüttenmän. Z.*, **25**, 38, 86.

Brooke, H. J. (1823). A description of the crystalline form of some new minerals. *Ann. Phil.* [2], **5**, 381.

Brooke, H. J. (1837a). On the crystallographic identity of certain minerals. *Phil. Mag.*, **10**, 170.

Brooke, H. J. (1837b). On the identity of two minerals from Vesuvius named biotine and anorthite. *Phil. Mag.*, **10**, 368.

Chrustschoff, C. (1894). Holokristalline makrovariolitische Gesteine. *Mem. Acad. Sci., St. Petersbourg* [8], **42/3**, 25.

Delamétherie, J. C. (1797). *Théorie de la Terre*, Vol. 2. Maradau, Paris. p. 200.

Delesse, A. (1847). Sur la constitution mineralogique et chimique des roches des Vosges. *Ann. Mines* [4], **12**, 283.

Des Cloizeaux, A. (1862–1874). *Manuel de Mineralogie* I, Paris, 1862; II, Paris, 1874.

Des Cloizeaux, A. (1870). La véritable nature d'Esmarkite. *Ann. Chim. Phys.* [4], **19**, 176.

Des Cloizeaux, A. (1875). Mémoir sur les propriétés optiques birefringentes des quatre principeaux feldspaths tricliniques. *Ann. Chim. Phys.* [5], **4**; *Compt. Rend.*, **80**, 364.

Des Cloizeaux, A. (1876). Mémoir sur l'existence; les propriétés optiques et cristallographiques, et la composition chimique du microcline, nouvelle espèce de feldspath tricliniques á base de potasse, suivi de remarques sur l'examen microscopique de l'orthose et des divers feldspaths tricliniques. *Ann. Chim. Phys.* [5], **9**, 433.

Des Cloizeaux, A. (1883). Nouvelles récherches sur l'écartement des axes optiques, l'orientation de leur plan et de leurs bisectrices et leur divers genres de dispersion, dans l'albite et l'oligoclase. *Bull. Soc. Mineral. France*, **6**, 89.

Duparc, L. and Reinhard, M. (1924). La détermination des plagioclases dans les coupes minces. *Mem. Soc. Phys. Hist. Nat.*, *Geneve*, **40**, 1.

Fischer, H. (1871). *Kritische Mikroskop.-Mineralogische Studien.* Freiburg i.B.

Flink, G. (1886). Kraflit från Krafla, Island. Bihang *Kgl. Svenska Vetenskaps. Handl.*, **12**, 2, No. 2, 64.

Forchhammer, G. (1842). Analyser af Mineralier fra Island og Færöerne, etc. *Skand. Naturforsk. Möde. Danske Videnskap. Selskabs. Forh.*, 43.

Genth, F. A. (1848). Untersuchung der Eruptionsproducte des Hekla. *Ann. Chem. Pharm.*, **66**, 18.

Gerhard, D. (1861). Über lamellare Verwachsung zweier Feldspathspecies. *Z. Deutsch. Geol. Ges.*, **14**, 151; *Z. Ges. Naturwiss.*, **19**, 475, (1862).

Glocker, E. F. (1844). Ueber den Saccharit. *Pogg. Ann. Phys. Chem.*, **61**, 385; *J. Prakt. Chem.*, **34**, 494 (1858).

Hausmann, J. F. L. (1813), (1847). *Handbuch der Mineralogie*, Göttingen (2nd ed., 1847).

Hausmann, J. F. L. (1817). Lecture 4/9: Göttingische gelehrte Anzeigen, *Kgl. Ges. Wiss.*, **1817**, 1401.

Haüy, R. J. (1801). *Traité de Minéralogie*, II. Paris. p. 590.

Haüy, R. J. (1822). *Traité de Minéralogie*, III. Bachelier, Paris. p. 101.

Hayden, H. H. (1819). Extract of letter to the Editor. *Am. J. Sci.*, **1**, 306.

Heddle, M. F. (1877). Chapter on the mineralogy of Scotland II: The feldspars. *Trans. Roy. Soc. Edinburgh*, **28**, 197.

Hessel, J. F. (1826). Ueber die Familie Feldspath. Taschenb. gesammt Mineralogie; *Z. Mineral.*, **1**, 289.

Hintze, C. (1897). *Handbuch der Mineralogie* II, *Feldspathgruppe*, Leipzig. pp. 1332–1554.

Hoffmann, C. A. S. (1812). *Handbuch der Mineralogie*, II. Graz., Freiberg. p. 369.

Hunt, T. S. (1855). Analyses of various feldspars. *Phil. Mag.*, **9**, 354.

Jenzsch, G. (1853). Amygdalophyr, ein Felsitgestein mit Weissigit, einem neuen Minerale in Blasen-Räumen. *Neues Jahrb. Mineral.*, **1853**, 396; **1854**, 405; **1855**, 800.

Kobell, F. von. (1873). Über den Tschermakit, eine neue Mineralspezies der Gruppe der Feldspäthe. *Sitzber. K. Bayer Akad. Wiss.*, 6 Dec.

Krenner, J. A. (1884). Über den Zygadit. *Math. Termeszettudomanyi Ertesito*, **3**, 146.

Lasaulx, A. von. (1878). Ueber den Saccharit. *Neues Jahrb. Mineral.*, **1878**, 623.

Lasaulx, A. von. (1881). Ueber einige ätnische Mineralien. *Z. Krist.*, **5**, 326.

Laves, F. (1952). Phase relations of the alkali feldspars. *J. Geol.*, **60**, 436.

Laves, F. (1960). Al/Si Verteilungen, Phasen, Transformationen und Namen der Alkalifeldspäte. *Z. Krist.*, **113**, 265.

Lea, I. (1866). *Proc. Akad. Philadelphia*, May, 1866.

Levy, A. (1827). On a new mineral substance, proposed to be called Murchisonite. *Phil. Mag.*, **1**, 448.

Mallard, F. (1876), (1881), (1884). Explications des phénomènes optiques anomaux que présent un grand nombre de substances cristallisées. *Ann. Mines*, **10**, 187 (1876); *Bull. Soc. Mineral, France*, **4** (1881); *Traité de Cristallographie*, II. Paris (Dunod), 1884. p. 263.

Michel-Lévy, A. (1879). Identité probable du microcline et de l'orthose. *Bull. Soc. Mineral. France*, **2**, 135.

Michel-Lévy, A. (1883). Sur les positions d'égale intensité lumineuse de deux minéraux juxtaposés en plaque mince. *Bull. Soc. Mineral. France*, **5**, 219.

Michel-Lévy, A. (1894), (1896), (1904). Etude sur la détermination des Feldspaths dans les plaques minces. Boudoy, Paris, 1894, 1896, 1904.

Milton, D. J. and De Carli, P. S. (1963). Maskelynite: formation by explosive shock. *Science*, **140**, 670.

Mohs, F. (1839). *Leichtfassliche Anfangsgründe der Naturgeschichte des Mineralreichs*, II. Gerold, Wien.

Monticelli, F. and Covelli, N. (1825). *Prodrome della Mineral. Vesuv.* p. 428.

Nöggerath, J. (1808). *Mineral. Studien d.Gebirge Niederrhein.* Bonn. p. 25.

Nordenskiöld, A. E. (1853). *Beskrifning öfver i Finland funna Mineralier.* Helsingfors. p. 129.

Nordenskiöld, A. E. (1857). *Bull. Nat. Moscow*, **30**, 225.

Pini (Pater). (1783). Mémoir Feldspath. *Mem. Soc. Ital.*, **3**, 688 (Milano).

Rammelsberg, C. (1850). Über den Hyposklerit von Arendal. *Pogg. Ann. Phys. Chem.*, **79**, 305.

Rammelsberg, C. (1860), (1875). *Handbuch der Mineralchemie.* W. Engelmann, Leipzig. p. 595 (2nd ed., 1875).

Rath, G. vom. (1868). Über die Winkel der Feldspathkrystalle. *Jahrb. Chem. Phys.*, **30**, 324.

Rose, G. (1823). Über den Feldspath Albit, Labrador und Anorthit. *Ann. Phys. L. W. Gilbert*, **73**, 173.

Rose, G. (1829). Über den glasigen Feldspath. *Pogg. Ann. Phys. Chem.*, **15**, 193.

Rose, G. (1833). Über die chemische Zusammensetzung des glasigen Feldspaths und des Rhyakoliths. *Pogg. Ann. Phys. Chem.*, **28**, 151.

Rose, G. (1839). Beschreibung einiger neuen Mineralien des Urals. *Pogg. Ann. Phys. Chem.*, **48**, 567.

Rose, G. (1852). *Das Krystallochemische Mineralsystem.* W. Engelmann, Leipzig. p. 88.

Schaller, W. T. (1910). La barbierite, un feldspath sodique monoclinique. *Bull. Soc. Franc. Mineral.*, **33**, 320.

Scheerer, Th. (1845). Untersuchung des Sonnensteins. *Pogg. Ann. Phys. Chem.*, **64**, 153.

Schneider, T. R. and Laves, F. (1957). Barbierit oder Monalbit? *Z. Krist.*, **109**, 241.

Seal, I. (1850). In Dana, *Mineralogy*.

Smith, J. L. and Brush, G. J. (1853). Reexamination of American minerals II. *Am. J. Sci.*, **16**, 43.

Tenne, C. A. (1891). Über den Sigterit Rammelsberg's und über den Albit von Sigterö. *Neues Jahrb. Mineral.*, **2**, 206.

Thomson, T. (1836). *Outlines of Mineralogy, Geology and Mineral Analyses*, I. London.

Thomson, T. (1843). Notice of some new minerals. *Phil. Mag.*, **22**, 188.

Tilas, D. (1740). Tanckar om Malmletande, i anledning af löse gråstenar. *Vet. Akad. Handl. Stockholm*, **1**, 198–201.—*See also* Zenzén (1925).

Tschermak, G. (1864). Chemisch–mineralogische Studien I: Die Feldspath-gruppe. *Sitzber. Akad. Wiss.*, *Wien*, **50**, 526.

Tschermak, G. (1872). Die Meteoriten von Shergotty und Gopalpur. *Sitzber. Akad. Wiss.*, *Wien*, **65**, 122.

Tschermak, G. (1883). Beitrag zur Klassifikation der Meteoriten. *Sitzber. Akad. Wiss.*, *Wien*, **88**, 347.

Viola, C. (1899). Über Bestimmung und Isomorphismus der Feldspathe. *Z. Krist.*, **30**, 23, 232.

Waltershausen, W. von. (1853). Über die vulkanischen Gesteine in Sicilien und Island und ihre submarine Umbildung. Dietrich, Göttingen.

Wiik, F. J. (1883). Mitteilungen über finnische Mineralien. *Z. Krist.*, **7**, 16.

Wiik, F. J. (1884). Mineralogische Mitteilungen. *Z. Krist.*, **8**, 203; **23**, 379 (1894).

Zenzen, N. (1925). On the first use of the term Feltspat by Daniel Tilas in 1740. *Geol. Foren. Stockholm Forh.*, **47**, 390.

Zirkel, F. (1863). Mikroskopische Gesteinsstudien. *Sitzber. Akad. Wiss.*, *Wien*, **47**, 226.

Zirkel, F. (1893). *Lehrbuch der Petrographie*, I. W. Engelmann, Leipzig. p. 238.

Author Index

Aberdam, D., 26
Abich, H., 241, 245
Allen, E. T., 31, 159, 160, 161
Allman, R., 201
Andersen, O., 20, 40, 41
Anderson, G. H., 8
Ansilewski, J., 120
Antun, P., 45
Aoki, K., 44

Bächlin, R., 71, 72
Baier, E., 43, 79
Bailey, S. W., 90, 102, 106, 108, 109, 112, 152
Bambauer, H. U., 31, 115, 118, 119, 120, 138
Barber, C. T., 79
Barbier, P., 123, 242
Barnes, H. L., 202, 205
Barrer, R. M., 50
Barth, T. F. W., 4, 13, 20, 35, 45, 46, 66, 70, 73, 90, 104, 114, 120, 124, 127, 129, 130, 155, 158, 211, 225, 227, 231, 242
Baskin, Y., 50, 71, 133
Battey, M. H., 82
Becke, F., 20, 34, 240, 241
Beckenkamp, J., 177
Becker, G. F., 160
Bell, P. M., 214, 215
Bentor, Y. K., 36, 37
Berek, M., 66
Berman, H., 154
Bertrand, E., 240
Berzelius, J., 10, 239
Bichowsky, F. R., 192
Birch, F., 214, 228
Bloss, F. D., 14, 135
Boettcher, A. L., 231
Böggild, O. B., 38, 245, 246
Bollman, W., 9, 39, 43
Bondam, J., 201

Bonnickson, K. R., 195
Boone, C. M., 35
Born, M., 189, 190
Bottinga, Y., 34
Boudette, E. L., 45
Bowen, N. L., 33, 120, 135, 166, 167, 171, 186, 191, 195, 197, 201, 210, 211, 212, 217, 222, 223
Bown, M. G., 136
Boyd, F. R., 171, 214
Breithaupt, A., 4, 17, 239, 240, 242, 243, 244, 245, 246, 247
Brögger, W. C., 6, 19, 20
Brooke, H. J., 242, 245
Brousse, R., 46
Brown, B. E., 90, 106, 109, 152
Brown, W. L., 38, 39, 60, 127, 135, 161
Brush, G. J., 242, 244
Bunch, T. E., 4
Burnham, C. W., 202, 216
Burri, C., 61, 62

Calkins, F. C., 30
Cannon, R. T., 35, 81
Carman, J. H., 14, 28
Carmichael, I. S. E., 45, 159, 163, 164, 220, 225
Carstens, H., 27, 36, 37, 42, 82
Catanzaro, E. J., 8
Chaisson, U., 9, 118, 120
Chandrasekhar, S., 90, 135
Chao, E. C. T., 226
Chao, S. H., 91
Chen, W. T., 202
Christie, O. H. J., 38, 39, 40, 117
Chrustschoff, C., 247
Chudoba, K., 153
Cole, W. F., 90, 91, 94, 152, 157, 159
Compton, R. R., 49
Corlett, M., 31

Cornelius, H. P., 36
Correns, C. W., 202
Cott, H. C., van 38
Covelli, N., 249
Crawford, M. L., 38, 39
Crump, R. M., 159

Darbyshire, J. A., 88
Davis, G. L., 134, 224
Day, A. L., 31, 159, 160, 161
De Carli, 244
Deer, W. A., 37
Degens, E. T., 50
Delametherie, J. C., 241
Delesse, A., 247
Des Cloizeaux, A., 4, 8, 241, 243, 244, 245, 247
De Waard, D., 38, 49
Dietrich, R. V., 117
Doman, R. C., 43, 138, 161
Donnay, G., 126, 128, 132, 134, 152, 154–159, 224
Donnay, J. D. H., 75–78, 126, 128, 132, 134, 152, 154–159
Donnelly, T. W., 48
Douglas, J. A., 167
Drescher–Kaden, F. K., 18
Drugman, J., 63
Duffin, W. J., 14
Duparc, L., 4, 63, 70, 241

Edgar, A. D., 218
Ehlers, E. G., 14, 134
Eitel, W., 190, 193, 196, 197
Elliott, R. B., 48
Elliston, J., 5
Emerson, D. O., 8
Emmons, R. C., 34, 66, 79
Endo, Y., 24
Engelhardt, W. von, 150, 226
England, J. L., 171, 214
Ernst, E., 44
Euler, R., 79
Evans, B. W., 38

Fedorow, E. V., 60
Ferguson, R. B., 90, 112, 121, 159
Finney, J. J., 90, 102, 106, 108, 109, 152

Fischer, H., 247
Fizeau, H., 172
Fleet, G., 9, 39, 90, 100, 135, 138, 157, 158, 159
Flink, G., 243
Forchhammer, G., 243
Ford, A. B., 45
Förstner, H., 43, 126
Fouque, F., 31
Franco, R. R., 168, 219
Friedman, G. M., 36
Füchtbauer, H., 12, 67

Gabis, V., 29
Gahn, J. G., 10, 239
Garrels, R. M., 202
Gast, P. W., 8
Gates, R. M., 62, 79
Gay, P., 41, 76, 120, 134, 136, 140
Geier, P., 18
Genth, F. A., 247
Gerhard, D., 17, 246
Gibbs, G. V., 102
Gielisse, P. J., 147, 148
Gilkey, A. K., 36
Glauser, A., 60, 65
Glocker, E. F., 246
Glover, J. E., 50
Goldich, S., 20
Goldschmidt, V. M., 127
Goldsmith, J. R., 14, 109, 114, 115, 117, 133, 134, 135, 136
Goldsztaub, S., 69
Gonnard, M., 62
Gorai, M., 79, 81
Goranson, R. W., 216, 232
Gottardi, G., 64
Greenwood, H. J., 227
Greig, J. W., 125, 211
Grundy, H. D., 123, 127, 179, 180
Gubser, R. A., 178, 179
Guitard, G., 117
Gysin, M., 8

Haber, F., 190
Hafner, St., 112, 115, 133
Hahn, Th., 101
Häkli, A., 156
Hall, K. M., 127

Hargreaves, A., 91
Harloff, C., 34
Hart, S. R., 114, 117
Hausmann, J. F. L., 243, 245
Haussühl, S., 150
Haüy, R. J., 241, 243
Hayden, H. H., 245
Hays, J. F., 215, 232, 233
Heald, M. T., 50
Heddle, M. F., 245
Heide, F., 73
Heier, K. S., 117
Hellner, E., 79, 201
Hemley, J. J., 202, 204, 205
Herz, N., 36
Hess, P. C., 202, 203
Hessel, J. F., 30
Hewlett, C. G., 108
Hinds, L., 50
Hoffman, C. A. S., 239, 243
Holmquist, P. J., 147, 149
Homma, F., 34
Hosemann, P., 50
Howard, P., 202
Hubbart, F. H., 28
Hunahashi, M., 49
Hunt, T. S., 246

Iiyama, J. T., 39, 227
Irving, J., 34
Ito, T. I., 75, 124

Jagodzinski, H., 136
Jahns, R. H., 202, 216, 223
Jenzsch, G., 247
Jones, J. B., 90. 102, 106, 109, 112, 152
Jones, W. R., 202, 204, 205
Jung, D., 24

Kani, K., 166, 168, 185, 186
Kano, H., 10
Kapustinsky, A. F., 189
Karl, F., 38
Kayser, G. E., 62
Kazakov, A. N., 8
Kelley, K. K., 191, 193, 194, 195, 196
Kempster, C. J. E., 90, 101, 135
Kennard, O., 90, 91

Kennedy, G. C., 213, 227, 228, 229, 230, 231
Ketner, K. B., 159
King, A., 148
Kinser, J. H., 21
Kizaki, K., 109, 117
Kleber, W., 147
Knoop, F., 148
Kobell, F. von, 247
Köhler, A., 37, 66, 78, 79
Korekawa, M., 136
Kozu, S., 24, 172, 175, 177, 179
Kracek, F. C., 130, 195, 197, 198, 199
Kralik, J., 50
Krebs, B., 11
Krenner, J. A., 247
Kretz, R., 233
Krushchov, M. M., 148
Kuno, H., 45

Lachance, G. R., 17
Lacroix, A., 4, 62
Lacy, E. D., 208
Lagache, M., 202
Lande, 189
Larsen, E. S., 34, 154
Lasaulx, A. von, 242, 246
Laves, F., 9, 12, 21, 38, 43, 46, 73, 74, 75, 79, 92, 99, 104, 106, 109, 112, 114, 115, 117, 118, 119, 120, 124, 126, 133, 134, 135, 136, 152, 159, 241, 242, 245
Lea, I., 242, 244
LeComte, P., 214, 228
Leedal, G. P., 34
Levy, A., 245
Limbach, D. von, 74, 76, 120, 121, 122, 123, 127, 131, 133, 155, 157, 174, 175, 176, 180
Lindsley, D. H., 214, 215, 229
Loewenstein, W., 88, 137
Luczizky, W., 8
Luth, W. C., 129, 223
Lyons, J. B., 49

McConnell, J. D. C., 110, 123, 195
Macdonald, G. A., 45
MacGregor, G. A., 36
Machatschki, F., 88, 224

MacKenzie, J. D., 66,
MacKenzie, W. S., 21, 66, 73, 74, 107,
    113, 114, 120, 126, 131, 159, 163
McKie, D., 110, 123, 195
Maclelland, D. D., 8
Maillard, P., 115
Major, A., 231
Makart, H., 8
Mallard, F., 4, 244
Mann, V., 34, 79
Manolescu, G., 65
Manus, R. W., 201
Marfunin, A., 114
Marmo, V., 117
Martin, R. F., 120
Mason, B., 12
Mawdsley, J. B., 21
Megaw, H. D., 90, 96, 97, 98, 99, 100
    101, 121, 135, 137, 140, 157
Mehnert, K. R., 47
Mellis, O., 43
Merwin, H. E., 120
Michel–Levy, A., 4, 241, 244
Michot, J., 4
Milton, D. J., 244
Misch, P., 50
Misik, M., 50
Mitchell, R. L., 36
Mohs, F., 147, 148, 239
Monroe, E. A., 39
Monticelli, F., 242
Mookherjee, A., 148, 151
Morey, G. W., 202, 218
Mügge, O., 73
Muir, I. D., 13, 44, 45
Mulert, O., 193

Neuhaus, A., 231
Neumann, H., 40
Neuvonen, K. J., 130, 195, 197, 198,
    199
Newton, R. C., 228
Nieland, H., 44
Niggli, A., 138
Niggli, P., 10
Nilsson, C. A., 43
Nissen, H. U., 9, 43, 114
Noble, D. C., 38
Nockolds, S. R., 36

Nordenskiöld, A. E., 243
Nowakowski, A., 120
Nowakowski, A., 120

Offret, A., 178
Oftedahl, C., 65
Oftedal, I., 8
Ohta, Y., 49, 109, 117
Olsen, E., 4
Orville, P. M., 126, 129, 130, 132, 133,
    152, 155, 201

Paliuc, G., 33
Parker, R. B., 8
Parker, R. L. VI, 10
Parsons, I., 30
Pense, J., 43
Penta, M., 90
Perrenoud, 66
Perry, K., Jr. V, 15
Phemister, J., 34
Phillips, E. R., 14, 28
Pichamuthu, C. S., 36
Pini (Pater), 241
Pittman, E. D., 34
Plendl, J. N., 147, 148
Poldervaart, A., 36
Posnjak, E., 90
Prasad, E. A. V., 82
Preisinger, A., 8
Prost, A., 123, 242
Przibram, K., 8

Quareni, S., 127
Quin, J. P., 32

Raaz, F., 66, 79
Radoslovich, E. W., 90
Raman, C. V., 9
Ramberg, H., 20, 28, 192, 194, 197,
    198
Rammelsberg, C., 243
Rao, Y. J., 37
Rath, G. vom, 13, 68, 69, 244
Reinhard, M., 8, 63, 70, 71, 72, 241
Reynolds, R. C., 50
Rhodes, J. M., 103
Ribbe, P. H., 9, 38, 39, 90, 100, 102,
    106, 121, 140, 157

Riecker, R. E., 183
Rimsaite, J., 17
Ringwood, A. E., 230, 231, 233
Rinne, F., 178
Robie, R. B., 191
Rose, G., 4, 13, 239, 242, 243, 246
Roseboom, E. H., 214
Rosenholtz, J. L., 172
Rosiwall, 147
Ross, J. V., 79
Rossini, F. D., 192
Rottenbach, E., 153
Rutland, R. W. R., 38

Sabatier, G., 9, 14, 28, 29
Sadanaga, R., 21
Saenz, I. M. de, 21, 50
Sahu, K. C., 148, 151
Saiki, S., 172
Saplewitch, A., 172, 174, 175, 177
Sarbadhikari, T. R., 82
Sass, D. B., 39
Saucier, H., 69, 172, 174, 175, 177
Scarfe, C. M., 229
Schairer, J. F., 167, 168, 171, 211, 212, 219
Schaller, W. T., 242
Scheerer, Th., 241
Schiebold, E., 88, 192, 194, 197, 199
Schloemer, H., 202
Schmidt, E., 31, 69
Schneider, T. R., 12, 124, 242
Schwantke, A., 14
Schwarcs, H. P., 25
Seal, I., 242
Sederholm, J. J., 18
Seifert, K. E., 183
Seki, Y., 229, 230
Selby, S. M., 192, 194
Sgarlata, F., 90
Shaw, H. R., 222
Shimizu, J., 45
Simmons, G., 183
Smith, D. T., 21
Smith, J. L., 242, 244
Smith, J. R., 167
Smith, J. V., 29, 31, 70, 73
Smithson, S. B., 117
Soldatos, K., 21, 24, 26, 74, 75, 124

Sommerfeld, 192, 197
Sörum, H., 90, 91, 100
Spencer, E., 28, 29, 120
Srinivasan, R., 157
Starkey, J., 66, 81, 82
Startsev, V. J., 82
Steiger, R. H., 114
Stenstrom, R. C., 29
Stern, P., 37
Stewart, D. B., 74, 76, 120, 122, 123, 127, 131, 133, 155, 157, 159, 160, 174, 175, 176, 179, 180, 223
Streckeisen, A., 62
Stishov, S. M., 8
Stöffler, D., 226
Strunz, H., 88
Sugi, K., 45
Suwa, K., 82

Tabor, D., 147
Takéuchi, Y., 134
Tane, J. T., 9
Tatekawa, M., 14
Tauson, L. V., 190
Taylor, E. W., 148
Taylor, W. H., 88, 90–92, 97, 99, 106, 112, 114, 134, 134, 138, 152
Tenne, C. A., 246
Tertsch, H., 66
Thomson, T., 38, 242, 243, 244, 245, 246
Thoresen, K., 70, 73
Thorez, J., 4
Tilas, D., 239
Tilley, C. E., 45
Tobi, A. C., 66, 81
Tomisaka, T., 114
Tschermak, G., 17, 18, 30, 31, 62, 226, 240, 244, 245, 246
Tsuboi, S., 4
Tsuji, S., 39
Traill, R. J., 90
Tunell, G., 69
Turner, F. J., 79, 81
Turon, M., 29
Tuttle, O. F., 14, 20, 28, 120, 129, 134, 213, 217, 222, 223, 224

Ueda, J., 14, 175, 177, 179

Vance, J. A., 34, 35, 78
Vernon, R. H., 66
Viola, C., 63, 241
Vogel, T. A., 66
Vogt, J. H. L., 197
Voll, G., 28

Wager, L. R., 37
Waldbaum, D. R., 192, 193, 195
Waltershausen, W. von, 242, 243
Wang, S. W., 66
Washington, H. S., 12, 13
Weiss, M. P., 50
Wenk, E., VI, 38, 42, 49
Wenk, H. R., VI, 42, 157
Werveke, L. van, 80

Wiebe, R., 34
Wiik, F. J., 243, 244
Williams, P. P., 90, 100–121
Wollast, R., 202
Wright, F., 12, 13
Wright, T. L., 115, 117, 126, 157
Wülfing, E. A., 70
Wyart, J., 9, 14, 28, 29
Wyllie, P. J., 217, 231

Yoder, H. S., 129, 216, 218, 219

Zambonini, Z., 3
Zavaritsky, A. N., 8
Zhirov, K. K., 8
Zirkel, F., 240, 245.

Subject Index

Abrasion hardness 147
Adinoles 48
Adinolization 48
Adularia 8, 118, 241
Albite 10, 71, 98, 194
Albite pegmatites 48
Albitites 48
Albitization 12, 47
Alkali feldspar 15, 125, 154–158, 199
Aluminium avoidance rule 137
Amazonite 8
Amphodelite 247
Analbite 241
Andesine 30, 44, 241
Anemousite 12, 44, 241
Anisotropic temperature vibration 101
Anorthite 13, 95, 100, 134, 197
Anorthoclases 16, 43–36, 73
Anorthoït 241
Anorthomer Feld-Spath 239
Anorthosite 42
Antiperthite 16–17
Antiphase domains 137
Antitomer Feld-Spath 239
Atomic coordinates 98
A-twins 81
Authigenic feldspar 4, 12, 50, 66, 67
Aventurine 40, 241
Avogadro's number 153, 189

Banater Verwachsungen 62
Barbierite 123, 242
Barsowite 242
Baulite 242, 243
Biotine 242
Body-centred anorthite 100, 135, 139
Born-Haber cycle 190
Bytownite 30, 44, 139, 242

Carnatite 242
Cassinite 242

Cathodoluminescence 29
Celsian VI
Chess-board albite 82
Chesterlite 242
Christianite 242
Clevelandite 12, 242
Clouded plagioclases 35
Coexisting plagioclases 38
Compressibility 181
Compressional velocity 183
Coronites 36
Cottaite 242
C-twins 81
Cyclopite 242

Delawarite 242
Desmosite 48
Diaplectic glasses 226, 244
'Difference reflections' 93
Diffusive transformation 104, 106
Diploite 247
Disorder 90, 101–113, 136, 140
Disorder space 105
Displacive inversion 104
Distorted M-twinning 74
Distribution of feldspars 46
Districtive transformation 135
Domain texture 137
Dulong and Petit rule 191

Edler Feldspath 243
Eisspath 243
Elastic constants 182
Empyrodoxer Feld-Spath 239
Ersbyite 243
Erythrite 243
Esmarkite 243

Feldspar glasses 151, 165, 206
Felsit 243
Fenitization 47
Frequency of plagioclases 49

Gladstone and Dale's equation 154
Glasses 151, 165, 207
Glide twins 80

Hafnefiordit 243
Hardness 147
Hecatolite 241, 243
Heliolite 241, 243
Heterotomer Feld-Spath 239
Hexagonal $CaAl_2Si_2O_8$ 134, 191
High albite 74, 121
High plagioclases 158
High sanidine 107
Huronite 243
Hypo-orthoclase 107
Hyposklerit 243

Indianite 242, 243
Intermediate plagioclases 41
Internal optical scatter 66
Isomicrocline 8
Iso-orthoclase 4

'Kantengesetz' of Tschermak 63
Kieselspath 243
Krablite 243
Kraflite 243

Labradorite 30, 41–43, 139
Lasur-Feldspath 243
Latrobite 247
Lattice energy 189
Lepolite 247
Lime anorthoclase 44
Lennilite 244
Lindsayite 247
Linseite 247
Long-range order function 107
Low albite 74, 120
Low plagioclases 161
Loxoclase 240, 244

Madelung constant 189
Maskelynite 226, 244
Mauilite 244
Mauite 244
Megaw's notations 96
Melting 209
Mesoperthite 16, 17

Microcline 4, 71, 98, 102, 112–114
Mikroklase 244
Mikroklin 244
Mikrotin 254
Mohs' hardness 147
Monalbite 123, 242, 245
Monoclinic sodium feldspar 123
Moonstone 9, 245
Mornite 245
Murchisonite 245
Murchisonite parting 3, 32
Myrmekite 17

Natronorthoklas 43
Necronite 245
Neumann-Kopp rule 191

Olafite 245
Oligoclase 30, 37–40, 44, 139
Order/disorder 101–113, 136–140
Order function (S) 107
Orthoclase 2, 102, 112–114
Orthotomer Feld-Spath 239

Pantellarit 245
Paradoxit 245
Parorthoklas 245
Pegmatolith 245
Pericline 12, 245
Peristerite 37–39, 139, 246
Perthite 16–29, 246
Plagioclases 30–43, 70, 135–140, 158–171
Polyargite 247
Polychromatischer Feld-Spath 239
Polymorphism 102–112, 224
Potassian andesine 44, 45
Potassian oligoclase 44, 45
Primitive anorthite 100
Pseudoleucite reaction 232
Pseudosymmetry 60

Radauit 246
Reciprocal lattice values 92
Redmergnerite VI
Rhombic $CaAl_2Si_2O_8$ 134
Rhombic section 68
Rhomb feldspars 45
Rhyacolite 243

Rhyakolith 246
Roselite 247
Rosellan 247
Rosite 247

Saccharit 246
Sanidine 2, 93, 102, 112–114
Schiller 42, 43
Schwantke's molecule 14, 28
Shear strength 183
Shear velocity 185
Sigterit 246
Silicite 246
Smeared transformation 110, 123
Soda hornfels 48
Soda orthoclase 44
Soda sanidine 16, 45
Solubility 201
Solvus 16, 129
Spilitization 48
Spilosite 48
Spinodal curve 16
Split atoms 101, 135, 137
Strain 182
Structure energy 189
'Stuffed' plagioclases 36
Sundvikite 247
Sunstone 40, 241, 246
Superlattice reflections 93
Synneusis 35, 79

Tankite 247
Tensile strength 183
Ternary feldspars 43–46, 163, 164
Tetartin 246
Thermal expansion 171 f.f.
Thjorsauite 247
Transitional anorthite 139
Triclinicity value 109, 116, 131
Tschermak molecule 233
Tschermakit 247
Twinning laws 61
Twin, boundaries 65, 66, 97
  elements 75
  genesis 75
  growth 66
  index 76
  lamellae 76–78
  lattice 75–97

Twin—*contd.*
  laws 62–64
  obliquity 76–78
Twins, Ala 62, 63
  Albite 62, 63
  Acline 63
  Breithaupt 62
  Baveno 62
  Carlsbad 62, 63
  Complex 63
  Cunnersdof 62
  Diagonal association 74
  Estérel 62
  Four-la-Brouque 62
  Goodsprings 62
    by inversion 7, 79, 126
  M- 73
  Manebach 62, 63, 97
  Mechanical 73, 79–80
  Nevada 63
  Normal 62
  Parallel 62
  Pericline 62, 63
  Petschau 63
  Primary 79
  Prism 62, 63
  Roc Tourné 63
  Scopi 63
  Secondary 79
  X- 62, 63

Übergeordnete Symmetrie 65
Unionite 247
Unit cells 91, 92
Unstable mixed crystals 133

Valencianite 247
Variants of potassium feldspar 112
Velocities of compressional waves 183
Vicker's microhardness 148
Viscosity 166, 185
Vitrification (by shock waves) 226
Vosgite 247

Weissigit 247

Zoning 32–35, 50
Zygadite 247